THE CHURCH CONFRONTS MODERNITY

RELIGION AND AMERICAN CULTURE

RELIGION AND AMERICAN CULTURE

The Religion and American Culture series explores the inter-action between religion and culture throughout American history. Titles examine such issues as how religion functions in particular urban contexts, how it interacts with popular culture, its role in social and political conflicts, and its impact on regional identity. Series editor Randall Balmer is the Ann Whitney Olin Professor of American Religion and former chair of the Department of Religion at Barnard College, Columbia University.

A complete series list follows the index.

THE
CHURCH
CONFRONTS
MODERNITY

───

CATHOLIC INTELLECTUALS

AND THE PROGRESSIVE ERA

───

Thomas E. Woods Jr.

COLUMBIA UNIVERSITY PRESS

NEW YORK

COLUMBIA UNIVERSITY PRESS
Publishers Since 1893
New York   Chichester, West Sussex

Library of Congress Cataloging-in-Publication Data
Woods, Thomas E.
The church confronts modernity : Catholic intellectuals and
the progressive era / Thomas E. Woods, Jr.
p. cm. — (Religion and American culture)
Revision of the author's thesis (doctoral)—Columbia University.
Includes bibliographical references (p.) and index.
ISBN 0–231–13186–0 (alk. paper)
1. Christianity and culture—United States—History—19th century.
2. Catholic Church—United States—History—19th century.
3. United States—Church history—19th century.
4. Civilization, Modern—19th century.
5. Christianity and culture—United States—History—20th century.
6. Catholic Church—United States—History—20th century.
7. United States—Church history—20th century.
8. Civilization, Modern—20th century.
I. Title. II. Religion and American culture (New York, N.Y.)

BX1406.3.W66   2004
282'.73'09034—dc22   2003063536

Columbia University Press books are printed
on permanent and durable acid-free paper.
Designed by Lisa Hamm
Printed in the United States of America
c 10 9 8 7 6 5 4 3 2

TO HEATHER

CONTENTS

ACKNOWLEDGMENTS

THIS BOOK IS AN EXPANDED VERSION of my doctoral dissertation, which I wrote at Columbia University under the direction of Professor Alan Brinkley. I am indebted to Professor Brinkley for the meticulous care with which he reviewed and commented upon my chapters, as well as for his kindness and professionalism. Indeed, I am grateful to my entire defense committee: Professors Kenneth T. Jackson and Casey Blake of Columbia University, Professor John McCarthy of Fordham University, and Professor Randall Balmer of Barnard College. I am particularly indebted to Professor Balmer, the editor of this series, for his interest in this project since reading the dissertation version several years ago.

I also wish to thank Professor James Hitchcock of St. Louis University, who read the entire manuscript and made helpful comments. Although Professor Hitchcock and I disagree on some important matters, he was kind enough to do this enormous personal favor for someone who was, in effect, a total stranger. That is real scholarly camaraderie, and I am very grateful.

Dr. David Gordon read my introduction and chapter 1, and I benefited from his usual attention to detail and his enormous wealth of knowledge. Needless to say, neither Dr. Gordon nor any other of these scholars is responsible either for my interpretations or for any errors of fact.

A special word of thanks is owed to the Earhart Foundation of Ann Arbor, Michigan, which provided me with financial assistance over the course of writing and preparing the manuscript. I am humbled by and grateful for the foundation's support.

Over the past several years I have been fortunate to be part of a department whose members genuinely rejoice in each other's accomplishments. It has been a pleasure to work with such colleagues. My department chairman, Professor Robert de Zorzi, has been extraordinarily kind to me since my arrival at Suffolk, and I wish to thank him for creating an unusually pleasant environment in which to work.

After leaving Columbia University, I lost that treasured possession: a large university library. So I need to make particular mention of Dolores Perillo, who headed our library's interlibrary loan program as I was finishing up this book. She never complained about my numerous and often peculiar requests, and her contribution was absolutely indispensable.

Finally, I wish to thank Heather, my wife. Words cannot adequately express my gratitude for her constant encouragement and support, and for her unfailing confidence in me.

THE CHURCH CONFRONTS MODERNITY

1 / THE STAGE IS SET

WHEN FATHER THOMAS J. GERRARD opened the July 1912 issue of the monthly *Catholic World* with a lengthy article titled "Modern Theories and Moral Disaster," he conveyed the unease felt by American Catholic thinkers as they surveyed their intellectual milieu in the early twentieth century. From philosophy and economics to art and education, Gerrard explained, the modern world was growing increasingly antagonistic toward Christendom. The subjectivism that had begun with Descartes and that had become more pronounced over the following three centuries of philosophic thought was at last reaching its ultimate destination—not merely in atheism but also in radical individualism, self-indulgence, and even nihilism.[1]

Catholics were not alone, of course, in their alienation from modern developments; historians of American thought and culture have amply documented the apprehension and fear that many ordinary Americans felt when confronted with so much intellectual dislocation all at once.[2] It was indeed a time of disorientation. Darwin's theory of evolution, which according to one scientist "made it possible to be an intellectually fulfilled atheist," only grew in influence in the decades following the publication of *The Origin of Species* (1859). In place of Christianity's teleological understanding of an orderly universe created by a benevolent God, this new creed pointed to a cosmos born of chaos and chance, materialistic and purposeless. Pragmatism in philosophy not only subjected traditional metaphysics to attack and ridicule—and was not infrequently an explicit assault on medieval Scholasticism—but also seemed to strike at the very idea of fixed standards of right and wrong. Modernity's assault was indeed unrelenting, for no sooner were principles of morality said to be relative to time and place than Einstein, in 1919, demonstrated with his General Theory that time and place were themselves relative. Catholics' assessment of the age, writes historian Patrick Carey, "was not just a narrow-minded Catholic ghetto interpretation of events in the United States and Europe, but a reflection of post–Civil War realities."[3]

Much of the unease with modernity that Jackson Lears describes in his well-known study involved a revulsion against consumerism, materialism, and other even less agreeable aspects of industrialization. The Southern Agrarians, for their part, who would emerge as a serious intellectual force in 1930 with the publication of *I'll Take My Stand*, the celebrated agrarian manifesto, ranked among the most articulate critics; industrial society, they said, seemed to have forgotten where it was going. It was directed toward the production of more and more capital and consumer goods, but for what purpose? For the production of still *more* goods? Allen Tate, one of the contributors to *I'll Take My Stand*, felt unsatisfied with a society that seemed, at least to him and to his fellow agrarian critics, to be directed toward no higher end than that. He considered his own conversion to Catholicism—which attracted him by its sharp condemnations of many modern developments—to be the logical culmination of beliefs and principles he had always held.[4]

The Catholic critique of modernity thus overlapped considerably with the assessments of other social and cultural observers of the late nineteenth and early twentieth centuries. But it was often deeper, more philosophical, and—naturally—more concerned with the effects of modern intellectual life on the well-being of the Church. As a visible, corporate body identified not unjustifiably in the public mind with stability and conservatism, whose Magisterium had over the centuries restrained rash intellectual innovation, the Catholic Church viewed these developments with a special acuteness. The Church had already railed against liberalism for more than a century by the time these new challenges were emerging; and as the modern world upped the ante, the papacy responded in kind. In 1864 Pope Pius IX issued his famous *Syllabus of Errors*, a collection of eighty of the "principal errors of our day" that the pontiff had condemned in his earlier letters and allocutions. Filled with denunciations of the secular "isms" that had engulfed the West, the *Syllabus* seemed to anathematize an entire age. Condemned Proposition 80 read: "The Roman Pontiff should reconcile himself to liberalism, progress, and modern civilization."[5]

Yet the proper response of Catholic intellectuals, the popes of the period agreed, was not simply to denounce modern errors—although that was important—but also to hold out the splendor of the Catholic alternative. The Church had, for example, the riches of Scholastic philosophy, an approach that was both hallowed by tradition and easily adapted to address the issues occupying modern philosophy and the modern world as a whole. Pius IX had condemned in the *Syllabus* the proposition that "the method and principles according to which the ancient Scholastic Doctors cultivated theology are in no way suited to the necessities of our times and to the progress of the sciences."[6] His successor, Leo XIII, would take this theme much further, laying the groundwork of a full-scale Scholastic revival in his encyclical *Aeterni Patris* (1879). This seminal document urged Catholic teachers and philosophers to draw deeply from the riches of the Angelic Doctor, Saint Thomas Aquinas, whose doctrine and method were thought to be the surest path both to finding philosophic truth and to engaging the modern world with forthrightness and vigor. Leo's program was greeted with enthusiasm, but it would take decades to become firmly established.

During those decades—the years that would become known as the Progressive Era—the Church in America found itself at a crossroads. Two major theological controversies had at last been settled. "Americanism," a term that referred to an excessive eagerness to ease the Church's discipline and present its doctrines in such a way as to appeal to modern man, was condemned in Leo XIII's *Testem Benevolentiae* (1899). Modernism, the second of these, was a more complicated and less easily defined theological phenomenon, but under this designation Pope Pius X included such condemned ideas as dogmatic evolutionism, vital immanence, subjectivism, and historical relativism. In *Pascendi Dominici Gregis* (1907), the pope used what historian John Tracy Ellis has called "the harshest and most negative language employed by a papal encyclical in this century" to condemn Modernism as "the synthesis of all heresies."[7] By 1907, therefore, Catholic intellectuals could at last direct more of their attention to the American scene. By an interesting happenstance, it was during one of the most ideologically charged and intellectually vigorous periods of American history that Catholic thinkers at last became a presence, albeit a modest one, in the intellectual life of the United States.

To be sure, American Catholics did not encounter an intellectual monolith. The milieu was one in which intensely moralistic crusades for practical reforms coexisted with a desire on the part of some social scientists to speak in a value-free, "scientific" idiom. A variety of perspectives is evident within the Progressive movement, reflected most obviously in differences of opinion over some of the most contentious issues of the day (e.g., government policy vis-à-vis big business). All of this is true, and it should not be supposed that references to a single Progressive perspective are meant to suggest that all Progressive intellectuals were essentially interchangeable. They fought, sometimes bitterly, among themselves.

But it would be unreasonable not to acknowledge the existence among Progressive intellectuals—that is, thinkers who spoke about changes in American society much more far-reaching than this or that particular reform—of a considerable range of agreement at least on the basics of what the new America should look like. It is with this intellectual dimension of the Progressive Era that we will be concerned. And as historian Eldon Eisenach has demonstrated, a key aim of this aspect of the Progressive movement was to manufacture a kind of civic religion, a nondogmatic ethic that could serve as a national bond that would lift Americans out of the dual parochialism of geography and religion. The Progressive effort to remove ethics from the speculative field of moral philosophy and set it on a foundation of value-free, empirical science, a trend amply documented by Morton White, was emblematic of this effort.[8] Even more so was the attempt by the Progressive sociologist Albion Small to persuade his fellow intellectuals of the need to "invent" a new American religion.[9] As Eisenach explains, "By 1915, Small is really codifying the results of a long-standing theological-ethical enterprise when he concludes that the symbolic centerpiece of this 'new' national religion is the now historically recovered 'Weltanschauung of Jesus' excavated from barbarism, superstition, church, and dogma."[10] A corollary to such a national creed, so to speak, was the construction of a truly national community, of a social democracy in which the locus of people's affections and loyalties would be transferred from local authorities and various subsidiary institutions to the central state. According to Eisenach, Progressives held that "all social knowledge deserving a hearing must be cosmopolitan in origin and national in import." They "invented a conception of citizenship," moreover, "that stipulated that the possession of social knowledge entailed the duty of reflecting on and articulating ideas of national public good unmediated by party, interest, region, or sectarian religion."[11] Social Gospel Christians could be considered allies by secular Progressives and could play an important role in the Progressive movement precisely because they portrayed Christ's message in a naturalistic way that posed little threat to the new secular ethic that Eisenach describes. Gone was the cry "No salvation outside the church." "The candid democrat," stated the New Republic, insists that "no one has a monopoly in salvation."[12]

The whole spirit of the new creed was positively hostile to any sectarian group claiming possession of absolute truth. What Eisenach does not mention, however, is that the Catholic Church was precisely such a "sectarian group." Catholics considered their dogmas binding not merely on themselves—in which case they could have had less of a quarrel with Progressives—but ultimately on the entire human race. In such areas as education and sociology, they were prepared to employ modern findings where they were not repugnant to Church teaching and where they offered potential benefit to the Church. But Catholics could not accept a philosophy that they believed focused on means rather than ends, a theory of education that neglected the proper cultivation of the soul, or a practice of the social sciences that considered it possible to study man and to make recommendations for his happiness without any specific understanding of his nature and destiny. They were not prepared to be just another faction, with no more claim to men's allegiance than any other.

During the Progressive Era, however, the Church in America found itself in the midst of an intellectual milieu in which a variety of disparate (though perhaps distantly related) trends in thought were tending to the conclusion that attachment to dogmatic and moral absolutes was inimical to the democratic ethos. I have already mentioned Pragmatism's rejection of dogma in the sense that Catholics understood it. The Social Gospel movement in American Protestantism, while said to be an effort to bring Christian values to bear upon the social problems facing the United States in the late nineteenth and early twentieth centuries, was at some level also a rejection of the idea of Christianity as a system whose ultimate basis lay in dogma, creed, and ritual.[13] Its chief theologians, Walter Rauschenbusch in particular, were known to argue, for example, that Saint Paul, by preaching and promoting so supernatural a vision of Christianity, had already departed from the simplicity of its founder. Indeed, Rauschenbusch rather explicitly accused the Catholic Church and some of the more conservative of the Reformed churches of having betrayed the original intent of Christianity by introducing the dead hand of dogma, ritual, and authoritarianism into what was supposed to have been a primarily ethical religion, concerned mostly not with theological hairsplitting but with men's relations with other men. Philosophically distinct from and yet logically consonant with this critique were the effects on Christianity of the Enlightenment, which continued to be felt even at the beginning of the twentieth century. Those Enlightenment thinkers who were not altogether hostile to Christianity emphasized the urgency of retreating from aspects of the religion that were purely ritualistic or devotional and of stressing instead the rational and didactic. Immanuel Kant was the standard-bearer of this group.[14] And beyond all this there was, very simply, the unmistakable Progressive instinct for efficiency, centralization, and simple practicality, none of which was thought to be aided by attachment to the outworn dogmas and moral teachings of an authoritarian institution out of step with modernity.

What is especially striking about the Catholic Church during this period, especially at a time when reigning philosophical presuppositions tended to be so antagonistic to its own, is its self-confidence. Its apologists truly believed that it was "the greatest, the grandest, and the most beautiful institution in the world."[15] The Catholic faith was "the one immutable thing in a universe of ceaseless mutations."[16] Catholic writers spoke with great affection of Pope Pius X, who reigned from 1903 to 1914 (and who became the first pope to be canonized since the sixteenth century). Time and again Catholic periodicals pointed with pride to Pius's vigorous and uncompromising stance against modern political and intellectual trends, and indeed many authors considered the Church's willingness to stand alone against modernity as an important testimony to its divine foundation.[17]

Pius is so often remembered simply as the anti-Modernist pope that his positive program—"to restore all things in Christ"—is frequently overlooked. The Jesuit writer John J. Wynne, for example, founded the weekly periodical *America* in response to the pope's call.[18] *America* would cover news in the Church and in the world at large for a Catholic audience, always with the good of Church and country in mind. American Catholics also undertook the staggering project of assembling an entire encyclopedia of their own. While no more tendentious than the French *Encyclopédie*, the *Catholic Encyclopedia* did serve more than a strictly academic purpose. In a world that seemed increasingly adrift from its Christian moorings, the publication sought to provide a reliable compendium of knowledge to the curious and intelligent Catholic. It also served the explicit purpose of countering the *Encyclopaedia Britannica*, many of whose articles churchmen considered anti-Catholic. The extensive Catholic campaign against the *Britannica*, all but unnoticed by historians, was a potent symbol of this sense of distinctiveness that American Catholics felt during the early twentieth century.[19] It could come as no real surprise, therefore, when they declared themselves unwilling to go along with a philosophy that insisted that their faith was merely the result of subjective sentiment and not objectively demonstrable, or that the ideal for society was not the conversion of America to Catholicism but a toleration that encouraged only (in Dewey's terms) individual self-realization. "We have a vision that they have not," a Jesuit writer put it simply.[20]

Progressive education provides only the most obvious example of this conflict. Education in the Catholic sense, the educator Edward A. Pace wrote in the *Catholic Encyclopedia*, "aims at an ideal, and this in turn depends on the view that is taken of man and his destiny, of his relations to God, to his fellow men, and to the physical world."[21] John Dewey's schools did inculcate values, but they were largely procedural: tolerance, respect for the democratic process, and the like. In an article critical of Catholicism, the *New Republic*—described by one scholar as given to "a continuing, though normally low-key anti-Catholicism"[22]—insisted that "freedom and tolerance mean the development of independent powers of judgment in the young, not the freedom of older people to impose their dogmas on the young."[23] More recently, Jacques Maritain wrote that Dewey's philosophy "proposes *no rules of conduct, but teaches rules and procedures of investigation* to be used in determining the value of various possible modes of conduct in a given situation."[24]

The philosophy of Pragmatism, which lay just beneath the surface of Progressive education, sociology, and the like, also contributed to an animosity toward dogma. William James and John Dewey, like many post-Kantian philosophers, were skeptical of the efforts of traditional philosophy to attain absolutely true knowledge. Pragmatism, based as it was on human experience, sought to render philosophy more democratic and individualistic; James even called it "philosophic Protestantism." Here again, substantive content gave way to procedure: the ends to be pursued by man became less the object of philosophy than the means of achieving them. James stated explicitly that Pragmatism had no dogmas or doctrines save its method. This apparent retreat from a commitment to objective standards seemed to many Catholics to be at the root of the problems besetting the modern mind, and churchmen would strike at Pragmatism with particular vigor—whether they found it expressed in pure philosophy or saw it manifested in education, the social sciences, or elsewhere.

Standard histories of American Catholicism have had little if anything to say about the intellectual battles in which Catholics were engaged during the Progressive Era. Several studies exist of the intellectual history of American Catholicism during the interwar period,[25] of the American contribution to the Modernist controversy,[26] and of the so-called "Americanist" debate of the 1890s,[27] but the period from roughly 1900 to 1920 still constitutes an odd gap in the literature. Treatments of this period confine themselves to issues that were peculiar to Catholics: the development of the parochial school system, the challenges of massive Catholic immigration, and so forth. Catholic efforts to grapple with issues in American intellectual life as a whole are limited to the question of labor unions and the application of Pope Leo XIII's social encyclical *Rerum Novarum*. Since this area was one in which Catholic thinkers, albeit for somewhat different reasons, found considerable common ground with their secular counterparts, the exaggerated emphasis on the issue has distorted the much more ambiguous relationship that Catholics enjoyed with the intellectual milieu of the Progressive Era.

This book, on the other hand, while addressing itself to the questions of labor and "social justice," will look more broadly at important intellectual developments of the Progressive Era and will consider the Catholic response to each. Eldon Eisenach's argument that beneath each of these individual trends lay a larger trend—namely, the construction of a national ethic that discouraged excessive attachment to competing creeds or sources of authority—will serve as a useful tool for understanding the period as a whole as well as the Catholic place in it.

Chapter 1 will discuss the philosophical chasm that was ultimately fundamental to Catholic-Progressive disagreements throughout the period under examination. The Pragmatism of William James and John Dewey helped to set the tone for the intellectual life of the Progressive Era; the editors of the *New Republic*, which became the most important and influential Progressive periodical, were all deeply influenced by it, and it provided an intellectual and philosophical rationale for the scientific and experimental ethos of the time. As Catholics were beginning to promote Pope Leo XIII's program of neo-Scholasticism, with its teleological view of man and its systematic metaphysical apparatus, many Progressives were imbibing a philosophy that despaired of man's ability to answer vexing metaphysical questions and that viewed philosophical truth in terms of its practical consequences. Such a philosophy challenged such ideas as natural law, a human nature constant across time and space, and indeed many of the metaphysical categories of which Scholasticism made extensive use. It threatened, Catholics feared, to lead all men to retreat into a lonely subjectivism, utterly closed to the idea of an absolute truth. This chapter will doubtless seem somewhat technical to some readers, but it serves the indispensable purpose of setting out much of the philosophical basis on which Catholic-Progressive differences rested.

Chapter 2 considers the discipline of sociology, which was continuing to come into its own as a distinct social science during the Progressive Era. Although Catholic intellectuals saw the potential for good in this developing discipline, they directed withering criticisms toward secular sociologists, whose inductive, "scientific" approach to knowledge often contained a more than implicit rejection of the Christian moral tradition as an a priori guidepost for the ordering of human society. Some were Pragmatists and others positivists, but all generally discounted the idea of natural law. Instead, they attempted to derive ethics from evolutionary imperatives or simply by observing social phenomena and determining what kind of behavior conduced to social comity. Catholics insisted that any true "science of society," if it were not to be mere materialism in the guise of social science, had to be based on a genuine philosophy of man.

Chapter 3 moves on to a topic of crucial importance not only to Progressive sociologists but also to Progressive thinkers in general: education. Here we will examine Catholics' selective appropriation of Progressive innovations in education, and their insistence that Progressive education alone, without the foundation that Catholicism could provide, led to an empty humanism and potentially even to nihilism. While Progressive education taught such democratic procedural norms as toleration and a dislike for dogma, Catholics insisted that education had to possess more substantive content, basing itself on man's nature and his exalted calling.

Chapter 4 explores some of the economic issues that animated both Progressives and Catholics. It is true, of course, as historians have pointed out, that Catholic thinkers had much in common with their secular counterparts on matters of labor-capital relations. This agreement has all too often given the impression that the two sides were ideologically closer than they actually were. Their agreement on these issues in fact obscured the deeper philosophical differences that continued to separate the two camps. Catholics were speaking the language of natural law, deducing the duties of the state and the meaning of the common good in step-by-step fashion, beginning with absolute truths about man revealed by both faith and reason and culminating in practical policy. This chapter serves, therefore, to demonstrate that even here Catholics were grounded in a specific natural-law tradition and that even when Catholic and Progressive paths converged their respective philosophies remained clearly distinct.

Chapter 5 looks at a relatively unexamined aspect of the Progressive Era, but one that flows directly from the period's basic premises. A project that was both implicit and explicit throughout the era was an effort to found American nationality on a nonsectarian ethic. Since most intellectuals appreciated the need to encourage moral conduct, but since at the same time an explicitly religious appeal to morality would undermine the dogmatic nonsectarianism of Progressivism, exhortations to virtue would have to be divorced from revealed religion and built on a wholly new foundation. This chapter will examine various efforts to accomplish that, and the Catholic response to those efforts.

With the Catholic perspective excluded, as it so often is, from the intellectual history of the Progressive Era, important features of the period are obscured. But in the same way that Saint Thomas Aquinas proposed that we learn about God by means of the *via negativa*—that is, by contemplating all those things God is *not*—we can, paradoxically, gain a fuller and more thorough understanding of Progressive principles by considering the response of a group to whom those principles were, quite literally, anathema.

The lack of sympathy of many Church historians and even some modern Catholics for a period in which the anti-Modernist crusade was launched throughout the Catholic world has tended in practice to give the impression that the early twentieth century was a time of regrettable stagnation in the Church's life. Such a picture is at best misleading. In fact, surveying the "astonishing growth of the Church" during this period, Theodore Maynard could write:

> The Catholic population of America had increased from about seven millions to nearly twenty millions, the number of priests—secular and religious—from 7,000 to 20,000, the bishoprics from fifty-five to over a hundred. And this does not take any account of auxiliaries or coadjutors or vicars-apostolic. Meanwhile the religious orders had grown so rapidly, both with regard to the number of orders working in this country and to the houses they had, that it would be impossible to tabulate concisely what had happened. But taking one fact that will perhaps reveal the extent of the work of organization, the Age of Gibbons closed with about seventy orders of men in the United States, including teaching and nursing Brothers, and about two hundred orders of women.[28]

As an intellectual history, this study will not be a history of the American hierarchy during the Progressive Era. For one thing, histories of American Catholicism have if anything focused too much on the bishops and the battles in which they were involved—immigration, public versus parochial schooling, and the like. The very fact that there exists no other book-length treatment of the Catholic *intellectuals* of the Progressive Era is clear enough evidence that the Church's intellectual life, especially in this critical period, has been curiously neglected. While our story, therefore, comes not from episcopal conferences and chancery offices, some kind of institutional contextualization of the Catholic intellectual project during the Progressive Era seems necessary. Again, the institutional life of the Catholic Church in the United States has received ample treatment by historians, and the interested reader is directed for further reading to the sources mentioned in this chapter. What follows is a brief recapitulation of a few key events in American Catholicism that will doubtless seem rather conventional to scholars of the American Church but that are all but unknown to most readers.

One path that American Catholicism might have taken is personified in John Carroll, the first American Catholic bishop. Carroll favored a host of innovations in Catholic practice that would, he hoped, accommodate the Catholic Church to the American milieu and give less credence to the common dismissal of his faith as a foreign religion unsuited to a republican people. Thus long before the vernacular was introduced in the Mass throughout the Roman Rite following the Second Vatican Council (1962–1965), Carroll favored replacing Latin with English in the liturgy as a necessary adaptation to the exigencies of ecclesiastical life in North America. He was relatively liberal on the question of religious liberty, and while in principle he was committed to the spread of the Catholic religion, in his preaching he appears to have been fairly diffident in setting forth the need for the conversion of his fellow countrymen.

Another model of a Catholic bishop might best be illustrated, curiously enough, in a man who never so much as touched American soil—Cardinal Paul Cullen, archbishop of Dublin, and thus primate of Ireland, from 1849 until 1878. Amid the waves of immigration that began to hit the United States in the mid-nineteenth century, none was more numerous than that of the Irish. This is not merely an incidental fact of ethnic composition, but rather one pregnant with implications for the future of American Catholicism, since the Irish brought with them something of the spirit of the primate of their country at the time of their great migration. Cardinal Cullen looked upon his country with a mixture of frustration and impatience. Ireland in the mid-nineteenth century felt itself humiliated and despised. The victims of devastating famines as well as of the ongoing and relentless cultural aggression of Anglican England, the Irish people felt the acute sting of national degradation and were uniquely prepared to respond to a vigorous call to spiritual arms. Thus it was to a badly shaken and disoriented Irish population that Cullen set forth his challenge. The Catholic faith that lay at the root of Irish culture and that had been a principal source of strength from which the Irish drew in resisting English domination was to be revived in still greater splendor. It is worth quoting at length from one historian's description of the Cullen program and its fruits:

> He pushed Catholic financial resources to the limit to build proper churches everywhere, as well as rectories, convents, chapter houses,

retreat centers, shrines. National jubilees and days of atonement were accompanied by an almost endless stream of new devotions—processions, the Forty Hours, novenas, the *Via Crucis*, benedictions, vespers, special devotional exercises for the Sacred Heart and for the Blessed Virgin, perpetual adorations, mass rosaries—coordinated, as far as possible throughout the nation. He cajoled, ordered, embarrassed his fellow hierarchs to improve the quality of preaching and singing, to regularize ritual, to follow ceremonials to the letter. He would not brook the kind of wooden cross that greeted him in Armagh. He wanted glittering plate, candles, flowers, beautiful music, hair-raising sermons—a total sensory experience, like the ceremony in his own procathedral that, as he recounted with satisfaction, was celebrated "with great pomp and magnificence. The Church is ornamented with damask . . . and what is better," he added, "crowds of people are attending." He did not exaggerate, for the Irish reaction to his reform program was stupendous. People flooded the churches, making their first confessions in years, begging to regularize their marriages, finally having their children baptized. It took all the resources of the religious communities—the Jesuits, Dominicans, Vincentians—to handle the upsurge in parish workloads.[29]

This was the spirit that waves of Irish Catholic laity would bring with them to their new country. More important, it was the spirit that many Irish prelates adopted as well. Thus amid the continuing specter of nativist suspicion of and even violence toward Catholics, New York archbishop John Hughes could proclaim that Catholicism

> will convert all Pagan nations, and all Protestant nations, even England with her proud Parliament. . . . Everybody should know that we have for our mission to convert the world—including the inhabitants of the United States—the people of the cities, and the people of the country, the Officers of the Navy and the Marines, the commander of the Army, the legislatures, the Senate, the Cabinet, the President and all.[30]

The American bishops had in common an apostolic zeal as well as a firm belief that the Catholic Church was the one Church established by Christ and that it alone could guarantee one's eternal salvation. From the point of view of dogmatic and moral teaching, all were conservative, and they were, in general, considerably closer in style and substance to Cullen than to Carroll. Within this overall framework, two distinct postures could be identified. One group favored rapid assimilation of Catholic immigrants into the mainstream of American society and were generally friendly and positive in their views of the United States itself. In matters not touching on dogma they were relatively accommodating, such as in their approach to the Catholic school question (more on which below). In a country that in the past had not been especially friendly toward Catholics, they wished to combat the impression that Catholics were a foreign, unassimilable group unsuited to life in a modern republican state. Thus they were unsympathetic to the demands of many German American Catholics for ethnic parishes staffed by German-speaking clergy. The sooner American Catholics could assimilate, the better. The other group was more aloof from, and perhaps somewhat suspicious of, American society; their more liberal counterparts seemed to them to be too accommodating, even naïve. They were less optimistic about the compatibility of the values of the modern age with those of the Church, and tended to adopt a more confrontational approach toward the surrounding society and indeed toward modernity itself.

It so happened that two of the best-known and most influential American prelates were of the more liberal, or Americanist, party: James Gibbons, cardinal archbishop of Baltimore and the first American cardinal, and John Ireland, archbishop of St. Paul. Gibbons, in fact, was the direct representative of the American Church before the pope until an apostolic delegate took up residence in the United States in the 1890s. Probably the two most prominent and outspoken opponents of the Gibbons-Ireland approach were Bernard McQuaid, bishop of Rochester, New York, and Michael Corrigan, archbishop of New York City. The cast of characters was at once more numerous and more colorful than this brief sketch would suggest, but there can be no real doubt that these were among the principal actors in the American drama.

One of the primary sources of division between the parties involved the question of education. As the nineteenth century progressed, it was becoming clear to Catholics and to Christians in general that the country was moving toward a secular curriculum and ethos in its system of public education. Christians were therefore faced with a critical choice. They could send their children to public schools and supplement the secular education that they received there with religious education in the home or in a church setting, or they could establish a network of schools of their own. As we know, the Catholic Church decided on the latter course of action, though our familiarity with the Catholic school system has perhaps served to obscure the staggering amount of effort and expense that the undertaking entailed. And it was the overwhelming demands that Catholic schools made on the finances and manpower of both clergy and laity that prompted Archbishop Ireland to look around for some less taxing arrangement.

We can date precisely when Catholic parochial education became the subject of bitter contention among the American faithful: July 10, 1890. It was on this day that Ireland addressed the National Education Association, which was meeting in St. Paul that year. "I am a friend and advocate of the state school," he said. "In the circumstances of the present time I uphold the parish school. I sincerely wish that the need for it did not exist. I would have all schools for the children of the people to be state schools." The reason that Catholics had chosen to establish their own schools was that in the current climate the state schools tended "to eliminate religion from the minds and hearts of the youth of the country." Ireland could point to the example of a compromise plan that had been implemented in Poughkeepsie, New York, by which Catholic schools were subject to state control during normal school hours, but were free after hours to supply religious instruction. The Vatican, in fact, when later apprised of the controversy, replied that the arrangements reached in Poughkeepsie, and later in Ireland's own archdiocese in Faribault and Stillwater, Minnesota, might in fact be tolerated; the issue was ultimately one for the American bishops themselves to decide.[31] (As we shall see, Father Thomas Edward Shields, the most influential Catholic educational theorist of the Progressive Era and a man who is routinely and rather carelessly described by historians as a "progressive," could not have objected more forcefully to the suggestion that religious education could be treated as a mere adjunct to the rest of the material the child was learning.)

It is true that Ireland sought a friendlier relationship between the Church in America and the surrounding society, but that was by no means his only motivation in setting forth his plan. Much of it had to do with sheer practicality. An Ireland supporter wrote privately that the archbishop thought he was only being realistic in the face of a seemingly impossible situation. Ireland "understood better than many other Bps. in the country, that the burden of our parochial school[s] was crushing our pastors, that [male] teachers could not be found for the boys, that our people were growing tired of pressure and that our public schools were far better than the schools frequented by the children in Italy and France."[32]

The controversy that erupted over the school question in the wake of Ireland's address had less to do with the content of the Faribault and Stillwater plans than with the tone and lines of argument that Ireland employed in defending them. The dispute crossed ideological lines, with the bishop of Peoria, John Lancaster Spalding, who was generally sympathetic to Ireland, opposing what he perceived as the St. Paul bishop's denigration of the parochial school system.[33] Immediately after the archbishop's National Education Association address a print battle broke out between sympathizers and opponents, with the initial volleys originating from Catholic University's Thomas Bouquillon, a professor of theology, and Jesuit ethicist René Holaind of Georgetown and Woodstock College. Bouquillon maintained that the state possessed an important claim to play a role in education inasmuch as it had an interest in guaranteeing the literacy and basic skills of its future citizens. Holaind shot back in a pamphlet called *The Parent First* (1891) that the right to educate lay with parents and that it was therefore an error to suggest that the state could have any intrinsic right to educate. Insofar as the state interfered with education at all, it could do so only by virtue of authority delegated by the parents themselves. The controversy continued through the summer of 1891 with "a veritable storm of articles, brochures, editorials, and reviews, of varying length and quality." With European Catholics struggling contemporaneously to preserve the Church's right to educate at all, Ireland's posture, which seemed to reflect Bouquillon's principles (and indeed Ireland was a firm supporter of the Catholic University theologian's ideas) appeared to be a dangerous capitulation.[34]

The school issue was fairly typical of the types of issues that divided Americanists from their opponents. It did not involve any Catholic dogma. It had to do instead with the practical question of how Catholics in the United States ought to interact with the society in which they lived.

When something called "Americanism" was condemned by Pope Leo XIII in 1899, its connection to these issues was not immediately obvious. The precipitating event in the controversy between the two sides was Abbé Félix Klein's introduction to the French translation of Walter Elliott's *Life of Father Hecker*, a biography of Isaac Hecker, the founder of the Paulist Fathers and a man whose goal it was to demonstrate that it was the Catholic faith above all others that comported best with the American spirit. Klein's introduction raised eyebrows when it seemed to suggest that fairly significant changes in the life of the Church might be called for in response to modern conditions. Controversy immediately surrounded Klein's comments, and in France, where sullen conservatives still had difficulty accepting the *ralliement*, the resulting debate was especially heated. It was at this stage that Rome made the decision to intervene.[35]

Testem Benevolentiae was Pope Leo XIII's 1899 apostolic letter on Americanism that was intended to address the issues that the controversy over the Hecker biography had raised in Europe. In the letter the pope congratulated and praised the Church in America for its outstanding growth and continuing success. This praise was not merely perfunctory; the pope was genuinely pleased and impressed with most of what he saw in American Catholic life. He went on to warn, however, that certain trends in American Catholicism that had come to his attention were in no way acceptable to the Holy See and had to be halted immediately. The pope allowed that the Church "has been accustomed to so yield that, the divine principle of morals being kept intact, she has never neglected to accommodate herself to the character and genius of the nations which she embraces." It was in this concession of Leo XIII that the Americanist party could take the greatest comfort; they were, it could be said, suggesting a few minor adaptations of the Church's life in line with what the pope himself in his encyclical had expressly allowed and called for. Such a posture could, however, easily evolve into something much more problematic. "The underlying principle of these new opinions," the pope explained,

> is that, in order to more easily attract those who differ from her, the Church should shape her teachings more in accord with the spirit of the age and relax some of her ancient severity and make some concessions to new opinions. Many think that these concessions should be made not only in regard to ways of living, but even in regard to doctrines which belong to the deposit of the faith. They contend that it would be opportune, in order to gain those who differ from us, to omit certain points of her teaching which are of lesser importance, and to tone down the meaning which the Church has always attached to them.

It would be difficult to convict even the most liberal American prelate of this latter charge—and, again, the pope was not accusing any specific individual of anything. Cardinal Gibbons has more than once been taken to task for false irenism because he claimed that his 1876 book *The Faith of Our Fathers*, an exposition and defense of the Catholic religion, contained nothing that would cause offense to a Protestant; this was said to be evidence that he was watering down Catholic teaching for the sake of ingratiating himself with his largely non-Catholic audience. Gibbons could have avoided much of the later misunderstanding of his position if he had said that his book contained nothing that could cause *gratuitous* offense to a Protestant. On no point of doctrine did he compromise in that book. He simply made sure to explain the Catholic faith without acrimony or invective, and with the charitable tone that he thought his countrymen would find most accessible.

Apart from this overall posture, the pope condemned several specific teachings under the heading of Americanism, all of which could be traced to the controversial introduction to the biography of Father Hecker. It would be wrong, Leo said, to disparage the contemplative virtues in favor of the active virtues. It would likewise be wrong to suggest that the vows and rigorous discipline of the religious life were unsuitable to an age—or a country—that prided itself on liberty and freedom from restraint. And it would certainly be dangerous to wish for the United States a Church unlike that which exists in the rest of the world—a desire that Leo also detected. The pope concluded by remarking that while an Americanism that referred merely to the filial piety that we owe to the country of our birth was worthy of praise, he was certain that the American bishops would be the first to condemn and repudiate the variety of Americanism of which he was speaking.

The response to the pope's letter, as has been recorded many times before, was exultation on the part of the conservatives and denial on the part of the Americanists themselves.[36] The latter group agreed that the condemned propositions listed in the encyclical were evils to be avoided and deplored, but insisted that no Americans with whom they were familiar actually held any of these views. The conservatives, on the other hand, while perhaps slightly disappointed that Leo had not taken a harder line, thanked the pope for his salutary intervention, which, they insisted, had headed off a potentially serious crisis. It was probably true, as many observers pointed out at the time, that the most unabashed and thoroughgoing adherents of Americanism were a small minority of liberal clerics in France. The ideas that Leo condemned, after all, could indeed be found in what Abbé Klein had written.

Although it is difficult to point to precise consequences of the Americanist controversy, it was surely a matter of some significance. For one thing, many German Americans exulted in Rome's pronouncement even though it took no concrete position on the specific issues of schooling and Americanization that so concerned them. To them, it was enough that those forces in American Catholic life who had in their view been so obnoxious in forcing the Germans along in the process of cultural assimilation had suffered at least an apparent rebuke from the Holy Father.

Archbishop Ireland's association with Father Hecker, whose biography had sparked the controversy, may have tended to discredit Ireland's initiatives (Ireland had written an introduction of his own to the Hecker biography). The mood that resulted from *Testem Benevolentiae* tended therefore to discourage aggressive Americanization efforts and allowed this process to take place more at the pace of those involved.[37]

Furthermore, while the episode demonstrated that fairly significant disagreement existed among American prelates at the turn of the century, it also illustrated a fairly critical fact: none of the issues separating the antagonists, as important as they were, really touched on the substance of the Catholic religion. Both sides were united in unfailing loyalty to Rome, to whose judgment neither side hesitated to have recourse. For that matter, Ireland and McQuaid got to know each other much better in their later years and found that they rather liked one another. Beyond this, in the aftermath of the pope's apostolic letter the controversy, at least in its public manifestations, disappeared almost entirely. Thomas McAvoy speculated at some length in *The Great Crisis in American Catholic History* as to why a matter that had been a source of such contentiousness and ill will should vanish from public view so quickly.[38]

Part of what the whole incident revealed, furthermore, was that the vast majority of American bishops were profoundly conservative and that all of them were basically united on fundamentals. Historian Charles Morris has described post–World War I American Catholicism as "an immense and flourishing enterprise. Its leaders enjoyed a remarkable unanimity of purpose and direction."[39] Another historian has suggested that it was precisely because the American hierarchy was in profound agreement in matters theological and dogmatic that such great importance should be placed on external and "nonessential" matters.[40] Even among those prelates themselves who might be loosely described as Americanists, it is nevertheless the case that "at no time in their writings was there any suggestion that the non-Catholic would be converted to anything but traditional Catholicism."[41] Thus following the Third Plenary Council of Baltimore in 1884, whose decrees were published in Latin only, then-Archbishop Gibbons distributed an English-language pastoral letter describing the council's decisions. And what had the council decreed? In addition to its pastoral directives regarding preaching, the sacraments, and other aspects of Catholic life in the United States, the council identified and condemned what it considered the two principal errors of the day: rationalism and materialism. Likewise, it declared that the decrees of the Second Plenary Council remained in force except where revised by the Third; this earlier council had singled out for particular reprobation still more unacceptable positions: religious indifferentism, Unitarianism, Universalism, Transcendentalism, pantheism, spiritism, and others. A few of these were especially pronounced in the United States, and thus their condemnation hardly suggests a Church eager for compromise. And it was Gibbons himself who went out of his way to publicize the teachings of the council.

Moreover, even the most outspoken of the Americanists cannot fairly be accused of doctrinal compromise. As historian James Hennesey put it, "During the Modernist crisis which developed in the new century's first decade, the leading Americanists could not have been more orthodox." Thus in 1908, the year following the papal condemnation of Modernism, Denis O'Connell, rector of Rome's North American College and a figure associated with the Americanizers, reported Charles Grannan, a professor at the Catholic University of America, to Pope Pius X for liberalism in biblical exegesis.[42] In the popular *North American Review*, Archbishop Ireland penned ringing defenses against the Modernists of the reality of the supernatural order and of the dogmatic authority of the papacy.[43] He was, says one scholar, "one of the foremost American episcopal opponents of Modernism."[44] This bespeaks a fundamental unanimity that would inspire envy in the modern conservative Catholic.[45]

Most American bishops, it should be noted, did not weigh in on the matter at all, their hands more than full with the daunting tasks of administration—constructing and maintaining schools, hospitals, and orphanages, soliciting funds, maintaining discipline, and the myriad other responsibilities that rest with the bishop's office. Historian Thomas McAvoy estimates that perhaps sixty of the eighty-seven American bishops took no interest in the issues associated with Americanism. Neither nationalism nor liberalism seemed enough of a real threat to distract them from the crucial and much more immediate work that impressed itself upon them in their dioceses. The controversies in which the hierarchy became involved in the 1890s thus fell to "but a handful of Catholic prelates."[46] As for the Catholic laity, McAvoy adds that "it is quite clear also that the rank and file of American Catholics were not much aware of these dissensions between the bishops."[47]

It may also be helpful in this context to recall an episode involving Cardinal Gibbons during the conclave that elected Giuseppe Sarto, patriarch of Venice, as the next pope. Sarto, a man of peasant background, had served as bishop of Mantua and then, in 1893, was appointed patriarch of Venice, at which time he was also named a cardinal. When he heard in 1903 from a number of sources that his name was being seriously entertained as a papal candidate, his first reaction was to mutter: "The cardinals are enjoying themselves at my expense." Learning that his supporters were in deadly earnest, he begged the conclave that his name be forgotten. "Forget me. I have not the qualities requisite for a pope."[48] One evening several cardinals paid Sarto a fateful visit. All urged him to accept. Significantly, among them was Cardinal Gibbons, who, fully aware of the future Pope Pius X's profoundly traditional and anti-Modernist background, assured the hesitant Sarto that the Church in America would be a source of strength for him.[49] For this reason one historian has claimed that it was "really Gibbons, more than any other man, who made Pius X Pope." In fact, when Cardinal Gibbons arranged to lead a group of Americans for an audience with the new pontiff three days later, Pius X would not allow Gibbons to kiss his ring, instead embracing him vigorously and kissing him on both cheeks.[50] (He later told Gibbons: "I love these Americans. They are the blooming youth of Catholicism. Convey to them how gladly I impart my apostolic blessing to their whole country."[51])

More important than any of this is the simple fact that the divisions that arose among certain members of the hierarchy during the Americanist controversy do not seem to have been replicated to any significant degree in the Catholic intellectual world. This is quite a claim, but one that can nevertheless be supported. The "remarkable unanimity of purpose and direction" of which Charles Morris wrote in reference to Catholic leaders after World War I is still more evident among Catholic thinkers. To be sure, it is not impossible to find disagreement among Catholic intellectuals on this or that issue, or to detect figures who were not as enthusiastic as others regarding, say, the Scholastic revival. In those days, though, those who disagreed strongly with their colleagues on matters of fundamental importance to the Catholic faith were either disciplined or left the Church of their own volition (as did a handful of churchmen after the condemnation of Modernism). Indeed, among men of prominence and good standing in the Church it is next to impossible to find anyone who dissented from what might be described as the Catholic program during the Progressive Era: (1) a refusal to be assimilated into the ideological syncretism, nondogmatic and nonsectarian, that they believed Progressive intellectuals were at least implicitly recommending; (2) a willingness, tempered by caution and prudence, to appropriate for the Church's benefit whatever good features the modern world had to offer; and (3) the desire, expressed again and again, to convert America to Catholicism.[52]

This kind of unanimity, though, while perhaps difficult for some historians to imagine, can hardly be surprising to the thoughtful observer.

Recall that the clergy, especially around the time of the Modernist crisis, were admitted to the seminary and approved for ordination only after their theological conservatism and sober judgment had been established to the satisfaction of their superiors. By 1910 all clergy, preachers, confessors, religious superiors, and seminary professors had to take the anti-Modernist oath established by Pope Saint Pius X. That pope had warned earlier: "Far, far from the clergy be the love of novelty!"[53] The very small minority of Catholic writers who favored a more thoroughgoing accommodation of the Catholic faith to the modern world and whose sympathies were with the Modernists were of little consequence in these years, whatever their long-term influence may have been in planting the seeds for the theological pluralism of the post–Vatican II period. Since the campaign against Modernism was prosecuted with such vigor, it became impossible for Modernist clerics to get published in Catholic periodicals or to secure the necessary imprimatur for their books. Again, since this book is concerned with Catholicism as an institutional phenomenon, its subject matter necessarily revolves around Catholics who were in good standing with the Church. And the very fact that historians have again and again bemoaned the crackdown against Modernism and the chilling effect it is said to have had on Catholic intellectual life is a good indication that for all intents and purposes all serious dissent vanished from the public eye in the wake of *Pascendi*. Those relatively few Catholics who could not in good conscience accept the teachings of Pius X as they pertained to Modernism simply left the Church.

Of course there were differences of opinion among Catholic thinkers. But as this is a study of the posture of Catholic intellectuals vis-à-vis the Progressive Era rather than a simple chronicling of Catholicism per se, the overwhelming range of agreement among these intellectuals is of far greater importance and significance for our purposes. Pope Leo XIII had summed up the widespread consensus of the Catholic intellectuals of the Progressive Era when he wrote in his encyclical on Americanism: "We, indeed, have no thought of rejecting everything that modern industry and study has produced; so far from it that we welcome to the patrimony of truth and to an ever-widening scope of public well-being whatsoever helps toward the progress of learning and virtue. Yet all this, to be of any solid benefit, nay, to have a real existence and growth, can only be on the condition of recognizing the wisdom and authority of the Church." This was a sentiment with which quite literally all Catholics in public life agreed. They may have differed over this or that application of this more general principle, but the suggestion that ideas and learning taken from the secular world might be selectively appropriated by the Church in order to further its mission was one that all of them shared. This impressive area of agreement extended to the further principle that despite the fact that there existed tremendous pressure within the intellectual milieu of the Progressive Era to abandon dogmatic systems, the need to emphasize the unique and irreplaceable nature of Catholicism seemed to Catholic writers to be greater than ever. These are the main issues that this study will examine and that ultimately resolve into the larger question of the reaction of a decidedly nonpluralistic institution to an increasingly pluralistic intellectual environment.

2 / THE CHALLENGE OF PRAGMATISM

"**T**O-DAY THE APPROACH TO GOD is made difficult in many ways," the weekly Jesuit periodical *America* declared in 1912. "And, sad to say, modern philosophy does its part to obstruct the path that leads to Him."[1] It was a statement with which few Progressive Era Catholics would have disagreed. The subjectivism of modern philosophy, from what they could see, seemed to be causing man to retreat within himself, to cut himself off not only from God but even from objective reality itself.

But before considering the philosophical school known as Pragmatism—the most prominent example of the intellectual trends that Catholics deplored and the school of philosophy that during the Progressive Era they would come to see as their principal intellectual antagonist—it is necessary to recall the state of philosophy within the Catholic Church itself during the late nineteenth and early twentieth centuries, and how the popes sought to respond to what they considered the erroneous philosophies they watched gaining currency.

The year following his election as pope in 1878, Leo XIII issued one of the most important encyclicals of his twenty-five-year pontificate: *Aeterni Patris*, or *On the Restoration of Christian Philosophy*. With this document the pope launched what became known as the neo-Scholastic movement, the systematic promotion of the thought of the medieval schoolmen and in particular that of their most illustrious representative, Saint Thomas Aquinas, the Common Doctor of the Church. The tradition of Scholasticism, having fallen largely into desuetude, was to be revived—not as a museum piece or as a reactionary throwback of a romantic medievalism, but as a living philosophy that would both lend an indispensable support to the Catholic faith and provide an alternative to those systems of modern philosophy that denied man's ability to use his reason to attain metaphysical truth. As one American Catholic expressed it, "To the philosophy of negation and doubt we must oppose the philosophy of affirmation."[2]

American Catholic reaction to the pope's encyclical was favorable, but it was not until the 1920s and beyond that a serious neo-Scholastic move- ment would take root in the United States.[3] Still, by the early twentieth century an enthusiasm had begun to appear for the pope's initiative as a sound and dynamic way to confront modern thought with the kind of sys- tematic reply that, more than any mere polemic, might bring their fellow countrymen to consider the claims of the Catholic Church more seriously. The major Catholic periodicals commended the movement to their read- ers and spoke up in favor of the project, what *America* called "a recovery of our brightest Catholic tradition, a reillumination of the heights whereon the Catholic mind is most congenially at home, an intrepid step forward."[4] The *American Catholic Quarterly Review* praised the "far-sighted policy of Leo XIII," which would "take shape and steer the bark of human wisdom clear from the dangers that beset it"; and *Catholic World*, the monthly journal of the Paulist Fathers, expressed confidence that "the same essential method that secured the successful synthesis of human thought with Christian teaching when science was in its infancy will secure a like success today."[5]

This was the spirit behind *Aeterni Patris*, a document in which the pope explained that much of the reason behind the Scholastic revival he desired, great as its benefits would be to the formation of candidates to the priesthood, revolved around the need to respond to the Church's oppo- nents. For one thing, there were those "who, with minds alienated from the faith, hate Catholic institutions, [and] claim reason as their guide." Apart from God's supernatural help, the pope offered, there could be no surer way of persuading such people of the reasonableness of the Church's position than through the revival of a school that demonstrated with such force the "perfect accord with reason" that the Catholic faith enjoyed. Ultimately the Scholastic revival ought to help the Catholic people themselves to defend their faith effectively. "Since in the tempest that is on us the Christian faith is being constantly assailed by the machinations and craft of a certain false wisdom," Pope Leo warned, "all youths, but especially those who are the growing hope of the Church, should be nour- ished on the strong and robust food of doctrine, that so, mighty in strength and armed at all points, they may become habituated to advance the cause of religion with force and judgment . . . and that they may be able to exhort in sound doctrine and to convince the gainsayers."[6] From the beginning, then, the pope's resuscitation of the study of Aquinas, while tempered with philosophical rigor and scholarly reserve, was infused with a strain of combativeness against a hostile world.

Proponents of neo-Scholasticism repeatedly disclaimed any intention merely to retreat behind a medieval philosophical system as though modern conditions and new knowledge demanded no revision or adaptation of that system.[7] No system, however venerable, was invulnerable to salutary change or susceptible of no improvements or refinements. No one, for example, suggested that anything was to be gained from clinging obstinately to various Scholastic theories of physics where modern investigation had proven the schoolmen's position wrong. Neo-Scholastics would also have to address issues in philosophy far different from those faced by their medieval counterparts. Where, for example, Aquinas had taught the Aristotelian concepts of substance and accident and had applied these ideas to the Catholic theology of the Eucharist, modern philosophy cast a skeptical eye on the very concepts of substance and accident themselves, as well as of causality, of potency and act, and other traditional Scholastic categories. Aquinas's would-be revivalists also had to address themselves to the nearly ceaseless criticism to which for a century the traditional Scholastic proofs of God's existence had been subjected. On a practical level, neo-Scholasticism would also adapt itself to the conditions of the times in the way it was propagated; the compilation of systematic *summae* would give way to "modern forms of presentation" more likely to attract students of the present day.[8]

These adaptations notwithstanding, to its proponents the Scholastic system was the highest expression of the *philosophia perennis*, an edifice of philosophical truth whose core retained its validity and worth independent of the vicissitudes of time and history. Saint Thomas's project, of course, had been to reconcile Aristotle with the Catholic faith and in particular to rescue the man he referred to as "the Philosopher" from what he considered the tendentious interpretations of Muslim thinkers. Yet it was not enough simply to baptize Aristotle; the Scholastics also modified and developed his thought in light of the data of divine revelation.

It is difficult to define Scholasticism further in a way that does it justice, for simply to delineate its stances on the various philosophical controversies that have occupied man since antiquity is to obscure the unity that characterizes it as a comprehensive system. Still, it is perhaps useful at least to point out that Scholastic philosophy, eschewing pantheism, taught a dualism between God and his creation—on the one hand was God, the all-perfect being consisting of pure actuality, and on the other were his creatures, who were composed of actuality and potentiality, matter and form. The human soul, it held, was a spiritual substance whose existence could be proven by man's ability to perform intellectual functions of which mere matter was incapable: self-reflection, the ability to abstract universals from phenomena, and so on. It also taught a dualism of matter and mind, a strict delineation between the subject knowing and the object known—a position that would attract opposition from the critical philosophers of the seventeenth century and beyond. It took something of a middle-of-the-road position—"moderate realism"—on the question of universals, an issue that had occupied so much of the attention of medieval philosophers. Its ethics, like that of Aristotle, was eudaemonistic. Thus a revived Scholasticism, it was thought, was uniquely equipped to respond to the reigning philosophical systems that Catholics believed to be dangerously in error: empiricism, positivism, materialism, and Kantian idealism.

During the Progressive Era, however, American Catholics set their sights in particular on a homegrown philosophical system, namely Pragmatism, that was becoming increasingly influential in intellectual circles. Although not every Progressive was a Pragmatist, Pragmatism was certainly the most discussed and debated philosophical system of the Progressive Era. And in fact, whether or not a given Progressive embraced the specifics of the epistemology of James and Dewey, virtually all of them held certain subsidiary positions that follow directly from that epistemology. It is next to impossible, for example, to find a Progressive who was not profoundly affected by Darwinism and for whom evolution was not further impetus toward the substitution of scientific method for (scholastic) teleology in politics and the social sciences. The whole spirit of Progressive education, with its emphasis on training children in democratic ways of thinking, ran counter to the inculcation in children of knowledge, such as religious dogma, that could not be demonstrated by means of the scientific method. This spirit helps to account for the attitude of the *New Republic*, cited earlier, according to which "freedom and tolerance mean the development of independent powers of judgment in the young, not the freedom of older people to impose their dogmas on the young."[9]

Indeed, Progressives were united in the conviction that if there was one thing that modern social, economic, and philosophical conditions had to reject, it was dogma of any kind. Thus the social-political vision of Albion Small, which included the need to encourage the growth of allegiance to the new centralized state as the very font of democracy and to discourage excessive attachment to other sources of allegiance (by which were meant not merely local governments but also competing belief systems) was very much in line with the Zeitgeist. Part of his aim consisted of merging the Christian denominations into a single, nondogmatic system divorced from the supernatural. Social Gospel theologians, for their part, frankly admitted either that they were revolutionizing Christianity or—what was the same thing—at the very least tearing away the dogmatic Roman encrustations that over the centuries had become attached to the primitive Christian faith. What America needed, they insisted, was a religion adapted to modern needs. Thus Washington Gladden could write that religion in the modern era must be less concerned about "getting men to heaven than about fitting them for their proper work on the earth. . . . For any other kind of religion than this I do not think that the world has any longer very much use."[10] Walter Rauschenbusch held that mankind must reconstruct "its moral and religious synthesis whenever it passes from one era to another. . . . The gospel, to have power over an age, must be the highest expression of the moral and religious truths held by that age."[11] Regardless of where they stood on the murky questions of epistemology that occupied strict philosophical Pragmatists, such sociologists and theologians, with their rejection of dogma and their advocacy of syncretism and ecumenism, betray at least a small-p pragmatism that shares much in common with its more systematic and theoretical counterpart.

Although Charles Sanders Peirce is considered Pragmatism's founder, it was William James whose clear, straightforward writing popularized the new school.[12] The Pragmatists, and John Dewey in particular, tried to instill into philosophy a dynamism, a relevance for everyday life, and a forward-looking posture. Dewey's criticisms of traditional philosophy shared much with those of Francis Bacon, whose own jeremiads had clearly been directed against the Scholastic philosophers. Deploring what he considered the reduction of philosophy to a mere epistemology industry, sterile and divorced from real-life concerns, Dewey called for a "reconstruction in philosophy," as the title of one of his books put it. Dewey was no system-builder, and indeed, he ridiculed the systematic intellectual labors of the Scholastics. "The Scholastic," he once wrote, "was 'abstract'; he was the miser of philosophy; the man who wanted to save truth lest it should get away. The strong box in which he kept his riches was called 'system.'"[13] What was worse, these thinkers considered themselves to be in possession of a perennial philosophy; thus Dewey spoke of "a tendency which I have occasionally observed in some of these writers to assume that the truth is so finally and clearly stated in Scholasticism that most modern European philosophy is a kind of willful and perverse aberration."[14] Dewey and the Pragmatists were heir to a distinct if minority tradition within Western philosophy that spurned what it considered to be the fruitless search for pure metaphysical truth in favor of a more practical, action-oriented approach to philosophical thought. Thus, although James was not himself much of a political activist,[15] it is no coincidence that philosophical Pragmatism became generally associated with political reform.

Pragmatism, according to William James, "is a temper of mind, an attitude; it is also a theory of the nature of ideas and truth; and finally, it is a theory about reality." The Pragmatic "attitude," as it were, was one of "looking away from first things, principles, categories, supposed necessities; and of looking towards last things, fruits, consequences, facts."[16] Indeed, the Pragmatist "turns his back resolutely and once for all upon a lot of inveterate habits dear to professional philosophers." And in James's catalogue of these "inveterate habits," many Catholics doubtless thought they could see, perhaps in somewhat caricatured form, the outlook of Scholastic philosophy itself. The Pragmatist, James wrote, "turns away from abstraction and insufficiency, from verbal solutions, from bad *a priori* reasons, from fixed principles, closed systems, and pretended absolutes and origins." He was blunt in admitting that Pragmatism synthesized "anti-intellectualist tendencies" in philosophy and scoffed at the "pretension" of rationalism. Thus Pragmatists scorned the very idea of eternal or absolute truth and made no pretensions to possessing epistemological certitude. In place of these Dewey offered a more modest "warranted assertability," by which a statement could be held to be true were it efficacious. James agreed, arguing that with metaphysical certainty beyond the reach of the human mind, inherently insoluble philosophical arguments ought to be resolved on the basis of their practical consequences here and now:

> There can be no difference anywhere that doesn't make a difference elsewhere—no difference in abstract truth that doesn't express itself in a difference in concrete fact and in conduct consequent upon that fact, imposed on somebody, somehow, somewhere, and somewhen. The whole function of philosophy ought to be to find out what definite difference it will make to you and me, at definite instants of our life, if this world-formula or that world-formula be the true one.[17]

Thus James could say that Pragmatism "has no dogmas, and no doctrines save its method."[18]

The unfortunate and provocatively crude terminology that James often used to expound his philosophy seemed almost calculated to lead to confusion among his readers; thus in an expression that particularly irritated John Dewey, James spoke of the "cash value" of an idea as the determination of its truth. By cash value, of course, James did not intend to imply a straightforward utilitarianism as the criterion of truth.[19] The truth or "cash value" of an idea rested not so much in its direct practical results in the world of action—although true ideas were likely to have this effect—but in the subjective realm of the human consciousness, where it helped individuals to cope with anomalous experiences, thereby removing a source of confusion or disquiet. Pragmatists were manifestly *not* claiming that truth could be reckoned as whatever happened to be convenient for someone to believe. For one thing, for a proposition to be considered "true" according to the criteria of Pragmatism, it must be in agreement with the accumulated corpus of experience that the individual already possesses. It must also conform to what we know from experience about the natural world. Having met both of these requirements, which James believed ruled out the merely hoped-for qualifying as true under the Pragmatic schema, only then could a proposition be considered deserving of assent.[20]

Just as truth and values were thought to be in perpetual flux, external reality itself was not something fixed, simply to be grasped by the human mind. The medieval view that the human mind directly apprehended an antecedently existing reality external to itself gave way to a more dynamic view, in which the mind took part in the very creation of the reality it was apprehending.[21] "I, for my part," said William James, "cannot escape the consideration, forced upon me at every turn, that the knower is not simply a mirror floating with no foot-hold anywhere, and passively reflecting an order that he comes upon and finds simply existing. The knower is an actor, and co-efficient of the truth on one side, whilst on the other he registers the truth which he helps to create."[22] In an oft-quoted passage, John Dewey explained how the human mind came into possession of the idea of a rose:

> A sweet odor of a certain specific kind enters into my consciousness. I think immediately of a rose. That is, there comes to my mind the idea of a rose. This idea becomes forthwith a plan of action. It leads me to walk towards the source of the odor, to look at the object from which the odor emanates, to handle it, to examine it closely, until I have finally reached satisfaction in the conclusion that the object is a rose. The idea has removed the mental strain, it has put an end to inquiry, it has satisfied; only in that sense is it true.

Thus was the so-called correspondence theory of truth and knowledge set aside in favor of a dynamic discovery process by which "mental strain" was alleviated and problematic situations presented to the mind satisfactorily resolved. Indeed, even such apparently impregnable intellectual fortresses as logic and mathematics, Dewey argued, were not exempt from this ongoing reappraisal from the point of view of human utility; and it was not inconceivable that a day could come when our traditional understandings even of such architectonic fields could be changed, even radically.

It hardly needs pointing out that Pragmatism represented a direct challenge to the Catholic worldview. Its rejection of the aims and methods of traditional philosophy could win little sympathy from thinkers whose Church had built upon and sought to perfect that impressive compendium of thought bequeathed to the West by Plato and especially Aristotle—a tradition for which action per se was not the principal motivating factor. Beyond this, the Thomistic and indeed the traditional Christian position had held that God had created an orderly and intelligible universe whose structure the human mind could apprehend by abstracting universal forms and essences from the phenomenal world. Pragmatists considered such a claim to be a hubristic exaggeration of what reason could accomplish in the realm of metaphysics, thereby both implicitly denying the order that Christians had traditionally used as evidence of the existence of God (as in the argument from design) and circumscribing the boundaries of the intellect—a divine seed implanted in man, said the Scholastics—in its search for truth. Finally, the "pluralistic universe" to which James's and Dewey's emphasis on the priority of experience led seemed to throw moral philosophy into chaos and to contribute to the same kind of moral and intellectual confusion and disorder that had resulted decades before upon the introduction of evolutionary thought into philosophy. In a sense, they were extending the epistemological apparatus of science to all realms of knowledge. Science dealt in hypotheses, and a hypothesis was thought to be worthy of belief if it could account for the relevant data better than any competing model. But there was nothing abiding and final about such hypotheses, which in fact evolve and change with some frequency. New experiences, as it were, can throw a previously reigning scientific paradigm into disarray and call a new one into existence, one that possesses no more claim to represent absolute and final truth than the first one, but one that better accounts for the data. This was the model that the Pragmatists wished to apply not simply to the arena of scientific hypotheses but to all human knowledge. Claims of absolute truth and finality, they claimed, neglected the experiential aspect of truth, whereby what is accepted as true evolves with time and with new experiences.

Pragmatism, clearly, is a philosophy whose teachings are easy to caricature; some would say that James's own terminology invited such misunderstandings. Yet it is difficult to convict the overwhelming majority of Catholic philosophers during the Progressive Era of having distorted the teachings of their antagonists or of having taken aim only at straw men. Some Catholic observers were especially harsh in their condemnation of this new approach; thus Father Richard Tierney wrote of Pragmatism in America that its thought "is insurgent, revolutionary, anarchic," and that its principles "are logically destructive of all that is noble in action."[23] In general, Catholics were scholarly and fair in their engagement with Pragmatism and did not carelessly dismiss it as simple relativism and nothing more. They viewed it as an unsound basis for knowledge and in fact rather dangerous to the Catholic religion, inasmuch as the most it could say on behalf of religion was an endorsement of a nonspecific spirituality rather than of the dogmatic system of Catholicism.

Of course, Pragmatism was a controversial philosophical posture even among secular thinkers, and an impressive number of books and articles were written at the height of its fortunes regarding its validity or otherwise. But since by far the greater part of the Catholic objection to Pragmatism followed from distinctly Catholic concerns, it is important to acknowledge the uniqueness of the Catholic position and not to conflate this position with that of more general attacks on Pragmatism.

Catholics at the time were reluctant to view any deplorable trend, in philosophy or otherwise, as simply sui generis; instead they searched for the sources of the perceived evil, going back in time as far as necessary to pinpoint its ultimate origin. One potential source of Pragmatist thought, explained the American Catholic philosopher William Turner, derived from a relatively recent intellectual trend: an erroneous extrapolation into philosophy of conclusions reached by the methods of the natural sciences. Thus with the rise of the theory of evolution, scientists began to reach the conclusion that a hypothesis, as long as it accounted for the phenomena it was intended to explain, was as good as a certainly true or verifiable law. If the evolutionary hypothesis served to explain the natural world and the available data on plant and animal life, or if a hypothetical medium called ether served to explain phenomena related to light and heat, it was not necessary, strictly speaking, to inquire into the absolute truth of the theory of evolution or the existence of ether. These hypotheses served their purpose, and this was sufficient. Explained Turner: "A principle or postulate or attitude of mind that would bring about an adjustment would satisfy the mind for the time being, and would, therefore, solve the problem. This satisfaction came, consequently, to be considered a test of truth."[24]

Other philosophical antecedents of Pragmatism, according to Catholic thinkers, were much less benign, and the degeneration of philosophy that they believed they were witnessing was the logical outcome of trends that originated in at least the sixteenth century. This "tissue of semi-hysterical absurdities," as Father Tierney called Pragmatism, far from originating overnight, was the culmination of a progression of religious and philosophical errors.[25]

In a comprehensive series of articles that appeared in *Catholic World*, the monthly journal of the Paulist Fathers, Father Edmund Shanahan proposed to trace modern Pragmatism all the way back to the Protestant Reformation. Appropriately titled "Completing the Reformation," the series began with a discussion of the philosophical ramifications of the theology of Martin Luther.[26] From there Shanahan traced his argument to its startling conclusion: "The attempt now being made to deprive human knowledge of all rational foundation and character is but the continuation and completion of the movement set on foot by the Reformers to derationalize Christian faith."[27]

According to Shanahan, the Protestant reformers had, wittingly or not, set in motion what he called "the modern anti-intellectualist movement" by transforming faith from a matter of knowing to a matter of trusting—in Scholastic terms, they removed faith from the realm of the intellect and placed it entirely within the scope of the will. The Catholic understanding of faith—indeed, the definition that appeared in the popular Baltimore Catechism, approved by the nineteenth-century Third Plenary Council of Baltimore—was that it was "the virtue by which we firmly believe all the truths God has revealed, on the word of God revealing them, who can neither deceive nor be deceived." The reformers, Shanahan explained, misinterpreted the Church's position as being simply one of cold logic, whereby faith was reduced to the assent of the intellect to a series of formalistic syllogisms marching triumphantly to their conclusions. In fact, the Church was arguing simply that faith was *reasonable*, in that the intellect perceived that the authority proposing matter for belief was itself credible and trustworthy. Faith was "a total and complete act of self-surrender, if by [this] you understand an intellectual, truly human act, and not the mere promptings of unenlightened sentiment. There is light in it, as well as confidence and love." There was no artificial division made between the intellect and the will; in the act of faith they worked in concert.[28]

In Shanahan's view, an exaggerated and erroneous conception of original sin led Luther to adopt an extremely pessimistic view of the power of human reason—an error that would have consequences for philosophy. In the reformer's eagerness to attribute the entire process of justification and salvation to the activity and initiative of Christ and to denigrate the very notion of human cooperation with divine grace, Luther tended to portray the mind as "essentially passive and inert, capable rather of being acted upon than of acting." Shanahan did not enter into great detail in defense of the Catholic position on grace and justification, contenting himself with the observation that God's very decision to endow man, the summit of his creation, with intellectual faculties, was a good indication that mere passivity in reaching one's salvation was unlikely to have been the divine plan. The point he was trying to make was that God had granted reason to man as an active faculty, which could and should be used to attain real knowledge about the world and about his Creator.[29]

Immanuel Kant began the process by which in Shanahan's view the Reformation was ultimately consummated, whereby philosophy itself was to be shackled with the limitations of Lutheran theology. What, after all, had Kant been aiming at? Kant was sympathetic to pietism, a movement within Protestantism that emphasized individual spirituality and gave feeling priority over intellect. Moreover, while far from being an orthodox Christian, he was appalled at the rising tide of outright unbelief. Thus his goal was "to make both science and religion the results of *immediate sensible experience*, so as to cut the *supersensible*, or faith, entirely off from all continuity and connection with *scientific truth*; so as, in other words, to create for religion—in this case, pietism—a sort of charmed circle, within which it might enjoy a haven of refuge and a right of asylum from the persecuting attacks of the skeptics for all time to come."[30]

"Once safely intrenched behind the moral conscience and its mandatory ideals," Shanahan went on, "Kant set about transferring to philosophy the entire pietistic background and scheme of religion—its preference for the subject over the object, its dislike of externals, its distrust of reason, its autonomous individualism, its insistence of the primacy of the will and moral sentiment."[31] Indeed, having undermined the mind's ability to know the so-called thing-in-itself, Kant had left nothing on which to base religious conviction except subjective experience and the sheer exercise of the will. With the mind permanently and by nature turned in on itself, it was within oneself that one would have to look to justify religious belief.[32]

This increasingly radical trend toward religious subjectivism understandably alarmed Catholics. The Catholic Church had traditionally held that the existence of God could be proved by reason, a position that became the subject of explicit dogmatic definition at the First Vatican Council of 1869–1870.[33] Saint Thomas Aquinas's famous "five ways" of proving God's existence had relied on universal ideas. Thus God's existence followed, in one of the saint's proofs, from the principle of causality: everything that comes into being must have a cause, and a regression back through these causes must lead to an uncaused cause, or God. Another of Aquinas's proofs was an argument from contingency. The world is composed of contingent beings, that is, of things that owe their existence to another. Existence is not part of their essence; it is possible to imagine them as not existing. It is logically impossible, however, to account for the world we see around us if we admit the existence of *only* contingent beings, for if every object depended on another for its existence, nothing could ever have begun to exist. Hence the need for a being, God, for whom existence belonged to his essence, a self-sufficient entity whose nonexistence was impossible, on whom all subsequent and contingent creation depended. Kant's epistemology completely disrupted the method behind these proofs. For Kant, such ideas as causality and contingency were not actual relationships corresponding to extramental reality but mere categories that the mind imposed on the outside world to bring order to the data it perceived. If these categories in fact originated in the mind, they could no longer serve to prove the existence of God. For indeed how could causality be used to prove God's existence if causality itself were merely part of the mind's a priori apparatus whereby it made sense of phenomena, and not an actually existing relation between bodies in the phenomenal world?

Thus Kant inaugurated what he called a Copernican revolution in philosophy. Descartes, it is true, had given this trend a certain impetus by his use of methodical doubt, which made a tabula rasa of all inherited knowledge possessed by the human race that did not seem to him "clear and distinct," as he defined those terms. It was Luther and Kant, however, who in Shanahan's opinion had laid the groundwork for the retreat into a destructive individualism by their dismantling of man's mental apparatus by means of an artificial and impenetrable division between man's powers of sense and his powers of intellection. All man could really know were his subjective states. "The reality of the external world, its knowableness, the existence of God, the rational principles of morality—which are all common convictions and evidential data—went by the board."[34] William James, he wrote, took Luther and Kant equally to task "for having clung to some shreds of the ancient metaphysics, instead of throwing the whole cargo overboard, and admitting outright that religion was irrational from top to bottom, and the whole universe along with it, for that matter."[35] Thus Shanahan could say that "Luther, Kant, and James shake hands across the years."[36] It was not a lineage to which James would have wished to disclaim allegiance, for he himself had described Pragmatism as "philosophic Protestantism." Shanahan confined his commentary on this statement by James to noting simply that some anti-intellectualists were more frank than others in admitting that the aim they had in mind was to "complete the Reformation," as he put it, by turning the "wheel of negation" all the way around rather than resting content with the half-measures of the Protestant reformers.[37] To James the idea of "philosophic Protestantism" no doubt expressed the intellectual excitement and indeed the revolutionary nature of his philosophy; to Progressive Era Catholics, on the other hand, it was a terrible indictment of the Harvard philosopher's entire intellectual enterprise.

Just as Luther's religious errors had had consequences for philosophy, Catholic philosophers observed, James's philosophical errors would have consequences for religion. By the turn of the century new ideas of God were beginning to conceive of him as immanent in humanity; there was a sense that the new democratic age had no room for the distant, self-sufficient God of the theologians.[38] The Pragmatist view built on these trends. In his influential *Varieties of Religious Experience* (1902), James defined religion as "the feelings, acts and experiences of individual men in their solitude, so far as they apprehend themselves to stand in relation to whatever they may consider the divine." His idea of the divine was notably flexible. "We must interpret the term 'divine' very broadly, as denoting the object that is god-*like* whether it be a concrete deity or not."[39] So far James appears not to be excluding the standard theistic view but simply extending the scope of what constitutes religion and the divine. But he clearly departs from traditional Christian thought in his contention that God "has an environment, is in time, and works out a history, like ourselves. Thus, He escapes from the foreignness, the timelessness, the remoteness which theists ascribe to Him."[40] As William Turner explained, "Naturally, being a pluralist, the pragmatist will not admit that God is an all-including infinite reality, in the pantheistic sense. He will not bow to the theistic idea of a God Who made the universe for us." Therefore, Turner argued, the Pragmatist advances his own kind of pantheism, "according to which the universe is not part of God, but God a part of the universe."[41]

Since James insisted throughout his philosophical writings on the priority of experience in establishing a truth, it is not surprising that in his religious work he was unsympathetic to dogma. Dogmas, he explained, were simply "the buildings-out performed by the intellect into which feeling originally supplied the limit."[42] The origin of belief lay in what James called religious experience, which in turn has often led in practice to the emergence of dogma, but it need not and probably should not do so. Religious experience was an intensely personal and subjective phenomenon, not subject to anything so prosaic as empirical verification or Scholastic disputation.[43] The *Catholic Encyclopedia* explained the Catholic objection to this perspective: "If therefore you go as far as making the Divinity a belief, that is to say, a symbolical expression of faith, then docility in following generous impulses may be religious, and the atheist's religion would not seem to differ essentially from yours."[44]

These are harsh words. Certainly it is possible to imagine a scenario in which James's thought, carefully sifted, and his emphasis on religious experience, might have been embraced as a propaedeutic to faith in the Catholic sense, serving a function rather like that of Pascal's wager (which, incidentally, James rejected),[45] which was itself an attempt to justify belief rather than to prove that God in fact existed. A number of his arguments were, in themselves, acceptable from a Catholic perspective, such as his indignant dismissal of the claim that agnostics and unbelievers had some claim to deem themselves more "scientific" than their believing peers. Likewise, the existence in history of countless cases of apparently genuine religious experience (Saint Teresa of Avila was one of James's examples), while clearly not in itself a conclusive proof of the Catholic religion, might well stir a potential convert to enter the Church. And in fact, as we shall see, during the Progressive Era Catholics in other disciplines did not hesitate to make use of and to build upon the findings of their secular counterparts, always being careful to excise whatever aspects of modern thought and method may have been in conflict with the Catholic faith. Grace builds on nature, as the theologians put it, so the Catholic outlook has generally been that what is good in the natural order, whatever its source, can be fruitful for supernatural purposes as well. Of course, Catholic attacks on the naturalism of John Dewey, whose outlook obviously constituted a thoroughgoing rejection of Christian supernaturalism, can hardly be unexpected. But although Catholics may very well have had to reject much of William James's philosophy, that even James's arguments on behalf of religion should have been the objects of such scorn demands further explanation.

It should be recalled at the outset that what James was doing and what orthodox Catholic theologians were attempting to do at the turn of the century were not the same thing. James's work on religion attempted to justify belief in God with the evidence inconclusive. He was not attempting to prove God's existence. He was attempting to justify religious belief itself before an intellectual community, including his fellow Pragmatists, that was generally skeptical. Catholics, on the other hand, particularly in response to the Modernist crisis (on which more below) that afflicted the Church at the turn of the century, but more generally in reaction to the Kantian and post-Kantian rejection of the traditional metaphysical proofs for God's existence, were anxious to demonstrate the solidly rational basis on which their belief rested. Theirs was the task of demonstrating that the existence of God could be known with absolute certainty. An apologetic that rested on some foundation other than the purely rational, that entertained the possibility that the question of God lay beyond the province of reason entirely, was likely to be considered distinctly unhelpful in light of the task that Catholics had set for themselves during this period—namely, the rehabilitation of human reason as a bulwark of religious truth.

Catholic philosophers responded with such vigor to the claims of Pragmatism in part, no doubt, because they had seen the fruits of a similar line of thinking within their own Church during the Modernist controversy. Modernism was the source of tremendous confusion and tumult within the Catholic Church during the early twentieth century, until an especially severe 1907 papal condemnation—"the synthesis of all heresies," the pope called it—not only deprived the movement of respectability but also removed it entirely from visible Catholic discourse. The Modernists, since they shared the same Kantian presuppositions about the structure of the mind and the limitations of speculative reason that had so influenced the Pragmatists, possessed a strikingly similar perspective on the meaning of religious truth. As did his philosophical precursors, the Modernist, "like the voluntarist and pragmatist that he is, substitutes for pure reason the vital process by which the truth is, as he says, emotionally or sentimentally realized." Like the Pragmatist, moreover, the Modernist taught "the essentially fluid nature of all truth, dogmatic as well as natural." Revelation, to a Modernist, was not a manifestation of God's truth but merely an interpretation of widely shared religious sentiment. Dogma's true value consisted in "its capacity to satisfy a certain momentary need of the religious feeling." To the Modernist, no religious dogma could be considered absolute and unchanging since it was merely an intellectual expression of believers' preexisting religious sentiments—precisely James's position—and these sentiments, like everything else in the universe, were part of the ceaseless flux of evolutionary change that characterized the physical world. Dogmas were not absolutely true statements of belief presented for the assent of the faithful by an infallible teaching authority; they were merely the inchoate expression of an ineffable religious "sentiment" to be found within all men. George Tyrrell, one of the best-known Modernists, wrote: "Revelation is a supernaturally imparted experience of realities, an experience that utters itself spontaneously in imaginative popular non-scientific form; theology is the natural, tentative, fallible analysis of that experience."[46] From the idea of dogmatic truth as "realizing itself in the consciousness of the faithful" and thereby giving rise to the Church's Magisterium—a teaching authority thus now seen to come not from God but from the people—followed the idea that no particular religion could claim the kind of universality that Catholicism had claimed for itself. Thus came "the doctrine that Christianity is merely a step forward in the natural process of the evolution of religions."[47] It becomes impossible for the Modernist to imagine religious reconciliation as consisting of anything but a shared spiritual journey in which the religious sentiment common to the human race comes to its full realization in some new dispensation that is the exclusive possession of no single group.

Such an outlook naturally tended to undermine the foundations of the Catholic Church, which claimed to be not merely a repository of symbols and practices flowing spontaneously from an amorphous and ill-defined "religious instinct," or merely one stage in an evolutionary convergence of all religions, but the divinely instituted guardian of a fixed doctrine entrusted to her by Jesus Christ. Furthermore, if it were established that a dogma depended for its truth on its ability to nourish and sustain religious sentiment, anti-Modernists pointed out, then it would simply be cast aside as soon as it no longer continued to do so. Hence Pope Saint Pius X, in the oath against Modernism that he imposed on "all clergy, pastors, confessors, preachers, religious superiors and professors in philosophical-theological seminaries," demanded assent to the proposition that faith "is not a blind sentiment of religion welling up from the depths of the subconscious under the impulse of the heart and the motion of a will trained to morality."[48] The excessive subjectivism of the Modernists, the pope feared, would lead to an individualistic spirituality that would render the Church superfluous to the believer. Its tendency toward a nonspecific spirituality in place of the concrete, revealed dogmas of the Catholic Church especially troubled the pope in light of global trends he saw beginning to emerge. At work in the world, he warned the bishops, was "a great movement of apostasy being organized in every country for the establishment of a one-world Church which shall have neither dogmas nor hierarchy; neither discipline for the mind nor curb for the passions."[49] More than ever, then, it was incumbent upon Catholics to place due emphasis on the *objective* nature of religious belief and to recognize the role of the Church as the divine guardian and repository of the specific doctrines entrusted to her by her Lord.

On the occasion of Pius X's death in 1914, the *American Catholic Quarterly Review* published a very lengthy tribute to the late pontiff. The essay, written by one Daniel Dever, covered the whole range of the pope's accomplishments but devoted twenty full pages to the campaign against Modernism.[50] Revealingly, though, much of this discussion was in fact a polemical investigation of the link between Pragmatism and Modernism. It was not simply an abstruse theological error that Pius had condemned, the *Review* explained; the pope had hit upon something far broader in scope. To understand Modernism, then, one must also understand its primary intellectual antecedent, for indeed "all history shows" that "philosophical errors have ever preceded aberrations in faith."[51] "Restricted thus to appearances and to sense, it is not wonderful that both Pragmatism and Modernism should have a cognate list of knowable and unknowable things; and, as a matter of fact, both remand God, first of all, and then all spiritual things, to the dark void of an unknown that lies wholly beyond our view."[52]

The two schools of thought also share the acknowledgment that religion exists in fact and the corresponding need to account for such a phenomenon.

No exterior explanation being possible, they seek this explanation in man himself; and, since religion is a form of life, they seek it in the life of man. . . . But since, further, and still in the Modernistic sense, every effect must have a cause, the Modernists ask themselves why this fact of religion appears at all, and they answer that it is due to a "need" in man for religion; and then when they ask whence this need, they place their last foundation in subconsciousness, as occasionally revealed by the activity of a non-cognitive, material organ in a movement of the heart.

Modernists are forced into this position, he argues, because "like Pragmatism, they have explicitly and professedly turned away from all 'intellectualism' as from something intolerably useless and absurd."[53]

Furthermore, according to Dever, both systems aver that "whatever is not in man himself or in the visible world around him must remain forever unknown, even granting that anything outside of these could exist."[54] William James himself had said, "The essential contrast is that *for rationalism reality is ready-made and complete from all eternity, while for Pragmatism it is still in the making, and awaits part of its complexion from the future.*"[55]

These words from James assume their full import, Dever explains, only when we understand them to mean, as James himself intended them to mean, that God and religion are themselves only "in the making." To a Pragmatist "God and all that pertains to Him are only a partial phenomenon in the unfolding of man's creative activity." At this stage Dever goes on to catalogue some of the remarks from James's *Pragmatism* that would seem most offensive to a Catholic audience.[56] Thus James: "Pragmatism has to postpone dogmatic answer, for we do not yet know certainly which type of religion is going to work best in the long run."[57] Again: "She [Pragmatism] will take a God who lives in the very dirt of private fact—if that should seem a likely place to find him."[58]

The *Catholic World* also, in mourning the death of Pius X, pointed with evident satisfaction to the vigorous, uncompromising posture that the late pontiff had assumed vis-à-vis the Modernists. "A foremost characteristic of our times has been religious unrest," the *World* began, "the advance of intellectual and scientific endeavor in certain fields, notably in history, in comparative religion, and criticism, and the putting forth of new philosophies, and ever-new forms of undogmatic religion." It pointed out that Pope Pius X reprobated this particular foe of traditional Catholicism for, among other things, "the degradation of faith to the region of sentiment." After cataloguing a considerable list of the Vatican's specific censures and disciplinary measures against Modernism, including the anti-Modernist oath imposed in 1910—"almost unprecedented," said the *World*—the section closed with the matter-of-fact conclusion that "the faith, the future training of priests and people were in jeopardy, and the Pope knew that half-measures would not answer the requirements of such a crisis."[59]

Historians of Modernism have been all but unanimous in decrying the severity of the anti-Modernist crackdown. In some cases, antipathy toward the Vatican's position and sympathy for the Modernists have yielded scholarship long on moral outrage and short on scholarly detachment. That modern scholars find the anti-Modernist campaign distasteful is neither surprising nor especially interesting. To decide simply that Rome's program was "repressive" is about as useful from a historical standpoint as the conclusion that the medieval Inquisition was "intolerant." Much more important, and indeed more difficult, is to take the trouble to discover, without cliché or polemic, precisely *why* the Vatican acted as it did and what it saw as peculiarly threatening about the Modernist advance—and, of more relevance to the present study, why American Catholic intellectuals greeted the vigorous papal campaign with such enthusiastic support.

An obviously central preliminary question is the extent to which Modernism had taken root in the United States at the time of the condemnation. Theodore Maynard wrote in *The Story of American Catholicism* that "there were no Modernists in America, at any rate none of any prominence. No Father Tyrrell was excommunicated here. Nor was there even any Baron von Hügel or Wilfrid Ward. . . . The condemnation issued in 1907 fortunately did not apply to American conditions."[60] Although Modernism was certainly not as well developed or nearly as widespread in the United States as it was in parts of Europe, it is no longer possible to render quite so sweeping a judgment. It is true that one needed to look to Europe rather than the United States in order to find Modernists of prominence and distinction, but the absence of theological celebrity cannot minimize the extent to which American sympathizers with the movement, although very much a minority within the American Church, were taking public stands on an array of theological and philosophical matters. In his authoritative study of American Modernism, Scott Appleby described Modernism in the United States as having been "inchoate," consisting of a relatively small number of thinkers within a variety of disciplines exploring new approaches to theology, philosophy, biblical criticism, and the like.[61] It was rarer in the United States than in Europe for priests with such sympathies to have worked out all the implications of this new thought. "The professors at Catholic University who contributed many of these articles," according to Appleby, "did not recognize the heretical implications of these ideas" in the same way that priests like William L. Sullivan and John R. Slattery did (both of whom, in sharp contrast to their colleagues, left the Church altogether when it became clear that Rome would brook no dissent on matters pertaining to Modernism). When the condemnation came down from Rome, all but a very few scholars immediately desisted from such activity. The same William Turner cited in this chapter, for example, wrote in the *New York Review*—the chief American Catholic periodical in which modernistic ideas appeared—in 1906 that certain aspects of Kantian philosophy could bear real fruit within Catholic theology. Two years later, following the condemnation, Turner declared Kantianism to be little more than "philosophical agnosticism" and cautioned his readers against the incipient tendency to hold scholasticism in low regard.[62] The board of trustees at Catholic University set up a committee "empowered to make a survey of modernistic books in the library of the University and to make recommendations on the matter."[63] Modernism there was, at least in embryonic form, in the United States, but it was forced underground by the vigorous and systematic campaign launched against it from Rome.

Neither *Pascendi* nor the campaign against Modernism in general intended to suggest that there was no room in the Catholic understanding for "religious experience" as James described it. In his study of Modernism, Gabriel Daly makes the rather exaggerated claim that one of the principal consequences for the Catholic religion of the condemnation of Modernism was "the total outlawing of experience as a factor in religion, theology, and spirituality."[64] Scholasticism indeed recognized a category of knowledge that corresponded to the religious experience of James and the Pragmatists—*cognitio confusa*, or confused knowledge.[65] Then, of course, there was the example of the mystics, who placed an especially strong emphasis on inner experience. But what the mystics did not do, according to Father Shanahan, was to divorce faith from knowledge. "They admitted *external and objective* criteria by which to test the truth of their experiences," he said. "They submitted their private feelings to the judgment of the public Church. They went down into experience *with* conviction, not *for* it—the exact reverse of what they should have done to become the ancestors of the modern liberals."[66] Thus what the Catholic approach had never done, despite its acknowledgment of a subjective element in religion, was to exalt the direct experiential aspect of faith to such a degree as to denigrate or even discount altogether the role of the intellect and of objective standards. James's approach to religion, on the other hand, by removing the intellectual dimension from faith, threatened a radical subjectivism in which arguments, evidence, religious dogmas, and the like would possess no independent validity in and of themselves, but only if ratified by the necessarily subjective testimony of the individual's own experience. In his *Syllabus of Errors* (1864) Pius IX had condemned the proposition that "every man is free to embrace and profess that religion which, guided by the light of reason, he shall have come to consider as true."[67] What James with his Pragmatist conception of religion was proposing was even worse than the kind of relativism and subjectivism the pope had there condemned; for James did not encourage people at least to look to the "light of reason" in their quest for spiritual satisfaction—an approach that he in fact condemned repeatedly—but rather he directed them to experience, which by its very nature had to be purely subjective. Having recently endured the Modernist crisis and seen its baneful consequences for Catholic philosophy and theology, Catholics were thus acutely sensitive to what they considered the destructive potential of James's approach to spirituality. If philosophical Pragmatism had no dog-

mas save its method, as James had said, then the Pragmatist view of religion had no dogmas save what an individual would find to comport well
with his private needs and personal temperament.

As one might expect, James also rejected the traditional proofs for the
existence of God, partly because he doubted the mind's ability to reach
such conclusions (he believed that Kant's arguments against the proofs
had settled the matter) and partly because he found such a posteriori arguments for God stilted and distasteful. The proofs had fallen into disrepute,
he said, because "our generation has ceased to believe in a kind of God
that must be argued for."[68] For James and Pragmatism itself, not surprisingly, the question of religion ultimately came down to personal utility,
how a given faith system or religious tradition succeeded in accommodating and satisfying the individual's temperament and outlook. Thus James
could write, in *Pragmatism*:

> You see that pragmatism can be called religious, if you allow that reli-
> gion can be pluralistic or merely melioristic in type. But whether you
> will finally put up with that type of religion or not is a question that
> only you yourself can decide. Pragmatism has to postpone dogmatic
> answer, for we do not yet know certainly which type of religion is
> going to work best in the long run. The various overbeliefs of men,
> their several faith-ventures, are in fact what are needed to bring the
> evidence in. You will probably make your own ventures severally. If
> radically tough, the hurly-burly of the sensible facts of nature will be
> enough for you, and you will need no religion at all. If radically ten-
> der, you will take up with the more monistic form of religion: the plu-
> ralistic form, with its reliance on possibilities that are not necessities,
> will not seem to afford you security enough.[69]

Indeed, the very question regarding whether one should believe in the-
ism on the one hand or a strict materialism on the other was the subject
of a famous illustration in James's book. How, James proposed, may the
theism-materialism debate be settled? From the Pragmatic point of view,
of course, strictly metaphysical questions can be meaningful only if holding one or the other position bears some practical consequence in the real
world. And in James's view the issue at hand was indeed "intensely practical," as far as the world's future was concerned. If the question were
merely the academic one of accounting for the world as it had come to
exist in the past and developed into the form we see today, it, according
to James, would indeed represent the kind of fruitless metaphysical spec-

ulation that Pragmatists rejected. Whether divine intervention or the mechanistic operation of atoms had produced the world we see would be of no real consequence; and as Herbert Spencer suggests, the debate might best be settled by attributing an unknowable, quasi-divine power to matter itself, thereby avoiding either extreme. And, said James, "if philosophy were purely retrospective, he [Spencer] would thereby proclaim himself an excellent pragmatist."[70]

But philosophy is not simply retrospective; it is prospective. The world existed in the past and present, and it will also exist in the future. The further question must therefore be, "What does the world *promise?*" And if the materialistic hypothesis could produce a plausible scenario whereby its principles, if true, would ensure continuing human progress, it would have to be seriously entertained. "Give us a matter that promises *success,*" James proposed, "that is bound by its laws to lead our world ever nearer to perfection, and any rational man will worship that matter as readily as Mr. Spencer worships his own so-called unknowable power. . . . Doing practically all that a God can do, it is equivalent to God, its function is a God's function, and in a world in which a God would be superfluous; from such a world God could never lawfully be missed." Yet any such confidence in the promises of a purely materialistic world was misplaced, James argued. The sun would one day dim, and all human achievement, all the labor and toil of the centuries, would have been for naught. Thus materialism must fail the Pragmatic test, for it "is not a permanent warrant for our more ideal interests, nor a fulfiller of our remotest hopes."[71]

The so-called God hypothesis, on the other hand, possessed the virtue of guaranteeing the eternal existence of some kind of moral order. The need for such an order had roots deep within the human breast. The issue ultimately resolved itself in the fact that "spiritualistic faith in all its forms deals with a world of promise, while materialism's sun sets in a sea of disappointment."[72] Thus since James, an admitted "anti-intellectualist," denied the ability of human reason to attain metaphysical truth absolutely, he had to reduce the issues of God and religious belief to a calculus based on the relative hopefulness that one or the other position engendered.

What James was manifestly not saying was that mere wishful thinking could somehow effect God's existence; nor was he advocating belief in a pleasant fantasy. James did genuinely believe in God.[73] What the issue ultimately amounted to for him was the question of whether, in the absence of overwhelming evidence in the strict sense, belief in God could nevertheless be justified. James rejected the suggestion, advanced by a

number of philosophers, that since in their minds (and in his) the existence of God could never be proven conclusively, the withholding of
belief was absolutely incumbent upon the thinking man. Thus the British
mathematician W. C. Clifford had argued that it was actually *immoral* ever
to believe anything in the absence of conclusive proof, and that it would
be preferable to hold one's mind in a state of suspense forever than to run
the risk of believing something that was untrue. James spotted in this
argument the unwarranted invocation of Clifford's own value judgments:
"He who says, 'better go without belief forever than believe a lie,'" James
wrote, "merely shows his own preponderant private horror of becoming a
dupe."[74] James held that there could be no a priori presumption in favor of
either of these positions and that Clifford's own hesitation in the face of
an insoluble question could in no way bind those more daring souls who
were prepared to take intellectual risks in their search for the truth.[75]

To James, the decision to make the assent of faith rested ultimately on
a series of converging probabilities. In *Varieties of Religious Experience*
James explored further the question of religious belief and its justification.
In this case, he surveyed a considerable array of testimonies by people from
a wide variety of religious backgrounds who could discuss religious experience from a first-person point of view. One of the most careful modern
scholars of James describes his approach thus:

> It would be a complete misunderstanding of James' pragmatic view of
> religion to say that James merely chose a comforting doctrine as an
> alternative to skepticism. Instead, he gathered together all the evi-
> dence available from the literature of religious experience. With the
> logical skills honed by continual debates with his father and with
> logicians such as Chauncey Wright, Charles Sanders Peirce, and
> Josiah Royce, he formed his reconciling hypothesis. This was the
> great effort of his life. He pioneered a science of religions in which
> the evidence was collected and the investigator, without being
> coerced by any purely logical argument, but moved by the converg-
> ing probabilities disclosed by his investigations, framed his hypothe-
> sis. He then allowed himself to follow the trajectory of the evidence
> to his over-belief in the reality of God.[76]

It is true, though, that for James the certitude regarding God's existence
to which his investigations gave rise in his mind is not of a kind that
excludes all possibility of error. It is still possible for him to "imagine
vividly that the world of sensations and of scientific laws and objects may

be all." At such times, he reports, "that inward monitor" within his being can be heard "whispering the word 'bosh.'" He concluded by observing that "the total expression of human experience, as I view it objectively, invincibly urges me beyond the narrow 'scientific' bounds."[77]

Catholic writers were quite unsympathetic to James's approach. The Pragmatist, said one, "is the beginning and end of his own philosophy. Like the Modernists, he is a sentimentalist, a subjectivist."[78] James's apparent defense of religion, rejecting as it did universal and absolute religious truth, was thus founded on quicksand. One critic of Pragmatism pointed out that much of the support for this school of philosophy derived from the popular perception that in the war against atheism and agnosticism the Pragmatists had entered on the side of the religious believer.[79] The *Catholic Encyclopedia*'s entry on Pragmatism explained why this confidence in the new philosophy was misplaced. It was true, of course, that William James had lent support to religious belief, arguing from typical pragmatic premises: "On pragmatic principles, if the hypothesis of God works satisfactorily in the widest sense of the word, it is true."[80] The errors of this approach, the *Encyclopedia* explained, were twofold. First, the proposition that "works satisfactorily" in this case was not the existence of God, but merely the belief in God, and no agnostic denied that some men believed in God. Second, and more to the point, the only serious way to meet the agnostic's objections was by demonstrating that the existence of God, while not self-evident, rested on sound evidence and could be established through reason. Since the Pragmatist equated experience with reality, he could be of no assistance in such an enterprise. For "if we attach any definite meaning at all to the idea of God, we must mean a Being whose existence is not capable of direct intuitional experience, except in the supernatural order, an order which, it need hardly be said, the Pragmatist does not admit."[81]

Once again, what James had actually constructed was not, nor was it intended to be, a proof of God's existence; it was, instead, an argument in defense of belief. In an ecumenical age, some Catholics observed, such an argument could as easily be a hindrance to Catholicism as a help. If faith rested on experience, how could religious error ever be posited of anyone? Who knew a person's own experiences better than he himself? This was Pius X's argument. "What is to prevent such experiences from being met within every religion?" he asked. "In fact[,] that they are to be found is asserted by not a few. And with what right will Modernists deny the truth of an experience affirmed by a follower of Islam? With what right can they claim true experiences for Catholics alone? Indeed Modernists do not deny but actually admit, some confusedly, others in the most open manner, that all religions are true. That they cannot feel otherwise is clear. For on what ground, according to their theories, could falsity be predicated of any religion whatsoever?"[82] And as for faith resting in the final analysis upon a series of converging probabilities, the Church spoke authoritatively against any such supposition. Thus in *Lamentabili Sane* (1907), the list of condemned errors intended to give concrete expression to the anti-Modernist proscriptions of Pius X's *Pascendi*, included as its twenty-fifth condemned and proscribed error: "The assent of faith ultimately depends on an accumulation of probabilities."[83]

The Pragmatist assault, therefore, was twofold. Philosophically, in abjuring the search for absolute truth, it seemed to retreat into an individualism that in effect made each man the judge of intellectual propositions; for this reason James could call his system democratic. Speaking not in terms of Pragmatism in particular but of modern philosophy in general, the *Catholic University Bulletin* declared in 1908 that "the ultimate distrust of reason's power to acquire certainty about anything beyond our own subjective states is the most radical and the most dynamic characteristic of educated unbelief."[84] In religion the Pragmatist, if he admitted religious belief at all, again insisted on the priority of subjectivism, and in place of the dogmatic system of Catholicism substituted a "religious experience" that could be different for every individual. In both arenas, the logical consequence was a philosophical aversion to any form of dogmatism or any teleological conception of man that claimed to hold true for man as man. Such ideas were merely so many fetters to be set aside in the new pluralistic universe.

Since the intellectual developments of the Progressive Era took place within a distinctly Pragmatist milieu, the profound sense of alienation that Catholics felt toward the new philosophy would have repercussions across the social sciences. It was not possible, for example, for a philosopher sympathetic to Pragmatism even to entertain the idea of natural law. A natural-law approach evaluated moral choices in the light both of man's nature, which it conceived of as something fixed and constant across time and space, and of certain ends toward which the conclusions of reason and divine revelation indicated man ought to be striving. To the Pragmatist, on the other hand, natural law and its ideas of fixed ends and an unchanging human nature could be only a mere construct of the human mind superimposed on external reality and with no independent claim to acceptance; moreover, such an idea seemed distinctly out of place in a world characterized by evolution and change. The Pragmatist, according to Father Edmund Shanahan, shared with Henri Bergson the view that any kind of thinking "that would introduce repose or rest into the moving reality of the world, mutilates the latter's nature, destroys its character. Consequently, we must regard all speculative ideas as foolhardy attempts to catch perpetual motion at a standstill."[85] Moreover, in an intellectual atmosphere in which the powers of reason to attain metaphysical truth were widely denigrated, natural law was unlikely to receive much sympathy. As a top scholar of natural-law philosophy has put it, "The idea of natural law obtains general acceptance only in the periods when metaphysics, queen of the sciences, is dominant. It recedes or suffers an eclipse, on the other hand, when being . . . and oughtness, morality and law, are separated, when the essences of things and their ontological order are viewed as unknowable."[86]

By no means were all Progressive Era intellectuals fully acquainted with Pragmatist philosophy and its implications, but merely to carry out scholarly investigation in an academic milieu so suffused with theories of evolution, pluralism, and the meaninglessness or even impossibility of declarations of absolute truth derived from reason and metaphysics virtually guaranteed a certain sympathy with Pragmatist modes of thought and incomprehension or even outright antagonism toward the idea of natural law or a school of philosophy so comprehensive and seemingly rigid and absolute as neo-Scholasticism. And whereas Catholics were defending substantial goods, Pragmatism promoted a philosophical individualism in which each person could adopt as worthy those ultimate aims and that Weltanschauung that seemed to him most satisfactory. "In the words of its protagonist," one Jesuit reminded his readers, Pragmatism "has no dogmas, no doctrines, save its methods."[87]

Philosophy was for the Catholic more than a series of propositions and principles; it was an atmosphere, a milieu one could not avoid imbibing. For a person to absorb the teaching of the prevailing philosophy, formal training is unnecessary; one becomes acclimated to the Zeitgeist without even being aware of it. This holds for true and false philosophy alike, a Jesuit explained:

> To most individuals Kantism is but a name. The student finds his system puzzling. Yet, for all that, we live in a Kantian atmosphere and the Kantian habit of mind is universal. Hence the patient submission to empiricism, phenomenalism, agnosticism, evolution, pragmatism, to any doctrine ignoring the existence of definite, objective, substantial truth, and the adequacy of our perceptive faculties to grasp it, and

the impatience of what some good people look on as an impertinent intrusion, when Catholic philosophy comes to disturb them.[88]

The subjectivism of the Pragmatist outlook, moreover, was logically antagonistic to a creed that claimed to be true for everyone and was not content to be relegated to the status of just another intellectual proposition that the individual could accept or reject depending on its success in relieving mental unease. With the British Pragmatist F. C. S. Schiller, William James had boasted of Pragmatism that it was humanism applied to philosophy; that is, it represented the emancipation of man from arbitrary authority and allowed him to make his own imprint on the universe. No longer was metaphysical reality to be thought of as something existing "out there," something to discover and to which man had to conform his mind and his actions. Likewise, any institution or belief system presuming to speak for and to apply to all men had to succeed at the bar of experience. Since the mind was unable to render definitive judgments about extramental reality, individuals were left to rely exclusively on their own subjective states of mind in rendering judgments. From this naturally followed, paradoxically enough, a *dogmatic* insistence on political, intellectual, and religious pluralism—the logical counterparts of Pragmatist subjectivism. Again, though, American Catholics, who spoke routinely of converting the United States, were not content to be one sect out of many; and indeed the very logic of their position prohibited such a posture. Since they insisted on the universality of their creed and on the need to vindicate substantial goods and not merely procedural norms in politics, education, and the social sciences, they found themselves in a state of low-intensity civil war with the intellectual environment in which they lived.

The "logical outcome" of subjectivism, said Father Richard Tierney, "with which pragmatism reeks," was a narcissistic and self-centered view of the world. Catholics saw this as a principal feature of modern philosophy and indeed of the modern world as a whole—the emancipation of man from all those fetters, whether ecclesiastical or political, that in the past had presumed to impose order on him from without. From now on, man would impose an order originating from within himself, and would bind himself to no external authority that was not at least in some way the extension of his own will. This kind of religious and political radicalism was deplorable enough to a Catholic, but Pragmatism dared even to break the bonds that the *philosophia perennis* of Aristotle and Saint Thomas had presumed to impose on man in their depiction of the very structure of reality. Scholastic philosophy had taught him to lift himself out of the parochialism of his own mind, his lonely individualism, his idiosyncratic desires, and to perceive around him an objective moral order to which his life should conform. In short, "he must flee the turmoil of his soul and ascend in spirit to heaven."[89]

Thus just when the neo-Scholastic revival was beginning to take root in the United States, as Catholics were preparing to draw deeply from what they viewed as the perennial springs of the Scholastic tradition in order to defend better a specific dogma and to rescue sound philosophy from pretenders whose ultimate tendency they believed was toward a combination of skepticism, subjectivism, and radical individualism, American philosophy was issuing a clear retreat from the search for an objective truth to be observed and adhered to by all. To most Catholic observers, it was no coincidence that at the very time when theological Modernism was paving the way toward religious convergence and syn-cretism, secular forces were calling for the cessation of old dogmatic alle-giances in the name of a new national unity. Hegel was perhaps correct to suggest that each age possesses a certain "spirit" that will be found to per-meate its philosophy, education, art, letters, and the like; and indeed Pragmatism was a profound statement of the spirit of an age—a spirit that extended far beyond the bounds of formal philosophy. And wherever it went, Catholics would not be far behind, offering a specific outlook on man and his destiny—that of Saint Thomas Aquinas and the Catholic Church—in place of a Pragmatism that in effect rested content with extending the opportunity to each man to settle such questions for him-self.

3 / SOCIOLOGY
AND THE STUDY OF MAN

O THE EXTENT that man's social nature has always commanded the attention of political philosophers, what we now call sociology can be said to have originated in classical antiquity. Yet among the Greeks the ground was not particularly fertile for sociological analysis. The Greek intellectual tradition was not especially suited to either the inductive methods or the assumption of social progress that characterizes modern sociology. Greek thinkers often preferred the elegance of deduction from a priori principles to the mundane details of social observation. Worse, a static view of society—which hardly lent itself to the emergence of a science concerned with social development—held sway, both as a result of the monotony and routine of an agricultural society and because social institutions were thought to bear the imprimatur of an inscrutable Providence.[1]

The Christian view of progress defies simple distillation, but all Christians shared the view that the golden age, at least on earth, lay not in the future but in the past, forever lost as a result of man's rebellion in the Garden of Eden. Furthermore, man's corrupted nature ensured that grandiose plans for the perfection of man and society would come to naught. Social and intellectual developments that marked the modern era, however, too numerous and profound to discuss in detail here, would change the way many Westerners viewed the possibility of human progress and the desirability and feasibility of large-scale social reform.

Exhausted from the wars and bloodshed instigated by the Reformation, Western philosophers looked increasingly askance at theological speculation and at arguments from authority, finding refuge instead in the certainty and rigor of mathematical proof and in the empirical approach of the scientific method. Here at last were sanctuaries from the theological difficulties, perhaps insoluble, that had led to so much internecine struggle among Christians. The modern mind came into being looking for certitude amid a congeries of warring sects, each of which claimed exclusive possession of the truth.

Isaac Newton, one of the most admired thinkers of the Enlightenment, inadvertently gave modernity a push when he demonstrated how profoundly mistaken the classical and medieval understanding of the physical world had been. By challenging the presumptive authority of the past, he indirectly encouraged philosophers to take up the same challenge in their own spheres of intellectual endeavor. Moreover, Newton's discoveries, by penetrating the essential order of the universe and revealing the harmony and predictability of its operations, suggested an exalted role for man in that universe: having discovered how it functioned, he could now transform his world for the purpose of human betterment.[2]

Closely associated with this confidence in the possibility of social reform was an effort to universalize ethics and morality—that is, to found them on grounds independent of Christian revelation. Rationalists, while frequently citing the Bible and appealing to the example of Christ, aimed to transform the traditional concept of Christian charity into the naturalistic humanitarianism that inspired the French Revolution. The satisfaction of man's temporal needs came to be viewed as an end to be pursued in itself, quite apart from any concern for his supernatural destiny. Beyond this secularization of charity and good works, enlightened opinion sought more generally to evacuate religion of the external ritual and superstition that, the argument went, not only served no positive good but also created dissension among men and nations. The sectarian theologian introduced divisiveness into the human community; the philosopher alone, setting forth universal principles, could mend what theology and superstition had torn asunder. Kant summed up this perspective simply: "Everything over and above a good life which a man thinks he can do, in order to please God, is mere superstition and idolatry."[3]

When Auguste Comte proclaimed the beginnings of a "science of society" (which he was the first to call sociology) in the 1830s, he was heir to all these trends—a confidence in man's progress and in his ability to transform the world around him; a distinctly secular, this-worldly perspective on social reform and uplift; and an eagerness to re-found the principles of morality and ethics on a strictly "scientific" basis. His epistemology speaks volumes about the temper and method that the discipline of sociology would adopt.[4] His tripartite division of human history into theological, metaphysical, and positive phases is, of course, well known. According to Comte, civilization passed through the theological phase at the most primitive stage of its development, when it explained natural phenomena as well as the functions of society in terms of the more or less arbitrary whims of the divine. This immature phase was succeeded by the so-called metaphysical phase, when men looked to abstract philosophy to supply a metaphysical edifice that might bring order to observed phenomena. As with the medieval Scholastics—to say nothing of the Platonists and neo-Platonists before them—it was supposed that beyond the world of phantasm and sense experience there existed forms, essences, and natures that made the universe intelligible to the human mind. The final phase, the positive or "scientific" stage, was concerned not at all with such speculation but rather with the bare facts of experience, with the systematic observation and induction that would render both the natural and the social spheres predictable.

The positive phase put an end once and for all to the search for the inner essences of things and for an ultimate truth that explained and undergirded phenomena of the physical world. Herbert Spencer relegated God to the realm of "Unknowable." Only phenomena now mattered. With the superstition that marked the theological phase at last put to rest and the sterile speculation of the metaphysical phase finally abandoned, man could turn his energy not simply to the accumulation of knowledge that was empirically verifiable—a profound advance in itself—but also to a knowledge practical enough to have some bearing on the improvement of the human condition.

Late in life, Comte devised a "religion of humanity"—complete with priesthood, saints, and sacraments—which he considered necessary in order to stir the human heart to benevolent action.[5] It would be wrong to dismiss this exercise as merely a curiosity of an eccentric thinker. Comte was divided within himself: his "scientific" frame of mind led him to discount the supernatural, but his study of human society revealed a need among men for a religious sanction for morality. Whatever new system sought to supplant the beliefs of old therefore needed to possess something of the spirit of what it was replacing. Moreover, with the sacred no longer reposed in a transcendent deity, in the minds of Comte and some of his successors humanity itself would take on the trappings of the sacred. Albion Small, one of the founders of American sociology, remarked: "In all seriousness, then, and with careful weighing of my words, I register my belief that social science is the holiest sacrament open to men."[6] (It can hardly come as a surprise, in light of Small's language, that fully one-third of all instructors in the social sciences at the college level in 1900 had had some theological training.[7]) Although few of Comte's successors followed him in his flirtation with mysticism, most agreed with the substance of what he was doing: sacralizing good works in a world in which God's existence was uncertain.

For Comte, the purpose of sociology was to amass facts and statistics relating to the development of the human race in order to construct a complete scheme for the direction of individual and social conduct. More than implicit in this endeavor was a rejection of the Christian moral tradition as an a priori guidepost for the ordering of human society; mere custom and utility would henceforth substitute for tradition and natural law in determining the structure of social order and human conduct.[8] Montesquieu, one of the first self-conscious social scientists, had set out in his *Spirit of the Laws* (1748) to produce a strictly scientific and dispassionate discussion of the various forms of government extant in his time, but a lingering attachment to the Christian natural-law tradition made him unable to refrain from rendering normative judgments about despotism on the one hand and liberty on the other. Comte and his successors cut this umbilical cord, as it were, once and for all.

Secular Progressives and Social Gospel theologians alike joined Comte and his followers in their hostility toward a confessional, ritual-oriented Christianity. Its devotion to abstruse theological speculation only created dissension and drained energies better spent elsewhere; its primary emphasis on man's supernatural destiny, as well as its exclusive placement of the locus of sin in the individual rather than in economic or social institutions, seemed to them ill suited to the needs of modern society. Most looked forward to a radical restructuring of traditional Christian belief— a development that they welcomed as a natural, evolutionary response to the new social conditions that obtained at the turn of the century. Modern man having come of age, the so-called "vertical" dimension of religion, which focused on his relationship with God, would at last give way to a horizontal outlook in which the Christian's treatment of his fellow-man would become the supreme criterion for judging a man's religious sense.[9] Walter Rauschenbusch was at his most frank when he wrote:

Every step in the historical evolution of religion has been marked by a closer union of religion and ethics and by the elimination of non-ethical religious performances. This union of religion and ethics reached its highest perfection in the life and mind of Jesus. . . . It is clear that our Christianity is most Christian when religion and ethics are viewed as inseparable elements of the same single-minded and whole-hearted life, in which the consciousness of God and the consciousness of humanity blend completely.[10]

At the turn of the century sociology was thus still in its infancy, but its impulse toward horizontalizing religious belief, its confidence in the malleability of man and society under expert direction, and its emphasis on empirical research and scientific analysis all but guaranteed its continued growth and vitality during the Progressive Era.[11] Comte's view that all philosophy should be directed toward improvement of the condition of mankind resonated strongly with pragmatic currents in American philosophy during the period as well.[12]

For their part, Catholics by no means rejected this new science out of hand; indeed, Father Aloysius Taparelli (1793–1862) of Rome and Bishop Wilhelm Emmanuel von Ketteler (1811–1877) of Mainz, both contemporaries of Comte, had been pioneers in Catholic sociology.[13] Yet it was not without some apprehension that Catholics assessed the new discipline. They sensed in sociology a hubris peculiar to modern man—who, having penetrated the mysteries of the physical world, possessed an impious confidence in his ability to remake human society and to dominate that world.[14] They also could not fail to note its questionable philosophical lineage; as we have seen, the development of sociology as a separate field of study occurred along lines that, if not positively anti-Christian, were plainly secular.[15]

The new sociologists' disdain for metaphysics, moreover, also gave Catholics reason for concern. One of the strengths of the Thomistic system, from Catholics' point of view, was that it satisfied the human mind's yearning for a comprehensive system for apprehending ultimate realities. But having spurned the integrated whole supplied by *philosophia perennis*, sociologists might very well try to derive their own philosophy of man through the collection and analysis of social statistics. Indeed, Saint-Simon and Comte had been supremely confident of what this new field of study could achieve, and their successors were nearly as ambitious. Albion Small held that sociology could provide "a positive philosophy of visible human experience" as a substitute for "all the philosophies built upon preconceived notions of life."[16] Ethics "must have the richest possible experience as its basis," insisted L. T. Hobhouse. Still another commentator revealed a sympathy for the view of David Hume and the Scottish moralists when he explained that all ethical concepts "are ultimately based on emotions, of either approval or disapproval. The concepts of wrongness, rightness, duty, justice, goodness, virtue, merit, and so forth, refer to generalizations of tendencies in certain phenomena to call forth a moral emotion."[17]

This kind of speculation elicited a panicked response from many Catholics. The main practitioners of modern sociology "frankly avow their complete independence of what they would doubtless term the out-worn creed and morality of the Catholic Church," said Father Paul Blakely, associate editor of *America*.[18] Modern thinkers had "declared that the source of moral obligation was to be found, not in the mandate of any power above earth, but in man himself, or in society, or in the present state of human evolution," said another critic.[19] "Our entire view of life will obviously take shape and color according as we admit or reject a Divine plan," wrote the Jesuit Joseph Husslein, and modern sociologists, who fell into the latter category, do not "admit any unchanging laws of morality." Some, it is true, suggested certain broad guidelines for moral-ity—Harvard's B. M. Anderson, for example, defined the moral law sim-ply as "the will of the group"—but rarely any whose actual contents were constant over time (the will of a group, for example, is far from constant). Social theorist Simon Patten confirmed Catholic fears when he noted that "social morality gets its force from its consequences; it has no antecedent principle from which it is derived nor any authoritative sanc-tion by which it is enforced."[20] From the Catholic point of view, all this represented a "new creed, cunningly invented to displace Christianity."[21] Still another observer noted that "in the minds of almost all professors of sociology who are not Catholic, whatever has come down to us from the past must be condemned. Its very age is its death warrant."[22]

Polemics against modern sociology did not go unanswered. For exam-ple, in April 1917, John W. Maguire, C.S.V., took issue with Paul Blakely's wholesale denigration of recent developments and perspectives in social thought. Blakely had objected that "the Church is from God; modern sociology is not." To dismiss modern sociology on such grounds, Maguire explained, would be as absurd as dismissing modern biology, chemistry, physics, and a host of other disciplines simply because many of its practi-tioners were philosophical materialists. What Blakely was attacking as "modern sociology" was simply the aberrations of certain sociologists.[23]

A case can be made that Blakely's condemnation of "modern sociology" was indeed too sweeping, that it assumed a shared outlook among sociol-ogists that did not exist. Moreover, by the time the Social Gospel move-ment had begun to develop, some kind of Christian dimension was grad-ually added to what had begun as an expressly secular discipline. It was the Christian clergyman W. D. P. Bliss who assembled the *Encyclopedia of Social Reform* (1897), the volume that one scholar has called "the real pio-neer among sociological reference books."[24] Some professional sociologists themselves had begun to take a positive view of religion as well. Charles Ellwood, for example, noted that religion "exalts the life in which the individual merges his personal interests, desires, and aspirations with his group, or, as in the highest religion, with humanity as a whole." In his seminal *Social Control*, Edward A. Ross praised Christianity for having produced a movement of philanthropy unknown to the pagan world. The University of Missouri's William Wilson Elwang spoke of religion as the font of all altruism. And these testimonies could be multiplied.[25]

Yet such sentiments provided little consolation for Catholics. There can be no real question that a secular outlook dominated the mainstream of the discipline, and the overwhelming majority of scholars, activists, and theologians who took a favorable view of religion agreed that religious belief, while valuable, needed to undergo a radical restructuring if it was to perform the socially useful functions they envisioned for it. The same Charles Ellwood who praised the social utility of religion also published *The Reconstruction of Religion* (1922), whose very title reveals its thesis. The Christianity he envisions will all but dispense with theology. Beyond that, it will be "concretely ethical," social rather than theological, collective rather than individualistic, active rather than contemplative, affirmative rather than negative. Instead of hurling anathemas at the modern world, it will cooperate in constructing the good society with all men of goodwill.[26] Simon Patten's *Social Basis of Religion* (1911) likewise spoke of the need to "reconstruct religion in ways that meet modern needs" and reinterpreted all the elements of the Christian creed in naturalistic terms. Had Saint Paul not perverted Christ's message into one of personal sanctification and a preoccupation with otherworldly concerns, he argued, then "Christ to us would be a social leader, preaching salvation only in terms of love, cooperation and service."[27] The support of Bliss and his Social Gospel colleagues seems to be more a reflection of the gradual secularization of the Christian creed under Social Gospel guidance than a clear indication that the principles of the new sociology posed no difficulties for the orthodox believer. It may be true that the sociology of this period had its kind words to say for Christianity, and even counted among its students a great many people who considered themselves Christians, but this support was always conditional: *if* the churches would revolutionize their creeds in favor of a more or less exclusively social orientation, then they might play an active role in the new society that the reformers envisioned.[28]

It comes as little surprise, therefore, that none other than the standard-bearer of American Progressive thought, the *New Republic*, itself acknowledged that the curmudgeonly Blakely was on to something when he detected a fundamental antagonism between the principles of Progressive sociology and those of the Catholic Church. "Father Blakely deserves cordial respect for the candor with which he states the issue as seen by the clerical organization," the magazine's editors began. They went on, quoting Blakely with approval:

"Between the principles of Catholicism and the principles of modern sociology, upon which many unwary Catholics have looked with approval, there is an essential and irreconcilable antagonism. . . . The Church is from God; modern sociology is not; for like present-day non-sectarian education, *it has severed all relations with Him.*" *We gladly accept the issue as Father Blakely states it.* . . . The enemy, as Father Blakely so plainly says, is the *secularizing tendency of modern life.* . . . From its own point of view the Church is perfectly right in its antagonism, however unwise the tactics it pursues. *The secularization of philanthropy is one of the clear intentions of modern liberals,* and though liberals wish to proceed moderately and with all possible fairness, they *do intend to proceed.*[29]

The trend toward secularization to which the *New Republic* referred was indeed present in much of the philosophy that undergirded modern sociology. Aware of this, Blakely aimed his indictment of the discipline's modern practitioners at many of the top names in the profession, attacking Yale University's Henry Pratt Fairchild with special vigor. Fairchild's views enraged him. The origin of religion Fairchild traced to "mental reactions"—which, he explained, are "secondary and non-essential." Sin was exclusively "a matter of social standards, not of absolute and eternal verities."[30] On the question of marriage, the antagonism between Fairchild and the Church could not have been clearer. Pius IX had condemned the proposition that "in natural law the bond of matrimony is not indissoluble."[31] Fairchild, on the other hand, while admitting that "monogamy is regarded by many as the form of union approved by Nature herself," could find no reason that under the influence of modern conditions, especially in the economic sphere, a "readjustment" of this view might not be welcomed. We have progressed mightily, he wrote, from the time when it was "considered that the size of a family, after marriage, was a matter for which responsibility rested with the Lord." (Blakely observed wryly that this comment constituted the only instance in Fairchild's *Outlines of Applied Sociology* [1916] in which the author referred to God.)[32]

Blakely insisted that the secular philosophy that informed the work of not only Fairchild but also most of the top sociologists of the day exercised so profound an influence on their approach to sociology as to render their work a kind of social and intellectual poison. Modern sociology had no place in its methodological apparatus for the supernatural; it utterly rejected God, and it reduced natural law to an archaism whose strict precepts thwarted the fulfillment of human desire.[33] The Jesuit writer cautioned his fellow Catholics to recall the warning of Pope Pius IX, who in his *Syllabus of Errors* (1864) had condemned the proposition "Philosophy is to be treated without taking any account of supernatural revelation." The implicit and often explicit philosophy that informed all too much sociology did just that.[34] No philosophy founded on false premises, when translated into action, could ever yield social good but by accident.[35] A bad tree cannot bring forth good fruit, Christ himself observed; and if modern sociology took its cues from a philosophy that viewed God's existence as at best a matter of indifference, it should claim the allegiance of no serious Catholic.

Yet in rejecting the perceived errors and the anti-Catholic prejudice of what Blakely and many of his colleagues dismissed as "modern sociology," they were careful to distinguish between what they considered a perversion of a potentially valuable discipline on the one hand and "true sociology," a science properly informed by Catholic truth, on the other. Even Blakely, the most skeptical observer, believed that every Catholic university should have a school of sociology; otherwise, good Catholic students would have to go elsewhere, where they would doubtless be taught principles that ran contrary to their faith.[36] "For the thousandth time," demanded one Catholic thinker, "what about the future faith and morality of our Catholic young men and women who attend these secular universities?"[37] Joseph Husslein, who joined his colleagues in insisting that the Church's unique mission was the salvation of souls, argued that it was precisely a catholicized social science that in modern times had become a principal means for securing this end. Without a Catholic sociology, not only would Catholic students of social science wind up lost in a labyrinth of error, but also countless needy souls, ministered to by secular-minded social workers, would be fed the stones of naturalism instead of the bread of life.[38] Simply put, the "moral riot" introduced by modern sociology— Blakely called it "the ethics of the barnyard and the stock-farm"—would continue apace unless Catholics put the discipline on the proper track. "We must not only engage in destructive criticism," insisted John Maguire. "We must enter the field, and do constructive work."[39]

This was precisely what William J. Kerby, who joined the faculty of the Catholic University of America in 1897 as its first professor of sociology, sought to encourage.[40] Undergraduates described Kerby as "among the best loved men on the campus."[41] He possessed a broad educational background, having studied at Milwaukee's St. Francis de Sales Seminary from 1884 through 1892, followed by study at Catholic University, a brief stint in Berlin, and the completion of his doctorate from Belgium's University of Louvain. He became a charter member of the American Sociological Society when it was founded in 1905, and he served on its executive committee from 1918 to 1920. He was the key figure in establishing the National Conference of Catholic Charities (today Catholic Charities, U.S.A.) in 1910, serving as its executive secretary during the first decade of its existence.[42] Kerby's doctoral dissertation was an examination of the American socialist movement. He believed that the appeal of socialism would dwindle as Catholics sought to put their own social teachings into practice.[43]

Kerby was more optimistic than some other Catholics about sociology's potential for good, but he began the *Catholic Encyclopedia*'s entry on the discipline by frankly acknowledging its defects as currently practiced. He accused it of showing "a marked tendency towards Agnosticism, Materialism, and Determinism."[44] Too many sociologists "eliminate God from their social science" and "drop the word sin from their vocabulary"; the result is a one-dimensional view of the human person, one that fails to take into account both body and soul.[45] Elsewhere he warned:

Now just because the organic spiritual character of charity is so clear in the Gospel; just because it has been fundamental in the Church's consciousness throughout the ages and it remains so to-day, it is not always easy to keep this great truth in mind. Prevailing tones of thought and expression tyrannize over us. We catch the atmosphere of current discussion, and we find attractive what is new and conspicuous and popular. The sociological features of poverty command attention to-day. The world attempts to set aside, by either neglect or denial, the spiritual character of the problem of poverty and the spiritual law of its relief.[46]

The principal difficulty with modern sociology, Kerby explained, was that its practitioners, when not openly hostile to Catholic principles, sought to arrive at a metaphysics without the compass of the natural-law tradition, through mere social observation and the collection of data. Now if sociology limited itself to assembling and sorting social data, the philosophical perspective of the sociologist would be of no import. But since social observation that lacked an interpretive framework was "necessarily incomplete," the supposition that sociology might restrict itself in practice from rendering value judgments was illusory. For in practice, Kerby pointed out, even descriptive sociology engages in interpretation of the data under study; and in so doing "it often takes on a tone with which the Christian cannot agree."[47]

The Catholic's approach to the social sciences, on the other hand, was "one that carries with it always the philosophy of Christ." This philosophy has its origins not in induction but in divine revelation. A sociology worthy to be called Christian—the "true sociology" of which Blakely spoke—must not be limited to the mere observation of the functioning of society, but instead must always concern itself with the ideal, with the *ought* of human existence. When a sociologist concludes that human life will be made more commodious if families agree to limit their offspring to a certain number, or when in the name of human progress he speaks favorably of divorce, he has departed from the moral system established by Christ. The Catholic, on the other hand, cannot look with indifference on developments that are repugnant to the norms of Christian morality.[48] Even on a purely natural level, prescinding from the moral considerations involved, the Catholic sociologist insisted that attempts to evade the natural law would have terrible consequences for human society and individual happiness. For "the man who persist[s] in excluding God from his universe [is] not likely to secure peace and happiness . . . if he sought them in the impermanent things of time."[49] Pope Pius X himself observed that the more frankly Christian a civilization is, the more "lasting and more productive of precious fruit" it is, whereas "the more it withdraws from the Christian ideal so much the feebler is it to the great detriment of society."[50]

Kerby's article on sociology in the *Catholic Encyclopedia*, from which much of the above critique is drawn, devoted what was for Kerby an uncharacteristic amount of attention to sociological theory. It had not been as a sterile intellectual exercise that Comte had pioneered his science of society; he intended the findings of his new discipline to be applied to remedying social ills. Kerby shared this vision, both in his personal approach to sociology and in his conception of proper university training in the discipline. "Sociology as taught in the University," he wrote in the Catholic University yearbook for 1898–1899, "is neither a body of pure speculation, as the science is sometimes represented, nor is it merely identical with social reform. It embraces the general principles underlying social phenomena." These principles, Kerby went on, would not be studied "without careful and detailed application to social conditions, normal and abnormal"—though "to preserve the scientific character of the courses" no sociological research would be considered acceptable "without the constant guidance of the principles involved." A proper balance needed to be maintained between sociology's pure and applied branches.[51]

Kerby's own work tended almost exclusively toward the applied end of the field. Although he was perhaps the most accomplished and respected of the Catholic sociologists, one searches his work in vain for the kind of systematic exposition of human interaction, public opinion, or of social control, of trends in social development or evolution, that characterized the work of a Ross, Franklin H. Giddings, or Lester Frank Ward. In a word, Kerby was no system-builder; he bequeathed to posterity no systematic treatise or edifice of sociological thought.

This shortcoming was not unique to Kerby. During the Progressive Era, at least, there seems to have been no Catholic counterpart to Ward's *Dynamic Sociology* or Ross's *Social Control*. For all their criticism of the secular assumptions behind most sociological thought, Catholics made little systematic effort at the level of theory to substitute a Catholic vision for the standard one. For although Kerby insisted on the priority of sociological theory, what most intrigued him and his colleagues was *applied* sociology—the use of scientific methods in both a preventive and a post hoc way for the alleviation of human suffering.

For Kerby this approach translated into a desire for professional social-service training for Catholics, and from a distinctly Catholic point of view. Catholic institutions were slow to take up the challenge. By the end of World War I, only two Catholic universities, Fordham and Chicago's Loyola, could claim to offer courses in social service, the former in its sociology department and the latter in a separate School of Social Study that had opened in 1914. Kerby was convinced of the need for a specifically Catholic school of social service so that Catholics interested in the field could receive the professional training they needed in an environment that was not only not contemptuous of Catholic teaching (which he believed secular schools tended to be) but also had an outlook suffused with the faith. Like Thomas Edward Shields before him, who set his sights on a college for teacher training that would combine the highest professional standards with a firm commitment to the Catholic faith, Kerby was determined to make his social service school a reality—which he did, in 1921, with the opening of the National Catholic School of Social Service.[52]

The establishment of the school falls just outside the chronological bounds of the present study, but its emphasis on practical social service over the more technical and scholarly aspect of the discipline of sociology raises an important point. The relationship between sociology and social reform, particularly during the Progressive Era, was ambiguous. On the one hand, sociologists described themselves principally as practitioners of a *science*—one that synthesized and yet transcended all the other social sciences.[53] They sought to investigate the development of society, of social institutions, of human interaction. Albion Small tried to correct what he saw as a widespread misunderstanding when he explained in 1905 that while sociological principles might be applied in society's posture toward, say, criminals or delinquent children, sociology itself was a systematic science.[54] When Henry J. Ford attacked sociologists in *The Nation*—in an article later reprinted in the *American Journal of Sociology*—for advocating social reforms, the psychological sociologist Charles Ellwood immediately corrected him, and a spirited and memorable exchange ensued.[55]

Yet few sociologists limited themselves to such a restricted definition of their profession. In fact, the same Small who denied any necessary connection between sociology and reform had said earlier that "scholars might exalt both their scholarship and their citizenship by claiming an active share of the work of perfecting and applying plans and devices for social improvements and amelioration."[56] This seems to have been the standard view among most sociologists. The science originated and began to mature in the nineteenth century, at a time when social scientists were increasingly convinced of the potential their disciplines held for improving the condition of humankind. Pure "science," with no ameliorative potential, fell into disrepute. Richard T. Ely, for example, founded the American Economic Association with some colleagues in an effort to replace the existing body of economic theory—deduced from self-evident axioms rather than those derived from experience, and leading ineluctably to laissez-faire conclusions—with an empirical approach that looked to the collection of facts and statistics for guidance in formulating policy.[57] Old sciences were being made anew, and a new science such as sociology was expected to fit the new mold.

Catholics were not alone in coming to grips with these issues; much of the Protestant world was being forced to face them at the same time. The extent to which Christians ought to involve themselves either in political agitation for social reform or in private charitable activity was in fact a source of great and lasting controversy within the various Protestant camps. The source of the controversy was the increasingly visible Social Gospel movement, which began among Protestant clergymen in the late nineteenth century and included such figures as Washington Gladden,

Walter Rauschenbusch, and W. D. P. Bliss. Gladden, who served as a minister in Springfield, Massachusetts, and Columbus, Ohio, summed up the overall outlook of the new movement when he said that the essence of the Christian faith was not to be found in dogma or ritual, or even in religious communion with God. Instead, the Christian ought simply to remember the injunction to "love thy neighbor as thyself."

Now there was, of course, an array of perspectives within the Social Gospel movement, and one must bear in mind the usual cautions against hasty generalization. At the same time, it seems fairly clear that if we take Rauschenbusch's perspective as more or less representative of the movement as a whole, the Social Gospel represents a fairly striking departure from the accumulated corpus of Christian thought as well as a perspective radically different from that of the fathers and the councils. George Marsden maintains in his book *Fundamentalism and American Culture* (1980) that the influence of philosophical Pragmatism is abundantly apparent throughout the writings and perspectives of Social Gospel theologians. "The Social Gospel, at least in its classic form as represented by Rauschenbusch, did not deny outright the validity of specific beliefs, but took the pragmatist position that we cannot know anything about their validity until we see what they do." He argues quite plausibly that within the Social Gospel tradition "the prevailing tendency is to follow William James and John Dewey in regarding ideas as plans of action rather than as mirrors of reality." "To my mind," he concludes, "the test of a genuine example of the Social Gospel is whether other aspects of Christianity are subordinated to, and in effect incidental to, its social aspects."[58] The Kingdom of God in the Social Gospel's conception would increasingly come to be viewed in terms of the arrival of a truly just and human society on earth rather than as a supernatural goal toward which the Christian soul was striving.

It was not that the Social Gospel amounted to secularism pure and simple. Rauschenbusch retained a belief in the importance of individual salvation, and did not entirely neglect this dimension of the Christian faith. What he sought to do was to bring the ideas of individual and social salvation into what he considered a better balance. Others, like Washington Gladden, were less nuanced, more or less abandoning discussion of individual salvation altogether, or at least claiming that it could be conceived of only within a social context. Thus Gladden contended that no one "is soundly converted until he comprehends his social relations and strives to fulfill them." Says one scholar of the movement: "There was no doubt in the minds of its advocates that God intended to turn this world into a holy utopia."[59] In contrast to the orthodox Christian tradition, Social Gospel theologians held an optimistic view of human nature. This conviction, which amounted to an implicit (and frequently explicit) denial of the doctrine of original sin, developed logically from the Social Gospel's unanimous belief in and enthusiasm for Darwin's theory of evolution. Just as the process of evolution was leading humanity down a path of certain if gradual progress, so also could the moral conscience develop and progress with the passage of time. Gladden, who believed in the malleability of human nature, went so far as to suggest a kind of moral Lamarckianism— that is, that once a Christian family and milieu had forged a morally good individual, his good qualities could be transmitted biologically to posterity.[60]

Protestants of all sorts, Social Gospel sympathizers or otherwise, had as individuals done a great deal to alleviate social ills. What the new position sought to do was to modify Christian theology to reflect new realities. Rauschenbusch believed that he was not introducing any new teaching but merely recapturing the original teachings of Christ. The reaction of more conservative Protestants to the Social Gospel was, if not to abandon charitable work and social action altogether, at the very least to hold social concerns among Christians in considerable suspicion. Conservatives took Social Gospel theologians at their word when they began to make a sharp distinction between the older Christianity, fundamentally individualistic and concerned above all with the salvation of souls, and this newer, social variety. With Social Gospel theologians themselves articulating the chasm separating their own conception of Christianity from that of previous ages, conservatives tended to conclude that they were being faced with a tragic either-or: traditional Christian belief or the new program of social action.[61]

The Catholic response was rather different. For one thing, there was within the Catholic Church nothing comparable to the Social Gospel movement, nothing that would subordinate Catholic dogma to the demands of charity and social work. In his recent book *Christian Critics*, an otherwise interesting and useful study of twentieth-century Christian social thought, Eugene McCarraher is clearly overstating the case when he refers casually and repeatedly to "Catholic social gospelers."[62] There is some truth in this term, of course, if it is meant to refer to Catholics who believed that Church teaching ought to be brought to bear in the economic realm. But the ethos of the Protestant and Catholic conceptions of this project differed in critically important ways. Isolated mavericks like New York's Father Edward McGlynn can be readily adduced, it is true, but such figures obviously constituted nothing like a full-fledged movement. (In any case, McGlynn was excommunicated for his radical views.) Catholics interested in such matters went out of their way to point out that the Church was not a social service agency and that such enterprises as poor relief had to be understood within the context of the Church's traditional supernatural mission. In short, *there was no Catholic Social Gospel movement*. Thus Catholics never found themselves in the unhappy position of the conservative Protestants for whom earthly good works had been tainted with suspicions of outright naturalism or worse.

Second, within the Catholic intellectual tradition there was a posture of venerable lineage according to which the good things of the secular world could be selectively appropriated by the Church, since all good things were understood to come ultimately from the same divine source. Saint Justin Martyr was among the first to set forth this view. Saint Gregory of Nyssa, who had received the same classical education as the other Cappadocian Fathers, made it his aim to take the beautiful things of classical culture—poems, histories, and the like—and render them all in Christian form, again influenced by the idea that all beautiful things ought to be used by the Church for the further glorification of God, the very source of beauty.

For these reasons, Catholics believed that they did not need to flee from modern sociology and social work; they had only to suffuse them with Catholic principles.

A practical application of Progressive sociology appeared in the movement known as "scientific charity." The connection between sociology and philanthropy in general, one sociologist pointed out, was an essential one: "Sociology stands for pure science, while philanthropy stands for applied science." More specifically, sociology is "the systematic study of social conditions and processes, with a view to determining what is normal and what is abnormal in them." The philanthropist, on the other hand, desires "in the interest of humanity to enlarge the sphere of the normal and limit that of the abnormal; a matter with which abstract science does not concern itself." His outlook is therefore not as broad as that of the scientist; he is absorbed, rather, with social conditions at present. "The love of pure science for its own sake is not inconsistent with the wish to find applications of scientific discoveries . . . which will prove of benefit to mankind."[63]

Scientific charity, though it had antecedents in Scotland and Germany, originated in England and spread to the United States: first to Buffalo in 1859 and then gradually throughout urban America.[64] Its goal was straightforward: to put charitable work on a more intellectually rigorous footing by bringing organization and intelligent direction to the practice of philanthropy. It encouraged "the principle of channeling benevolence through an organization rather than giving directly to individuals."[65] Trained professionals with firsthand knowledge of the targeted poor could then allocate monies on a rational and efficient basis.

As one might expect, scientific charity has met with mixed responses from historians over the years. Some have claimed to see in the new methods the roots of modern casework, which relies heavily on individual evaluation of those in need.[66] Others, such as Michael Katz, have purported to see a somewhat less benign motivation: the creation of a docile labor force by means of the inculcation of middle-class values in the poor.[67] Paul Boyer has also suggested that alleviating social unrest was at the root of scientific charity, whose principal purpose, in his view, lay in reestablishing the bonds between rich and poor that the industrial age had dissolved.[68]

Though its origins predated the Progressive movement, scientific charity attracted the interest of Progressive thinkers not only with its concern for the amelioration of the human condition but also with its promises of efficiency. It appealed to the Progressive desire to centralize the decentralized, to coordinate the haphazard, to replace the sentimental with the scientific.[69] Progressives also appreciated its emphasis on the wider benefits and consequences of intelligent charity. Advocates of scientific charity drew, ultimately, on the thought of that quintessential American, Benjamin Franklin, who held that charity, far from being a private activity, was a prudent *social* act. A well-conceived act of philanthropy ultimately benefited all members of society.

Such purely naturalistic considerations were not sufficient from a Catholic point of view; for as Pope Leo XIII made clear, efforts at social amelioration must be directed primarily toward supernatural ends. Speaking in *Rerum Novarum* (1891) of Catholic workingmen's associations, the pope insisted that "moral and religious perfection" should be their primary goal. Reflecting the spirit of Catholic distinctiveness that animated American Catholic intellectuals of the Progressive Era, he pointed out that should the workingmen's associations fail to observe this aspect of their mission, "they would degenerate in nature and would be little better than those associations in which no account is ordinarily taken of religion." What would it profit a man to secure material goods in abundance if, through lack of proper nourishment, he should run the risk of losing his soul?[70]

This aspect of *Rerum Novarum* was so central to Leo XIII's teaching, explained *America*, that to neglect it or to downplay its significance was to distort the very meaning of the pope's "immortal document." The brilliance of the encyclical and the richness of Christian wisdom that it contained made it possible for virtually any man of goodwill to use it merely as a source of supporting quotations, that in expressing his own opinions he might thereby claim to be reflecting the mind of the late pontiff. Too often overlooked, for example, was the pope's insistence that workingmen's associations not simply be founded on Catholic principles but that they also be rooted in Catholic *practice*—as *America* put it, "in the practice of religion, of mortification and self-restraint; in the seeking first the Kingdom of God; in the manly contempt of passing sensual gratification, which enables one to practice thrift and thus lay by something for sickness and old age."[71]

What held for workingmen's associations applied a fortiori to Catholic charity and social work. "The great social work of the Church," *America* stated flatly, "always has been and still is the Christianizing of mankind."[72] Leo XIII was only reiterating the teaching of Saint Thomas Aquinas when he observed that for most men physical misery was destructive of the interior life and perilous to their supernatural destiny, and that the alleviation of such distress would conduce to the salvation of a greater number of souls.[73] Sound psychology taught that the condition of the body affects the operations of the soul; hence the Church's concern for both bodily and spiritual health.[74] One should, therefore, work to alleviate the extreme poverty that existed in America's major cities, but with supernatural ends in mind.

America cautioned that while the Gospel exhorts Christians to alleviate these conditions, it "nowhere even encourages us to look upon their absolute removal as possible."[75] On the contrary, the Church commends to her flock the patient endurance of suffering as the most sublime way of imitating and sharing in the sufferings of her divine founder and of reaching perfection in the interior life. She does not wish gratuitous sufferings on her faithful, of course, but she insists that the Catholic, when enduring privation in a spirit of expiation for sin and mindful of the agony of the crucified Christ, can supernaturalize and therefore give meaning to suffering. If the poor man's needs cannot immediately be met, he might at least be made aware of the ultimate value of his present hardships, thereby enabling him to turn "his earthly need into heavenly coin."[76]

One of the instructors at the new school of social work would be John J. Burke, the Paulist father and "moderate progressive" who headed the National Catholic War Council (which in 1919 became the National

Catholic Welfare Council, still under Burke's leadership) and edited the *Catholic World* from 1903 to 1922. A central point of his writing and lecturing concerned the supernatural element of charity.[77] For two millennia, Burke told the 1915 graduating class of New York's College of Mount Saint Vincent-on-Hudson, the Church had pursued as her "one great purpose" the leading of souls to the love of God. "Whatever other claims she makes as to her mission," he insisted, "are at best but secondary."[78] This was to be the outlook of the National Catholic Welfare Council for at least the first several decades of its existence. It was not sentimental humanitarianism that inspired the work that the new organization coordinated. The purpose and motivating force of Catholic charity was to sanctify souls as it alleviated human want. Merely to duplicate the work of other charitable organizations would have been to misunderstand the Church's mission and to forfeit an opportunity for evangelization. "We are in this cause not to do simply a negative work," said Burke. "We are in the cause not simply to do something after a non-Catholic organization has done it. We are in it as the cause of Christ, as Christian men possessing and alone possessing the truth of Jesus Christ."[79]

Burke warned Catholics about what he considered the modern superstition that "experts in the social sciences might well be trusted with our social betterment"—a view that encouraged the trend toward making religion "a private and an almost secret matter." "It is difficult to stand against such a tide," he admitted, but he insisted on these principles to his students at the National Catholic School of Social Service.[80] They responded warmly to Burke's counsel. "We have realized how favored we are in having your wealth of spiritual thought unfolded so generously," one student wrote to him, "and if we, as Catholics, are to do any worthwhile social service, surely that is the side we should stress—there are many humanitarians better equipped than some of us, if that were the one thing necessary."[81]

On one occasion, Burke felt it necessary to remind even his dear friend William Kerby of the need to emphasize the supernatural element above other factors in charity work. Since Kerby had always insisted on the centrality of charity's supernatural aspect, for indeed this was what made Catholic charity unique, he may have had reason to believe that his readers would take the point for granted. But several years before assuming his post as head of the National Catholic Welfare Council, Burke cautioned Kerby that unless he took pains to emphasize the spiritual and uniquely Catholic nature of his work, he ran the risk of sounding like just another advocate of secular philanthropy and social uplift. After receiving an article submitted by Kerby to Burke's *Catholic World* in the summer of 1912, Burke replied with a cordial yet critical letter. The article, he insisted, suffered from a glaring omission:

The paper presupposes motive. It deals with the human, natural agencies by which we may know how to help the poor. In other words, prayer and love and sacrifice are put aside and you present the means by which those who cultivate these things may be alive to their actual duties and responsibilities, and be moved to practical, intelligent action. But this distinction is not clearly defined in the paper, and even if there is no need for such distinction, the reader would not see that it is taken for granted.[82]

"On its face," Burke said, "the article gives too much to the intelligent, scientific relief of the poor. The impression received is that this is the be-all and the end-all—*unium necessarium*." He went on:

You say that among the modern champions of the poor there is keen vision; wide horizon, subtle interpretation, fine analysis, scholarship and personal force, but you say nothing of religion. There may or there may not be religion and it would seem that there is little difference as to effectiveness.[83]

Burke was, of course, sympathetic to Kerby's aim of arousing Catholics to a more intelligent approach to practical charity, but insisted "it would be better and more effective if this appeal gave credit more explicitly to the supereminent, appealing inspiration of Christian faith." Thus animated by a supernatural zeal, men would become sympathetic to the very scientific methods that Kerby sought to promote. Catholics would be eager "to use every means, every bit of knowledge, every possibility of legislation or organized effort, every bit of statistics by whomsoever gathered to promote intelligently the welfare of the poor."[84]

Aware, perhaps, that his message might be misunderstood, Kerby included in most of his writings, and most dramatically in his acclaimed *Social Mission of Charity*, reminders to Christians that in helping the poor they were engaging in a supernaturally meritorious action, one whose salutary effects were far from exhausted by the mere material comforts that they provided to those in need. He explained to his readers that the Church "meets with deep regret" all trends tending to "secularize the service of the poor or make it a merely natural phase of social progress."

Emphasis on the spiritual nature of charity as both attitude and action is in no direct conflict whatsoever with so-called scientific or systematic charity. The Church must use science and system to the utmost in doing the work to which she feels called. The motive in supernatural charity is static but the methods change. The impulses of Christian service operate through the terms and relations of their time. When science and system isolate the service of the poor and see it in merely a natural phase of social progress, it introduces a quality of motive and a tone that are foreign to the supernatural. It is not sufficient in the Christian view to recognize that religion is a good thing socially. We must insist that it is a divine power, carrying a divine message and that there is a divine warrant, divine compensation for everything that we do for the poor in the name of Christ.[85]

Catholic charity, according to Kerby, can be properly appreciated only in terms of its relationship to the Church's mission of sanctifying souls. "The social work of the Catholic Church is so intimately bound up with its whole view of life and its normal service of souls that one cannot understand its spirit, agencies or motives unless they are studied in their organic relation to the processes of spiritual life fostered in the traditions of the Church," he wrote in a secular periodical. "It is coordinated with prayer and fasting as a highly meritorious supernatural action, as a traditional form of expiation for sin and one of the noblest proofs of consecration to God."[86] It therefore redounds to the benefit of both the recipient and the giver.[87] On another occasion Kerby emphasized the superiority of prayer to almsgiving, since the former inevitably proceeded from a supernatural intention.[88] "Penetratingly scientific as he was in approach," an admiring pamphlet of the posthumously organized William J. Kerby Foundation later observed, "Dr. Kerby never failed to keep the supernatural note uppermost in charity." His students especially appreciated the fact that the spiritual element dominated his teaching.[89]

It was precisely the supernatural element of philanthropy that scientific charity neglected, often as a matter of principle. Some proponents of scientific charity acknowledged the contributions of such Catholic organizations as the St. Vincent de Paul Society, but others sensed a fundamental antagonism between secular and religious philanthropy. Samuel H. Bishop, of the Brooklyn Bureau of Charities, spoke of the history of Christian charity with respect and even awe; but in order to be truly effective, he insisted, charity "must be a primary and not a secondary activity; its reference must be relative to the causes of its problem and to the improvement and well-being of its human objects." Without this realization, he explained, the modern charity movement could not have developed.[90]

Catholics felt the same ambivalence toward scientific charity that the likes of Samuel Bishop felt toward Catholic charity. They praised Edward T. Devine, a key figure in scientific charity, for his insights and advice for improving the lives of society's least. And yet, "as Christians," explained the editors of America, they could not give "unqualified approval either to his ideas or his methods." Devine exaggerated the importance of the scientific approach to charity, in the process ignoring altogether "the fact that the Catholic Church has its charity, which is supernatural rather than scientific, with methods that rest on faith rather than upon statistics, and seeks first of all the Kingdom of Heaven and its justice, for the objects of its charity, and then their relief in the evils of time." And they insisted, finally, that if religious orders devoted to performing the corporal works of mercy, or such Catholic charitable organizations as the Society of St. Vincent de Paul, received anything like the support given to, say, the Red Cross, Catholic achievements would more than stand up to the levels attained by their secular counterparts.[91]

Paul Blakely took special exception to the spread of scientific charity, and especially to its implicit—and frequently explicit—denigration of more traditional forms of almsgiving. As he put it, in the past we had given, without the benefit of careful investigation, to those persons we deemed especially needy. If our money had in fact been poorly directed, we were at least "saved by a good intention" and could still expect a heavenly reward. Under the new dispensation that is scientific charity, we give to a few well-investigated poor—minus the good intention. Blakely's summary conclusion: "It is not supernatural. We do not aid our suffering brethren out of love of God, but because giving 'makes for social betterment.' That is the difference."[92] This was also the concern of Father John A. Ryan, a professor of political science and moral theology and perhaps the best-known Catholic Progressive. Ryan, who taught at Minnesota's St. Paul's Seminary and at the Catholic University of America, also founded and edited the Catholic Charities Review and directed the Department of Social Action of the National Catholic Welfare Conference. "There is grave danger," he warned, "that assistance to the neighbor for his own sake alone will be converted into the service of society as a whole, and the ignoring of the intrinsic worth of the individual."[93]

Kerby frankly admitted that certain "phases" of scientific charity, as with the discipline of sociology itself, had been associated with a philosophy that a Catholic would find objectionable.[94] The effort to secularize charity, he explained, was part of a modern drive to divorce things that rightly belong together. "Everything is nowadays to be separated from everything else," he observed: science from faith, education from religion, morals from dogma, State from Church—and now, charity from the supernatural.[95] Moreover, in an age that tends "to underrate everything old and overrate everything new," the Church proceeds with a caution and skepticism that, if not always fruitful, is at least understandable.[96]

But to refuse to apply modern methods to Catholic social work simply because in some of their manifestations they had been hostile to Christian truth was to relinquish a supremely useful tool for alleviating suffering and bringing people closer to reaching the supernatural end for which they were created. Methods, Kerby reminded Catholics, were not ends but means; they were "channels by which love travels from soul to soul."[97] Yes, charity is primarily a supernatural act. But "its supernatural character does not exempt it from the influence of the natural processes of mind and emotion."[98] No system could exhaust Christ's love, and merely to put charity on a scientific footing would do nothing to narrow the range of that love.[99]

True Christian charity, he explained, was informed by humility. It never supposed that it had nothing to learn, that its methods had so approached the level of perfection as to have no need to absorb the lessons that modern developments had to offer. Serving the poor was such an exalted calling that the authentic apostle of charity would fear to offer unworthy service. Humbled by the magnitude of the task, the charitable person would be willing to be instructed in the most effective ways to help the poor even by those "who admittedly occupy the lower plane of natural vision and impulse" and who could not pretend "to attain to [his] exalted motive or improve upon it."[100] The Church's history of assistance to the poor, the example of her saints whose devotion to the poor was so great as virtually to demand a supernatural explanation, was a useful apologetic for her divine foundation and a source of pride for all members of the Mystical Body of Christ. But merely to continue traditional methods of charitable work simply because they were traditional, especially when social and economic conditions had undergone such drastic change, was to fail the Church. New methods were not wicked simply because they were new.

A common theme in Catholic writing on charity is that people are expected, as in the parable of the talents, to make fruitful all the gifts that God has given them. Joseph Husslein observed that just as the early Christians built their churches with stones from pagan temples, modern Catholic social scientists "have borrowed for our own Catholic sociology whatever was true and good in the work even of men who may have been positively hostile to Christianity itself."[101] Kerby agreed, pointing out that Clement of Alexandria, the late-second-century bishop who encouraged Christians to use pagan learning and philosophy for the benefit of the faith, is recognized as a saint; Tertullian, on the other hand, who vigorously rejected any Christian effort to borrow from Greek philosophy ("What has Athens to do with Jerusalem?" he demanded), died outside the Church. Hence the need for Catholics to rise to the opportunity that scientific charity presented. He summed up his posture by quoting a statement uttered before the National Conference of Catholic Charities in 1918: "In relief work there is nothing static but the motive."[102]

According to Kerby, the question from the Scriptures—"Who is my neighbor?"—was of special relevance to the whole matter. Whenever someone of relative wealth comes across or is able to find a person or family in need, so long as he discharges his charitable work intelligently and with human warmth, nothing is wanting. This, indeed, is "the ideal relation."[103] But industrialism, economic concentration, and urban congestion have created a certain atomism among people; the small, face-to-face setting of the neighborhood has given way to an environment in which most of one's everyday interaction occurs with strangers. Charity work is no longer so simple. Those in a position to help the poor only very rarely encounter in the ordinary course of life cases of need that they might be able to address in such an intimate manner. Under these new conditions, Kerby argued, "we obey a universal law by creating organizations of benefactors and by some kind of system in rendering service."[104]

Even skeptics of modern methods of charity appreciated Kerby's point. Paul Blakely, for all his criticism of modern sociology and scientific charity, conceded the benefits of the new approach in his very efforts to defend the Church's charitable activity. It is not without significance that in his essays on Saint John Francis Regis (1597–1640), Blakely took special note of the organization and the statistical methods that the saint brought to relief work. The rudiments of "scientific charity," therefore, far from being foreign to the Catholic Church, were present in the work of some of her most beloved sons.[105] "If American sociologists would only wipe away a certain mist of prejudice from their mental vision," one Catholic thinker remarked acidly, "perchance they would find that the solution which they seek has been in the world for two thousand years and is even now under their very noses."[106]

More recently, Blakely and his colleagues could point to the example of Frederic Ozanam, the brilliant young law student who, in 1833, founded an enormously successful charitable lay organization, the St. Vincent de Paul Society.[107] Amid the lingering anticlericalism of postrevolutionary France, Ozanam determined to found an organization composed not of priests but of laymen, who would demonstrate the Church's inexhaustible generosity by giving to the poor not merely money or material sustenance but the fruits of a holistic approach to charity as well. As one sympathizer explained, "The Society was created to be a vindication of the Church by the exercise of charity in its widest sense, charity for mind, charity for heart, charity for the body, charity for the whole man—full and perfect service to our neighbor by charity of the spirit."[108]

Ozanam, who began with a mere eight men, found his entire enterprise derided by a friend influenced by the socialist Saint-Simon, who wondered what eight men could do for the suffering poor of Paris. It was with a mischievous delight that a writer for *America* observed that a mere quarter century after this incident the St. Vincent de Paul Society had grown to two thousand in Paris alone, while the Saint-Simonians had drifted into obscurity. The implications for the effectiveness of the two approaches, spiritual and secular, were obvious.[109]

Ozanam provided an especially happy example for Catholics, who noted that the Frenchman's approach took its cues from the scientific methods of modern charity: individual investigation of reported cases, personal visits to the poor at their homes, strict record-keeping, self-help, and attention to the ultimate causes of material want. Unlike the harshly scientific methods of some secular agencies, the society did not "set up an inquisition for card-indexing the unfortunates and their wants, but courteously and carefully inquired into their needs, being always considerate of their feelings."[110] Around the beginning of the twentieth century, when the ideas associated with scientific charity began to gain currency, the society began to place special emphasis on this aspect of its work and adapting it still further to the "scientific" model where that model seemed useful or appropriate. Some, in fact, began to argue that merely dispensing material aid could actually be a selfish act, in that while it sought the grace that charity brings to the giver, it gave no thought to the actual needs of the recipient. A speaker at the first meeting of the National Conference of Catholic Charities in 1910 advanced the argument that "a Catholic doing an act of charity . . . is looking at the spiritual benefit flowing back to himself rather than to the . . . practical benefit he confers upon the dependent." Society volunteers, then, should "give to the family in overflowing measure your time, your knowledge of the world, [and] your influence."[111]

At the same time, the society could boast an essential dimension that "modern charity is apt to overlook, spiritual aid and consolation."[112] Since the science of charity is not merely material—it is "above all a spiritual science"—it "differs from mere philanthropy, as much as grace from nature, as heaven from earth." Such was the science of charity "which can be learned only in the school of Christ."[113] For these reasons, Husslein pointed out, personal perfection and not the eradication of poverty per se was the primary goal of the society that Ozanam had founded. Ozanam himself wrote that his main purpose "was not to help the poor. This was only a means. Our object was by the practice of charity to strengthen ourselves in the Faith, and to win others for it."[114] A society member explained: "The charity or almsgiving feature was adopted as the best means of reaching the poor in their homes, means by which Vincentians can become more intimately acquainted with those to whom they are giving relief, thus learning the real cause of their destitution." This "real cause," society members found, was tied in many cases to "neglect of religion."[115] Aid is not predicated on membership in a particular church, but members "avail themselves of opportunities to bring stray sheep back to the Fold."[116] Pope Pius X praised the organization on these very grounds, telling its president-general in 1904 that he had seen the society "at work at Mantua, and at Venice, where it was rendering invaluable services to the poor by distributing alms, but still more so by bringing them spiritual aid."[117] In 1913, on the centenary of Ozanam's birth, the pope expressed his wish that the observances on that happy day "may develop among men a knowledge and a liking for his work," for Ozanam had devoted his life to proving "by his writings and deeds the salutary efficaciousness of the Catholic Faith, so much so that he has been ranked among the most distinguished champions of Christian science."[118] Another bishop observed that Ozanam perceived "that the spirit and teaching of the Church would be more beneficial to society than the spirit and teaching of unbelieving social reformers" and that the Church "contained all that there was of truth and value in the current schemes of social reform."[119]

Long before Ozanam, of course, there was Saint Vincent de Paul himself. An extraordinarily accomplished figure, Vincent surely boasts one of the most appealing and compelling stories of all the saints. In seventeenth-century France, devastated by the destruction and exhaustion of decades upon decades of warfare, both civil and foreign, and wracked by the epidemics that wars leave in their wake, he organized an extraordinary charitable organization that has provided a moving example to Catholics through the present day.[120] (Chapters of the St. Vincent de Paul Society

can be found in countless Catholic dioceses around the world.) Even
Voltaire, who helped to set the anticlerical tone of the eighteenth-century
Enlightenment, admitted: "My favorite saint is Vincent de Paul."[121] What
Catholic writers of the Progressive Era found especially relevant about
him was that in his methods he appeared to have anticipated the "scien-
tific" outlook in charitable work, but without the disadvantages that
Catholics saw in its secular variety. Thus the *Catholic World* argued that

> the most representative of Catholic social workers [namely, Vincent
> de Paul], was as thoroughly "scientific," and infinitely more success-
> ful in charity organization than the best of modern secular philan-
> thropists. There are signs that secular scientific philanthropy is
> developing on lines more and more opposed to the principles and
> practice of Catholic charity. If we Catholics are to meet our oppo-
> nents successfully, we must remember that the traditional charity of
> the Church is both supernatural and scientific.[122]

While the work of such organizations as the St. Vincent de Paul Society was admirable from a specifically Catholic point of view, it also had
much to recommend it, Catholics argued, purely on the grounds of efficiency. "A fact we never weary of insisting on," began an exasperated
America editorial in 1911, "is the efficiency of our Catholic organization
for charitable work."[123] Joseph Husslein pointed with pride to John D.
Rockefeller's praise in the *Saturday Evening Post*, on efficiency grounds
alone, of Catholic organized charity.[124]

There were reasons for the efficiency of Catholic social work. John
Burke explained that the Catholic who believes that every man is immortal, created in God's image, and renewed through Jesus Christ recognizes
the profound importance of helping the poor. "In such an individual, the
whole meaning of life deepens, and deepens with an intensity that never
reaches its limit. . . . His task is to perfect himself, and an essential element
of that perfection is the dedication of himself and what he possesses to his
fellow men."[125] Daniel Lord added that philanthropy may make him spend
his money for his fellowmen, but that that naturalistic inspiration may
well come from mere "prudent foresight"—the outlook of Franklin, Rockefeller, and Carnegie. But Christian brotherly love alone, with "its supernatural view of man's dignity and destiny, can make me spend *myself*."[126]
John Ryan also insisted on the superiority of the religious motive from the
standpoint of efficiency; it is, he explained, "a much more effective
motive than love of the neighbor for his own sake or for the sake of soci-

ety; for the human being in distress assumes a much greater value when he is thought of in relation to God."[127]

By 1915 a consensus had developed among Catholics: new methods of dispensing charity, if employed with a properly supernatural outlook, were not to be despised. The useful aspects of the scientific approach had no necessary connection to the naturalistic outlook of some of its prominent advocates, and could be harnessed for the good of the Church. "It is the best the world has to offer," said Joseph Husslein, "and we welcome whatever lifts, however lightly, the heavy burden of the poor."[128]

Yet there was more to Catholic misgivings about scientific charity than its failure to acknowledge the spiritual element in charitable giving. They discovered that applied sociology also suffered from the same defects as its theoretical counterpart—namely, the danger that social science, emancipated from the Christian natural-law tradition, would advocate remedies offensive to Catholic belief.

This concern became critically important when advocates of scientific charity urged investigation into the ultimate causes behind the widespread destitution that existed in the early twentieth century. One advocate, for example, listed the "two new expedients" of scientific charity as, first, "helping the poor to help themselves"—an innocuous and worthy sentiment with which Catholics could agree—but second, "preventing extreme destitution by prophylactic measures."[129] Indeed, many of its advocates considered the prudent use of contraception an essential element of the scientific approach to charity. Was it not obvious that large families created financial burdens that could lead to impoverishment?[130] Dr. John J. Cronin observed in the *American Monthly Review of Reviews* that a "very little study of sociology will convince the advocates of the 'race suicide' idea that a few perfect children are far better for the nation and the family than a dozen unkempt degenerates, who add pathos to the struggle for existence, and who sink under the inflexible law of the survival of the fittest."[131] Yet Father John A. Ryan, who ranked among the most progressive of Catholic thinkers in matters economic, spoke with fervor against what he saw as the despicable moral evil of artificial contraception.[132]

The reason was that Catholics refused to abide any evasion of the demands of the natural law. Catholic sociologists pointed out that, even prescinding from the wisdom and authoritative teaching of divine revelation, the perversion inherent in artificial contraception could be perceived on a natural level. All faculties have a certain end as their proper object. Eating, for example, has nutrition and the preservation of life as its object. In addition to serving a nutritive function, eating is a pleasurable activity. Yet one who subordinates the primary end of eating to the merely secondary end of sensual pleasure misuses and perverts one of his faculties, and is said to have an eating disorder. Likewise, marital intercourse, while pleasurable, has procreation as its primary end. Deliberate attempts to frustrate a natural and benign process are not only immoral from the Catholic point of view, but will also, in transgressing a law built into the human heart and designed for man's good, inevitably lead to misery and alienation.[133]

A more detailed exposition of the natural-law critique of contraception is neither possible nor desirable for our purposes; it suffices simply to demonstrate the qualitative difference between the Catholic and the non-Catholic approaches.[134] Catholics and secular sociologists were in a sense speaking past each other. Catholics persisted in a metaphysical outlook that viewed nature in terms of teleology; that is, each faculty and each being as a whole was thought to possess a nature, toward whose full realization its actions must be directed. The kind of argument that Catholic sociologists were making was unlikely to persuade their secular counterparts, for whom so-called metaphysical truths—among them natural law and the principles deduced from it—were of little value next to the scientific knowledge gained through social observation. Secular sociology was a science whose ultimate purpose was the improvement of man's material condition. Philosophical investigation into the natures and proper ends of things seemed antiquated and unhelpful. Blakely put the matter less kindly when he wrote that while the Catholic argument against contraception is "easily stated," it "has no appeal to any man who has determined to rule God out of his world, and very little to those who make self-gratification, or utility, private or communal, the norm of right and wrong."[135]

Yet while both Catholic and non-Catholic sought the good of man, secular sociologists all too rarely specified the particulars of that good. What *was* the good toward which man should strive? What kind of behavior would most conduce to his happiness? Sensual pleasure and physical comfort? Or reaching man's final end, the eternal enjoyment of the beatific vision?

At no level of sociology could these questions at last be evaded. Whether studying man at a distance, as in pure sociology, or seeking via applied sociology to improve his earthly lot, it was ultimately impossible for secular and Catholic sociologists alike to escape value judgments and first principles. Even an endeavor as ostensibly innocuous and free from controversy as relief for the poor turned out to be pregnant with spiritual and ideological ramifications. The kind of relief administered, as well as the method employed in extending it, must, from a Catholic point of view, be consistent with the demands of natural law and of the dignity of the human person. If relief were to aim at the genuine well-being of the recipient it must, moreover, be mindful of his supernatural end and through its offices bring him closer to its attainment. The Progressive or scientific approach, on the other hand, generally viewed relief for the poor without recourse to teleology, without an appreciation of the proper end of man's life. Paul Blakely noted for this reason that "we will soon realize to our cost and perhaps to the loss of immortal souls for whom Christ died, that the modern social worker constitutes a greater danger to faith and morals, than godless schools or the despicable ever-present proselyter."[136]

But, Catholics argued, if applied sociology were to live up to its purported goal of improving the human condition, it would have to proceed based on a true understanding of man and those norms of behavior that will bring him true happiness. The natural law, therefore, had to be admitted as a guideline for practical sociology. Secular sociologists of goodwill should have no objection to this stipulation, Father Daniel Lord noted, because, paradoxically enough, "it is only by teaching men to gain heaven and avoid hell that earth becomes more like the former and less like the latter." The very qualities that a man needs to cultivate in order to make himself fit for heaven are ones that make us "acceptable citizens of the earth that is"; Lord cites purity, honesty, and charity as examples. "Throw over the hope of heaven and the fear of hell, and paganism is the inevitable result. And paganism is a polite name for selfishness, pessimism, immorality, and despair."[137]

Without an appreciation for the spiritual dimension of man's existence, moreover, a cold materialism would triumph, by default. As John Burke explained:

> If the individual, for example, believes that he himself has no immortal soul for which he is answerable to a living, personal God, he will not believe that any other creature has an immortal soul. He will declare that human society and human beings may and should be well content if they are comfortably housed, fairly well fed, free from disease, and enjoy a fair proportion of time for leisure and culture and education.[138]

"Social values," he insisted, "are ultimately determined by *what we think the individual man is, what is his calling and what is his destiny.*"[139] Burke and his colleagues made clear what they thought man was—a creature composed of body and soul, made in the image and likeness of God, whose temporal happiness could be found in conforming his actions to that law of nature written in the heart of every man, and whose destiny and purpose was to enjoy eternal happiness in the presence of the beatific vision.[140] According to Paul Blakely, the modern social worker, for his part, failed to acknowledge either a supernatural end for man or a divine or natural law that could circumscribe or stand in judgment of sociological prescriptions for human betterment. The typical social worker, having been trained in "principles ultimately destructive of faith and morality," had a purely naturalistic outlook whose definition of human happiness, neglectful of matters of soul, was necessarily incomplete.

> "Whether or not there is a God," say some apostles of social reform, "we do not know. But this we know: that there is a world of misery to be relieved, of ignorance to be enlightened, together with practical means at hand to accomplish our work. If God does not exist, He does not seem to enter deeply into the problem. Certainly, we have not found that we greatly need Him. As far as we see, man can be happy and good without Him."
>
> It all depends on what one means by goodness and happiness. If goodness is conformity to a purely subjective norm of action, happiness the relief from the more grinding burdens of poverty, and if God does not exist, perhaps our social faith is vain, and these modern apostles speak the truth. Yet we feel that there is no field of human activity, however small, from which God can be safely excluded.

"If one is content," Blakely concluded, "to remain continually within the circle beginning with man and ending with him, and to make of himself dull clay, unlit by any aspiration after higher things, one may by degrees suppress the soul's yearnings for the Absolute Truth and Good." But those who recognize that man was destined for an existence higher than that of a mere brute could never rest satisfied with any such approach.[141]

The combination of a distorted and incomplete picture of the path to human happiness on the one hand and a refusal to submit to the laws of God or nature on the other led to moral disaster. "For what appears to be a temporal advantage," Blakely explained, the social worker "will counsel conscious birth restriction, sterilization, marriages forbidden by the Church, divorce, or legal remarriage after divorce."[142] Modern sociological theory, therefore, having emancipated itself from an a priori allegiance to the Christian moral tradition, had its direst consequences not in its systematic treatises, which were read by very few anyway, but in its baneful application in everyday life.[143]

For this reason the incorporation of Catholic principles into sociology and a concomitant emphasis on the supernatural element in social work and reform efforts were, for Catholic intellectuals, not mere adjuncts to an intellectually self-sufficient discipline. They were absolutely essential to the proper use and development of the social sciences. The two principles on which Catholic sociologists would admit no compromise were, first, that sociology, in both its pure and its applied forms, could not claim autonomy from the inherited moral tradition of the West; and second, that in the realm of applied sociology and social work the supernatural dimension had to be considered paramount. As Burke warned, "The cult of the intellectual alone, that is, the intellectual untempered by any spiritual sense, leads to the irrational, and the morally disastrous."[144]

There was, to be sure, a considerable difference in emphasis between the approaches to sociology of the skeptical, confrontational Paul Blakely on the one hand and the apostle of scientific charity, William Kerby, on the other. But we may still speak of a distinctly Catholic view of sociology. Blakely and Kerby, for example, were in perfect agreement that the philosophical underpinnings of much of modern sociology were irreconcilable with Catholic teaching. Quite apart from the materialistic prejudices of many individual sociologists, whose work either discounted the supernatural or relegated it to the realm of Spencer's "Unknowable," the discipline as a whole seemed so wedded to positivism that even the basic norms of Christian moral teaching were up for debate.

Even in the related area of applied sociology, and particularly in that of scientific charity, differences among Catholics between advocates and skeptics of modern methods of relief for the poor were more apparent than real. Kerby was well aware of the potential for abuse of the method of scientific charity, and for all his reputation as a "progressive," he condemned those scientific philanthropists whose absorption in the method of charity blinded them to its supernatural end. He insisted on this dimension with the same firmness as did other Catholics. His point was simply that this very end could be better met through the appropriation of modern approaches. He insisted, moreover, that these modern methods needed to be infused with Catholic truth to bear good fruit. Social work as a mere profession, divorced from spiritual considerations and "setting forth its own standards, formulating its own morality" would always remain utterly foreign to the Catholic Church. Proper moral direction was essential. Anticipating scientific charity, St. Vincent de Paul had emphasized the importance of providing good spiritual and moral counsel to the poor whom one served.[145] Kerby asked, "If wholesome environment, effective moral and mental training, vigorous home ideals and good example are fundamental in all life, who shall measure the extent to which lack of these results in every kind of delinquency that we find among the poor?" Since the fullness of spiritual truth and the moral law had been entrusted to the Catholic Church, Catholics alone could reliably perform for the poor the essential (and scientific) function of offering sound moral advice.[146]

For Catholics, therefore, values and first principles meant everything. The William J. Kerby Foundation observed in 1943 that the direction that American social work would take in the future would be determined "either by the materialistic or the spiritual views common to the leaders in the profession."[147] It was not merely that Catholics considered the Church a supernatural help in performing functions that civil society alone might just as easily carry out; as John Burke put it, "It is Christ or chaos, the Catholic Church or the yawning chasm."[148] Some, it is true, insisted on the value of modern scientific methods in the alleviation of poverty; and in this way they partook of the spirit of the Progressive Era—in its desire for order, its preoccupation with empirical study, and its confidence in the ability of experts in the social sciences to manage human affairs.[149] But their demand that the spiritual element of poor relief prevail over merely secular considerations could not have been more opposed to the technocratic outlook of the period.

Equally disquieting from the Progressive point of view, with its dislike of dogma and its emphasis on the construction of a unified national community, was what Progressive intellectuals would have considered the sectarian nature of the Catholic approach. Paul Blakely, in a parody of scientific charity that he wrote for America, pinpointed this developing antagonism, paraphrasing his opponents thus: "Private agencies, especially when dominated by the 'sectarian outlook,' can never hope to suppress public evils. This is the work of the State, committing its duty into the hands of capable persons possessed of the 'social outlook.'"[150] Catholic charities, moreover, "resolutely [oppose] race-suicide [that is, birth control], divorce, lawless marriages, sterilization, and such like evils, suggested by modern sociology to the consideration of man's supreme guardian, the State." The two positions were impossible to reconcile, and both Catholics and secular Progressives knew it.

Many Catholics, it is true, were eager to cooperate with Progressives where suffering might thereby be alleviated,[151] but mere material cooperation could not conceal the chasm separating the two philosophies. "No good can come from a 'cooperation' which disregards these differences, or involves a denial of essential principles," Blakely warned. "Cooperation is worse than barren gain, when it tends to obscure the principles which must underlie all profitable social work. . . . Black is not white, and the Church of God can enter into no true fellowship with any social force which denies or minimizes the absolute rights of God over men and nations."[152] When in their own charitable work, moreover, they deprecated the very secular ideals that constituted Progressive belief, and when they spoke of alone possessing the truth of salvation, Catholics threatened to undermine the emerging national creed that Professor Eisenach identifies as a crucial element of the Progressive program.[153]

Following the counsel of Leo XIII, Catholics in sociology, as elsewhere, accepted the good they found in modern thought. But, also following Pope Leo, they rejected anything that seemed to threaten Church teaching. "While welcoming all possible cooperation," Paul Blakely noted, "the present is surely no time for the Catholic social student either to hide his principles, or to gloss over fundamental differences. . . . No power of diplomatic speech can reconcile the radical antagonism of the two forces which today are aligned with Christ, and with what Christ called 'the world.'"[154]

4 / ASSIMILATION AND RESISTANCE: CATHOLICS AND PROGRESSIVE EDUCATION

I T STANDS TO REASON THAT EDUCATION should have occupied so much of the Progressives' attention and energy. Since the Progressive project consisted in part of implementing a series of social reforms and of creating a populace creative and flexible enough to accommodate ongoing change in the future, education had to be considered an essential arena for Progressive reform. No halfway measures could substitute for the systematic training of coming generations in the new kind of citizenship that corresponded to prevailing social conditions and to the democratic way of life that John Dewey and his colleagues advocated so vigorously. As Dewey himself once remarked, "I believe that all reforms which rest simply on mechanical or outward arrangements are transitory and futile."[1]

The reaction of Catholic intellectuals to innovations in educational theory was similar to their response to developments in sociology and other social sciences during the Progressive Era. A good deal of the specific methodology introduced via the new pedagogy, in particular its eagerness to conform educational practice to ongoing developments in biology and psychology, appealed to Catholics, especially in religious education. There, many Catholics had acknowledged for some time, the excitement of the faith was in danger of ossifying into an arid process of lifeless memorization. Some of the recommendations of the so-called new education seemed to offer a helpful remedy, one that engaged the child at all levels—the "whole child," as the Progressives put it.

Several of the most prominent Catholic educational theorists of the Progressive Era, in particular Thomas Edward Shields and Edward A. Pace, both professors at the Catholic University of America, have been referred to indiscriminately as "Progressives"; and while it is true that these men sought to incorporate new approaches into education, to refer to them without qualification as Progressives is more problematic. Progressive emphasis on allowing the child latitude for creativity and experimentation may have been intended to forge the type of fluid, tolerant, nondogmatic citizen that the Progressives envisioned for the emerging new republic, but these approaches themselves were not intrinsically ordered to such an outcome and indeed could be appropriated for other purposes. Thus many Catholics believed that in religious education in particular, the new methods could make their faith a living reality for children and thus help to steel them more effectively against the incursions of the modern world. Catholics wanted to transmit to children certain *substantial goods*, not simply to impart to them neutral procedural rules within which a variety of perspectives may be debated (as in the Progressive scenario).[2] Insofar as the Progressives were seeking through their educational innovations to inculcate in the child a national, secular, nondogmatic ethic of social democracy, one that placed a greater premium on the democratic ethos itself than on the vindication of specific goods, Catholics were adamant in their opposition. Hence when Catholics did avail themselves of modern educational methods it was the letter and not the spirit that they followed. It was the classic example of Catholic engagement with the Progressive milieu: selective appropriation of morally neutral elements of the Progressive program, for a purpose that tended to undermine that program's goals.

The Progressive education movement could claim many philosophical and historical antecedents, tracing itself at least to Jean-Jacques Rousseau's *Emile*, a book with roots in the Romantic tradition. Rousseau, who placed tremendous faith in human nature prior to the corrupting influence of social institutions, held the nature and innate capacities of children in especially high regard. Over and against the contrary view, prevalent if not universal in his time, whereby education served to conform what was thought to be the child's corrupted nature to a model of right conduct and moral enlightenment effected from without at the hands of the instructor, Rousseau encouraged his readers to think of education as a development from within.[3] The Progressives did not necessarily share the exalted view of the child expressed in *Emile*—indeed some considered it utterly ridiculous—but they would take up several of Rousseau's themes in their own work. These included in particular the need to conform instruction to the interests of the child and, on a broader scale, to render through education the kind of citizen who would be both self-supporting and inclined by a universal benevolence to assist his fellowmen in need—what has been called "the sociological tendency in education."[4]

Rousseau's direct influence on the Progressives is difficult to measure, but enough of the themes he introduced in *Emile* were adopted by subsequent theorists that they had become common currency by the time the Progressives emerged on the scene. Thus Johann Pestalozzi carried Rousseau's ideas into the nineteenth century, in the process concretizing and expanding them. Experiment rather than tradition was to be the benchmark of educational progress. The new education had to take into account the needs and capacities of the child's developing mind. Education should, moreover, further the cause of social reform. Many of Pestalozzi's themes thus had a familiar ring and indeed would prove influential well into the twentieth century.

Johann Herbart and Friedrich Froebel, in turn, elaborated on and developed in more systematic fashion the often tentative propositions of Pestalozzi, especially regarding the psychological foundations of the new education. Herbart, a native German, conceived of education as a formal process. Froebel, on the other hand, was convinced that since what the child craved was not learning but action, or play, then play ought to be accorded some significant role in the educational process. Thus it was Froebel who was especially interested in the education of young children and established the first kindergarten. The Prussian government, unsympathetic to Froebel's lack of regimen and structure, went so far as to forbid kindergartens in Prussia, and it was only because Froebel's educational ideas received a friendly reception when the Baroness von Marenholtz exported them to England that we know about them at all.

Herbert Spencer helped to accelerate the movement for educational reform in America even though he was not, strictly speaking, an educational theorist (or even an American). His laissez-faire political views, which would have precluded the use of public funds for educational purposes, were of course anathema to Progressives, but many still appreciated his philosophy of education, which smacked of, so to speak, the *via moderna*. Education's main function, Spencer explained, was "to prepare us for complete living." Accordingly, education needed to serve the principal subdivisions of "complete living": activities pertaining to self-preservation, securing the necessities of life, maintaining proper social and political relations, and the gratification of tastes and feelings.[5] Spencer's answer to all these concerns was characteristic of the nineteenth century: *science*. In his 1859 essay called "What Knowledge Is of Most Worth?" Spencer argued that science was of greater utility to students than the traditional curriculum of classical studies. This was the element that was missing from Rousseau's original scheme, and it would play a considerable role in the Progressive curriculum.

Spencer's faith in the new education and its redemptive potential for the human race was shared even by those Americans who held the rest of his philosophy in low esteem. Thus the sociologist Lester Frank Ward, who denied Spencerian determinism and seized Darwinian social thought for use by reform-minded Progressives, conceived of education as the great driving force in the progress of civilization.[6] A broad diffusion of knowledge was necessary in order for humankind to apply rational and intelligent guidance to the process of evolution.[7]

These strains of educational thought converged in the thought of the Progressives. Progressive education, in particular its American manifestation, "rejects the doctrine that certain collections of fixed, unchanging truths are to be transmitted by teachers to their students."[8] In an age of change and uncertainty, future citizens needed to be trained in a spirit that eschewed dogma in favor of a flexible outlook on the world. As Dewey explained:

So far as education is concerned, those who believe in religion as a natural expression of human experience must devote themselves to the development of the ideas of life which lie implicit in our still new science and our still newer democracy. They must interest themselves in the transformation of those institutions which bear the dogmatic and feudal stamp (and which do not?) till they are in accord with these ideas. In performing this service, it is their business to do what they can to prevent all public educational agencies from being employed in ways which inevitably impede the recognition of the spiritual import of science and democracy, and hence of that type of religion which will be the fine flower of the modern spirit's achievement.[9]

Although they favored a revision of the traditional liberal curriculum, Progressives did not advocate a strictly vocational training to replace it.[10] Such a solution, in John Dewey's view (and in a distinctly Veblenian analysis), would undermine the democracy the Progressives were trying to promote by reserving "culture" for the well-to-do and placing it beyond the reach of the common man. What they advocated was a curriculum more suited to modern social conditions, which would promote socialization and form the democratic citizenry of the future. What this meant in practice was that the "traditional curriculum," which "was a matter of routine in which the plans and programs were handed down from the past," would give way to a Progressive alternative "based upon a philosophy of experience" that had not been possible "before the rise of experimental science."[11]

For some, perhaps many, of its exponents, Progressive education was the logical outcome of a belief in the immanence of authority; that is, that the ultimate source of authority, indeed of the very moral law, rested not in some transcendent Being but in man himself. William H. Kilpatrick was particularly emphatic on this point. "The right of parents or other grown-ups to determine what children shall think must be essentially revised," he wrote. "In the new situation of ever increasing change, we cannot, try as we will, foretell what our children will need to think, while with the new philosophy of change and its ethics those who are at present in authority have no such right of control." The duty of the present generation, he went on, was to prepare the succeeding one to think for itself, even if that meant rejecting what the present generation held. "As soon as we take the lid off the universe our claim to fasten our conclusions on our children vanishes. We must free our children to think for themselves. Anything else is not only to refuse to accept the facts as to the unknown changing future, but is at the same time to deny democracy and its fundamental demand that we respect other people, even our own children."[12] (As an icy rejoinder to this point of view, a Catholic commentator cited Chesterton's assessment of modern education: "We cannot decide what is good, but let us give it to our children."[13])

In the field of morality, while Dewey did not advocate the hasty overthrow of inherited beliefs, he insisted that a moral system could no more be considered absolute and unchanging than could a scientific paradigm that was forced to give way in light of new developments and discoveries. Thus he held that

there is also a presumption in favor of principles that have had a long career in the past and that have been endorsed by men of insight; the presumption is especially strong when all that opposes them is the will of some individual seeking exemption because of an impulse or passion which is temporarily urgent. Such principles are no more to be lightly discarded than are scientific principles worked out in the past. But in one as in the other, newly discovered facts or newly instituted conditions may give rise to doubts and indicate the inapplicability of accepted doctrines. In questions of social morality, more fundamental than any particular principle held or decision reached is the attitude of willingness to reexamine and if necessary to revise current convictions, even if that course entails the effort to change by concerted effort existing institutions, and to direct existing tendencies to new ends.[14]

Dewey, furthermore, was a case study of how classical liberalism evolves into its modern counterpart, how the so-called negative liberty of the old liberals becomes the positive liberty of twentieth-century social democrats. Society, according to Dewey, if it were to be truly just and humane, needed to furnish its citizens not merely with the absence of restraint, as liberalism had traditionally held, but with what Dewey called "effective freedom," by which he meant the moral and material wherewithal by which individuals may achieve complete self-realization. This kind of freedom entailed "positive control of the resources necessary to carry purposes into effect, possession of the means to satisfy desires; and mental equipment with the trained powers of initiative and reflection required for free preference and for circumspect and far-seeing desires." The mere absence of restraint is "formal and empty," according to Dewey, for if a person is without "resources of personal skill, without control of the tools of achievement, he must inevitably lend himself to carrying out the directions and ideas of others."[15] For Dewey, then, the importance of education lay in its ability to develop within the child the habits and frame of mind that would make possible the neo-Hegelian self-realization that he envisioned for every citizen of a democratic state.[16] And if this self-realization were to occur, it would have to happen outside the constricting bonds of dogma.[17]

Hence the rise of a distinct Catholic school system was not a development that Dewey could support. He was surprisingly candid in his denunciation: "It is essential that this basic issue be seen for what it is—namely, as the encouragement of a powerful reactionary world organization in the most vital realm of democratic life, with the resulting promulgation of principles inimical to democracy."[18]

By the time of Dewey's rise to prominence, this system in the United States had already been firmly established. Aware both of the enormity of the task and of the opposition they had faced, American Catholics took considerable pride in the educational system they had erected. Thomas Edward Shields pointed with awe to an accomplishment that had been realized "under difficulties that to any but heroic souls would have proved insuperable."[19] Paul Blakely called the Catholic school "the most splendid monument ever reared by any people to testify to their belief in God, and their unswerving devotion to His Son."[20] It was indeed an impressive achievement, and one that reflected the self-confidence and sense of distinctiveness that characterized Catholics in the United States during the late nineteenth and early twentieth centuries.[21]

Yet despite this accomplishment, some Catholics, before even venturing an opinion on the innovations that were overtaking American education, began on the defensive, convinced that Progressives either considered the Church downright hostile toward education or were loath to concede her contributions to educational theory and practice over the centuries. All serious educational and pedagogical advances, it seemed, were being attributed to the post-Reformation period. In 1911 the *Catholic Educational Review* published a review essay of the available literature on the history of education, noting its anti-Catholic bias and suggesting avenues for research that might help to reverse what the author and his coreligionists considered the tendentious conclusions of many of the popular works on the subject.[22] Surveying the educational theory of the preceding century, another commentator declared: "Whatever is best in their educational doctrine is nothing more than modern and catchy phrasing of pedagogical tenets held by the Church for the two thousand years she has been exercising her God-given mission of teaching all men."[23] Article after article appeared in the Catholic press on the great strides the Church had made in the Middle Ages toward educating the masses, on medieval and Renaissance Catholic thinkers who anticipated principles of modern pedagogy, and the like.[24] Another essayist for the *Catholic Educational Review* was especially effusive in his praise for the Church: "To look into her past, to study her history, to recall her wonderful achievements for the spread of culture and the humanizing of the race, is to make the Catholic heart throb with joy for the glory of the ancient faith."[25] Frustrated by the failure of many standard histories of education to acknowledge Catholic contributions, one Jesuit writer tried pithily to set the record straight:

If there is any truth in the history of education, it is that the two millennia between Aristotle and Locke saw the solution of some of the greatest educational problems the world has ever known. Call it what you will, an education, or a philosophy of life, or a religion that accomplished the change; the conversion of the barbarian plunderers of imperial Rome into the makers of modern Europe was accomplished by one of the greatest educational means in the world. That system flowered in the thirteenth century, and produced almost simultaneously St. Louis the king, St. Thomas the philosopher, St. Francis and Dante the poets. It was the source and inspiration of such drama and poetry as the Mystery Plays and the Minnesingers. It built the universities; set on foot such enterprises as the Crusades, encouraged chivalry and founded the gilds. Such a system of education was surely more constructive and satisfactory than Rousseau's revolution-philosophy or Kant's transcendentalism, or Madame Montessori's talk about absolute freedom for three-year-olds.[26]

With such a history behind them, Catholics saw themselves in a position to evaluate the so-called new education. Simply put, they found it materialistic, and by design. Edward Pace, one of the most accomplished Catholic educational theorists, certainly thought so. Pace, who arrived at the Catholic University of America in 1891 as a professor of psychology, was a man of considerable erudition whose intellectual interests spanned several disciplines. After going on to found Catholic University's School of Philosophy in 1895 (and serving as its first dean), he became a guiding figure in the staggering intellectual enterprise of the *Catholic Encyclopedia*, helped establish the university's School of Education, and cofounded and coedited the *Catholic Educational Review*. His scholarship on Catholic educational principles and their relationship to modern trends was extensive. According to Pace, the Church's educational work in the modern period—carried out, he noted, with virtually no help from other Christian bodies—had consisted fundamentally in maintaining the proper union between the natural and the supernatural. But the tendency over the preceding several centuries had been to establish education on the basis of pure naturalism—"whether this be aesthetic culture or scientific knowledge, individual perfection or social service." Hence conflict was inevitable.[27]

This conflict took place against a backdrop of widespread secularization, a trend that had been set in motion well before the Progressives had emerged on the scene. While many Catholics looked forward with confidence to improvements in education in the coming years, this larger trend of the secularization of the schools continued to fill them with dread. Timothy Brosnahan, S.J., was amazed, for his part, that a country that still seemed to him basically Christian should suddenly find itself with a completely secularized school system.[28] His evaluation of this turn of affairs was ominous: "There is a national alliance to cut out of the curricula of our public schools those disciplines and studies that are essential to the formation of citizenship and the preservation of civilization, and that this alliance, so far as we can see, is directed slowly, cautiously and progressively towards the accomplishment of this purpose by some central agency unknown to us."[29] Paul Blakely compared the situation that obtained in his day with that of Julian the Apostate, the last Roman emperor to attempt to overthrow Christianity.

The popes themselves had drawn the battle lines clearly during the nineteenth and twentieth centuries, thundering against the evacuation of religious content from education and sternly rebuking those parents foolish enough to subject their children to the perils of agnosticism and indifferentism that modern public schools were thought inevitably to encourage. Pope Pius IX condemned the statement "Catholics may approve of the system of educating youth, unconnected with the Catholic faith and the power of the Church, and which regards the knowledge of merely natural things, and only, or at least primarily, the ends of earthly social life." "Full of danger," declared Pope Leo XIII, "is that educational system in which there is either a false religion, or, as is usual in the schools termed 'mixed,' no religion at all." Furthermore, the pontiff went on, it is not enough that certain hours should be set aside for religious instruction; the "whole system should be redolent of Christian piety."[30] These repeated papal urgings were reflected in the very law of the Church. Canon 1374 of the 1917 Code of Canon Law stated the matter flatly:

> Catholic children must not attend non-Catholic, neutral or mixed schools; that is, such as are also open to non-Catholics. It is for the Bishop of the place alone to decide, according to the instructions of the Apostolic See, in what circumstances and under what precautions, attendance at such schools may be tolerated, without danger of perversion to the pupils.[31]

Catholic prelates and intellectuals in the United States issued the same warnings. An impressive number of Catholic writers saw something diabolical in the ultimate aims of the new education. It was, as they saw it, part of an ongoing assault on Catholicism whose ultimate origin dated back at least several centuries. "The enemies of religion," explained Paul Blakely, "understand the importance of the receptive, impressionable years of childhood far better than many a Catholic parent."

> Are we preparing [children] to pass through [the world] unscathed, by entrusting them to schools whose highest religious effort is the furtive admission that any religion is good if one finds it helpful? Plainly, this miserable principle means the substitution of a primitive form of pragmatism for the acceptance, binding on every human creature, of a supernatural revelation. Can the Catholic parent who freely subjects his child to schools ruled by this base spirit, escape before the judgment seat of God, the condemnation of those who "scandalize these little ones that believe in me"?[32]

Judgments of this severity were not uncommon. The Second Plenary Council of Baltimore had declared in 1866: "Daily experience has demonstrated beyond doubt how grave are the evils, and how deep-seated the dangers to which Catholic children in this country are frequently exposed by attending the public schools." The Third Council reiterated these concerns, noting that "purely secular training" can "in no wise supply them with the necessary means for knowing and attaining their last end."[33] Joseph Husslein decried "the criminality of the Catholic parents who send their children to the so-called neutral schools and universities."[34]

Still, it would be incorrect to conclude that in the battle over the new education Catholics were concerned only with the parochial concerns of their own faith, or even exclusively with religion. They also evaluated Dewey's educational theories and proposals from the point of view of the common good and the benefits or ill effects that would accrue to the nation as a whole by their adoption. From the point of view of education per se, Catholic commentators, although by and large sympathetic to some of the scientific emphasis of Dewey's approach, feared the consequences of abandoning the traditional curriculum. As biographer Robert Westbrook points out, Dewey "had very little to say about the particular facts that children should learn."[35] His desire for an education that would equip children with the skills necessary to make critical judgments led him to place great emphasis on instruction in the sciences, less for the inherent value of scientific knowledge than for the benefits of training children in the exercise of "deliberative, practical reason in moral situations."[36] Dewey's emphasis on both socialization and practicality, combined with a contemporaneous drive for exclusively vocational training, left Catholics and other educational traditionalists wondering what would happen to education in the classics, a dimension of the curriculum that in their minds ennobled man and elevated him above the level of a mere brute.[37]

As for moral education, they believed that it was not only Catholic children who would be harmed by the use of a merely naturalistic creed but indeed all American students, who would be deprived of what had proven itself over centuries to be the greatest source of inspiration for the pursuit of moral conduct. Were an entire generation instructed thus, no one should be surprised to see Americans' entertainment grow more vulgar, their manners more coarse, and their society more violent. This kind of moral instruction was simply not strong enough to encourage virtue and quiet the passions.[38] (This theme will be developed at greater length in chapter 5.)

Yet the overwhelming majority of Catholic writing on the subject of education revolved around two principal concerns: a vindication of Catholic education against the theories of Dewey and the Progressives, and the question of incorporating modern findings into Catholic education. These were the matters of greatest urgency to them, for while they believed that their philosophy of education would, if heeded, redound to the benefit of the entire nation, their main concerns at this time were to defend and to perfect the school system that they had established with so much effort and that they sensed was under implicit attack.

The principles of education that Catholics defended were really quite simple. Edward Pace spelled out six basic ones in the *Catholic Encyclopedia*. First, intellectual education and moral and religious education must not be separated. The second built on the first: religion should not be a mere adjunct to education in other subjects but should be the focal point of the entire curriculum. Third, no real moral instruction was possible if divorced from religious education. Fourth, the welfare of the state demanded an education that united intellectual, moral, and religious elements, for it was only by steeping the child in such principles that he could be habituated "to decide, to act, to oppose a movement or to further it, not with a view to personal gain nor simply in deference to public opinion, but in accordance with the standards of right that are fixed by the law of God." The Catholic philosophy of education was thus "the most effectual preparation for citizenship." Fifth, advances in educational methods, far from rendering moral and religious training less necessary, accentuate it all the more; by the same token, the Church "welcomes whatever the sciences may contribute toward rendering the work of the school more efficient." And finally, Catholic parents have the grave duty to ensure that their children receive a good Catholic education, in order that both the intellectual and the moral dimensions of the child be properly cultivated.[39] As Catholic University of America rector Father Thomas J. Shahan put it, the Catholic teacher saw in the child "not only mental capacities that are to be unfolded, but a life that is to be shaped and a soul that is to be saved."[40] The difference between the two approaches lay chiefly in the fact that the Catholic school taught a "clear and solid philosophy of life"—the very kind of all-encompassing outlook on the world, the very essence of the closed and abstract systematization that Dewey's philosophy, and Pragmatism in general, explicitly rejected.[41] Another writer compared the Catholic and non-Catholic systems of education to two vessels, the latter of which was "without compass or rudder."[42] This, then, was where Catholic educators took their stand.

We should be careful not to miss the essence of Dewey's critique and thereby fail to comprehend the meaning and significance of the Catholic response. Dewey was far from being the first philosopher to look to mathematics and the sciences, with their verifiable certainties, as his models for knowledge, and to look with a jaundiced eye on the endless bickering of theologians and metaphysicians. If only the scientific method could be imported into the political and ethical spheres, he and others believed, dissension and discord might at last give way to unanimity. He had no patience whatever with sectarian infighting among Christians. In fact, it is not unfair to say that Dewey, while he seemed to appreciate the value of a kind of natural religion, wanted the ideas of the supernatural and transcendent more or less excluded from society or at least from serious intellectual discussion. As one Dewey scholar put it, "For Dewey, there is no room for the churches in secular society."[43] His desire for "unanimity" is precisely what Progressive intellectuals sought with such earnestness, and that unanimity, it seemed, would be accelerated by discouraging dogmatic attachment to one sect or another in favor of a greater national ideological convergence. The one thing, Dewey wrote, "which has done most to discredit the churches, and to discredit the cause . . . of organized religion [is] the multiplication of rival and competing religious bodies, each with its private interpretation and outlook."[44] The public schools provided a favorable contrast:

> Our [public] schools, in bringing together those of different nationalities, languages, traditions, and creeds, in assimilating them together upon the basis of what is common and public in endeavor and achievement, are performing an infinitely significant religious work. They are promoting the social unit out of which in the end genuine religious unity must grow. Shall we interfere with this work? Shall we run the risk of undoing it by introducing into education a subject which can be taught only by segregating pupils . . . ? This would be deliberately to adopt a scheme which is predicated upon the maintenance of social divisions in just the matter, religion, which is empty and futile save as it expressed the basic unities of life.[45]

Thus when Dewey studiously excluded religious instruction from his curriculum, and indeed discouraged it altogether as unhelpful in forming the spirit of scientific inquiry that he wanted to see inculcated in the new American citizen, it was easy for Catholics to see at work not the benign creation of a truly national community, as Dewey understood his project, but instead something rather sinister. Would they find themselves under pressure, in the name of this new national unity, to retreat from their position as a universal institution with a claim upon the consciences of all men and uniquely in possession of the fullness of truth? Only when Dewey's distaste for religious instruction in the schools is understood in this light can the intensity and vigor of the Catholic response be properly understood.

Thomas Edward Shields, a professor at Catholic University and one of the most important Catholic educational theorists of the Progressive Era, began by describing education as a way of restoring order to fallen man, of enlightening his mind and strengthening his will, of reestablishing the equilibrium between reason and the passions that was destroyed in Adam's rebellion.[46] Since grace built upon nature, the cultivation of the child's natural virtues helped to predispose him to respond to and benefit from divine grace.[47] Yet an education based on the natural virtues alone was still insufficient. Shields quoted favorably from Father James Burns's book on the American Catholic school to the effect that "it is the development of *Christian* character based upon the supernatural virtues and teachings of Christ, not distinct from the natural virtues, but including them and much more besides, which the Christian school places first among its duties, as the thing of most fundamental importance to the child."[48] The *Catholic Encyclopedia* described the matter this way: "When education is defined as 'preparation for complete living' (Herbert Spencer), the Christian can take no objection to the words as they stand; but he will insist that no living can be 'complete' which leaves out of consideration the ultimate purpose of life, and hence that no education really 'prepares' which thwarts that purpose or sets it aside."[49]

Education ought also to develop and refine the child's moral faculties; in Shields's words, it "must aim at bringing the flesh into subjection to the spirit."[50] The allure of temptation can often be great; and only a properly formed conscience can, for any length of time, render men and women truly honorable, chaste, and just. Indeed, purely temporal motives "are like straws before the violent winds of temptation."[51] An interior purification must take place within students; their "hearts and minds must be attuned to the message of a higher ideal than that of mere civic virtue, or social service, or patriotism." Shields wrote that the child who received a religious education was "better equipped for his future contact with the world than the child to whom no such education is given. For when religion is properly taught it fixes in the mind certain beliefs that steady it in the midst of doubt and certain principles of conduct which guide and protect it in the midst of temptation."[52] To educate in a Christian nation without reference to God is not only a "crime," Joseph Husslein wrote, but also "a gross and well-nigh irremediable pedagogical error," for even from a purely naturalistic standpoint, no other influence has a more sure and more salutary effect on the development of the human faculties. "There is no pedagogical substitute for the Ten Commandments," he said.[53]

Catholic commentators pointed out that the Progressive scheme, equating as it did the moral and the social, offered children an unacceptably truncated form of morality. "The social and moral quality of conduct are not identical, nor coextensive," the Jesuit John Reville insisted in a review of Dewey's book *Democracy and Education* (1916). Catholics must continue to insist, moreover, that that education which concentrates exclusively on the "social spirit" is immeasurably inferior to one that, while maintaining due respect for man's social dimension, does not fail to acknowledge his relationship with his Creator.[54]

At bottom, warned Reville, John Dewey's philosophy of education misunderstood "the inherent dignity of human nature." Were education merely socialized and democratized, it would be "truncated and shorn of its crown." "There is a life of the soul with its spiritual yearnings, its responsibilities, its destinies projected far beyond the range of mere social service."[55] While Catholics insisted on an education whose primary end was the cultivation of the soul that it might reach its last end—eternal beatitude—for Dewey, as historian Robert Crunden has argued, the school had replaced the church as "the key institution in the saving of souls for democracy."[56] The Dewey school sought, among other things, to inculcate in children a proper social spirit. Thomas Edward Shields, on the other hand, while pointing out at a meeting of the Catholic Educational Association that the Church recognizes "the indispensable necessity of educating for citizenship," added that she "can never accept it as the ultimate aim of the education given to her children" because "her vision of life is not bounded by the grave."[57] "Apart from participation in social life," Dewey had said, "the school has no moral end or aim."[58] To Dewey's insistence that "the child is for democracy" Catholics answered, "The child is for God."[59]

Although Catholics did not consider the civic aspect of education to be an end in itself, they did not thereby discount it altogether. Edward Pace argued that it was precisely the training that Catholic children received in the tenets of their religion that in an incidental way made them into especially outstanding citizens. The Catholic school had as one of its primary purposes "to shape the individual with a view both to his personal growth in virtue and to the discharge of his social obligations."[60] And by teaching her children the essentials of citizenship, he concluded, "the Church does more for the real prosperity of the country than can be done through any system of purely secular education." In fact, added Pace, it only stood to reason that Catholic schoolchildren should grow up to be among the finest American citizens, since their education had been thoroughly imbued with the ethical precepts and social consciousness that good citizenship demanded and since they had for their support a religious basis, which Pace believed was the only effective guarantor of right conduct.[61]

Educational reformers much more radical than Dewey did not escape the attention of the Catholic press. *America* reported in 1914 on the progress in New York of an organization called the Francisco Ferrer Association, whose philosophy only confirmed Catholic suspicions that the new education represented at heart an attack on all forms of external authority that presumed to bind the individual conscience. In the first issue of *Modern School,* the association's monthly bulletin, the editors boasted: "It is pleasant to think that the education we are giving the children at our school is anti-authoritarian in the real sense of the term; and for that reason, we hope, better than that at any school in America. . . . We wish men and women to be free, and to that end we are opposed to religion, war, property and all the things that divide men into camps and nationalities." Dewey himself would doubtless have been horrified at the anarchy of the Ferrer School; according to *America,* children came and went as they wished, with no given hour set for the beginning and end of classes. Ferrer educators, however, shared Dewey's conviction that education ought to lay the groundwork for social reconstruction by encouraging the development of critical minds that would scrutinize carefully the institutions under which they lived.[62]

Catholics did not completely discount Progressives' claims on behalf of the social aspect of education. Indeed, they considered it eminently proper for the school to inculcate in children the intellectual tools and the moral disposition to perceive the common good and to order their actions in conformity with it.[63] The only reliable way to do so, however, was by means of the one mechanism to which Progressive education had forsworn to have recourse: religious belief. Religious belief alone could supply a comprehensive and socially useful moral code as well as sufficient motivation to encourage men to observe it.

Take away the love of righteousness as a motive of conduct and a civil community becomes a pestilential congregation of freebooters, who have adopted some "laws of the game," keep up some appearances of well-behaved propriety, and publicly profess theoretic adherence to some principles of right. Now righteousness is a moral quality. An education, therefore, which does not primarily aim at the development of the child's moral nature and which does not ultimately effect this development, whatever other merits it may have, has this drawback, that it tends to produce a type of character against whom society must be constantly on its guard, and to whom the laws of God and man are tolerable only in so far as they subserve his personal interests, and failing in this are to be observed only when he cannot, through mental adroitness acquired from education, devise subterfuges and deceits to avoid their sanctions. Can this be the end to be attained through education?[64]

Yet in education, as elsewhere, Catholic thinkers acknowledged the genuine contributions of the modern era and spoke freely of the benefits to Catholic pedagogy to be reaped from a selective appropriation of certain Progressive principles. As authoritative a source as the *Catholic Encyclopedia* distinguished between the aims of education, which were constant, and the methods employed, which ought to be "based on the findings of biology, physiology, and psychology."[65] According to Edward Pace, one of the great virtues of Catholic education was that while its subject matter of course remained static over the centuries, divine revelation being unchanging, it adapted itself as circumstances dictated. The Church could, therefore, glean from the so-called new education those principles it found in harmony with its mission and liable to increase the effectiveness with which it transmitted the contents of its sacred deposit of faith. A writer for *America* who was critical of much of the new education insisted that he did not mean to give the impression that "the fads of modern education have no good in them"; they did possess some good, but this was precisely what made them potentially so pernicious. An obvious absurdity, he argued, was inherently less alluring and was less likely to seduce the well-meaning than an error containing an admixture of truth.[66] The Church would therefore have to proceed carefully. But even the tough-minded Paul Blakely conceded that modern pedagogy, "unconsciously perhaps, has suggested many a new and useful application of old principles to modern instances."[67]

Of course, it was not to modern scientific advances to which the Catholic turned first. "Those who know not God and who are indifferent to the teachings of the Church" may well so act, and "naturally turn in the first place to the underlying sciences of biology and psychology" in order to understand and justify a given principle set forth for improving the training of the child's developing mind. The Catholic had no objection to this method, but he of course "will naturally turn for enlightenment to Christ and to His Church. If he finds the proposed principle embodied in Our Lord's method of teaching and in the teaching activities of the organic Church, he will not need further confirmation of the validity of the principle, although he will turn to the sciences of biology and psychology in search of whatever light they may shed upon it and in the endeavor to find a common ground on which to discuss the matter with those outside the Church."[68]

A striking proof, according to Edward Pace, that there could be nothing inherently radical or undesirable about integrating sound modern psychological principles into Catholic education was that the Church's liturgy itself, which served a didactic as well as a devotional purpose, had from the beginning employed these very principles. Each item of the Mass, Pace explained, "conveys a lesson through eye and ear" to the highest reaches of the soul. "Sense, memory, imagination, and feeling are thus aroused, not simply as aesthetic activities, but as a support of intellect and will which thereupon issue in adoration and thanksgiving for the 'mystery of faith.'"[69] The iconoclastic tendency in religion, Pace was happy to report, appeared to be dying out; and at the same time the findings of modern psychology related to the use of imagery and sensory activities were vindicating the Church's approach.[70] "Sensory perception, image, pleasurable feeling and idea must all grow into a unity, and this must form, not a package of knowledge that the mind lays by for future use, but a living element in the living mind, a part of the mental tissue."[71]

Thomas Edward Shields never tired of making similar observations to the effect that the best modern principles of education had for many centuries already borne fruit—within the Church. "The Church, in her teaching, reaches the whole man: his intellect, his will, his emotions, his senses, his imagination, his aesthetic sensibilities, his memory, his muscles, and his powers of expression. She neglects nothing in him: she lifts up his whole being and strengthens and cultivates all his faculties in their interdependence."[72] This appeal to the whole man extended to the Church's liturgy as well. His discussion of this issue deserves to be quoted at unusual length, not only because it provides an elegant illustration of his point that the Church had in fact anticipated by centuries much that was valuable in educational principles erroneously labeled new, but also because it offers a fine example of the genuine affection for the Church and its institutions that was absolutely standard among Catholic writers of the period:

> Her liturgical functions themselves have a teaching power of a high order. The very edifice in which Catholic worship is conducted points heavenward and tends to gather up the successive generations of the Church's children into solidarity; it carries the mind back to the days of the basilica in ancient Rome and to the ages of faith which flowered forth in the medieval cathedrals; memories of the past look out from chancel and reredos, and the noble and disinterested deeds of the saints are called to mind by the stained glass of her windows and by the pictures and statues which adorn her temples; the stations of the cross recall the great tragedy of Calvary with its story of love and self-oblation, while the tabernacle draws all hearts to Jesus in the Sacrament of His love.
>
> The cloud of incense carries the mind of the worshipper back to the smoke of sacrifices which arose from the altars in ancient days of darkness and of struggle and of Messianic longing and helps to bring home a realization of the meaning of the great sacrifice of redemption. Its perfume reminds the worshipper of the sweetness of prayer, and its ascent indicates the way in which man is lifted up to heaven through the ministry of prayer and worship. The music from her organ and from her chanters stirs the feelings and the emotions of the worshipper and directs them heavenward that they may harmonize with the uplift that is being experienced by all of man's conscious life. Nor is the worshipper permitted to sit back and be a mere witness of this liturgical drama. He constitutes a living, moving part of it, by his song and his prayer, by his genuflection and his posture, he enters into the liturgical action which, in its totality, shows forth the divine constitution of human society by which man is made to cooperate with his fellow-man in fulfilling the destiny of the individual and of society.

In this manner of teaching there may be plainly traced many of the recognized fundamental principles of education. We find here embodied sensory-motor training, the simultaneous appeal to the emotions and to the intellect, the appeal to the memory of the individual and of the race, the authority of the teacher and the faith of the hearer, and the principles of cooperation and imitation.[73]

As Shields saw it, it had been through this kind of approach—an appeal not merely to man's intellect but to his whole being—that the Church had been so successful in inculcating in children and in her flock at large the values of civilized life. Thus the Church had succeeded even through the present day in imparting to her faithful "the great doctrines of revealed truth, not merely as apprehended by the intellect or stored in the memory, but as the living, active forces in their lives which lead them to prayer and to worship, which lead them to make their sacrifices, to offer their oblations, and to remain loyal to the Mother of civilization."[74]

More than the liturgy in particular, whose didactic purpose, according to Pace, was served by "modern pedagogical principles," was the Church's sacramental system in general. Thomas Edward Shields argued that although universities and schools founded on modern principles of pedagogy abounded, the sacramental system proved that it was not there but in the Catholic Church, "in which the Holy Spirit is the teacher," where "the perfect embodiment of sound pedagogical principles" could be found.[75] After a lengthy discussion of such abstruse psychological-pedagogical topics as affective consciousness, feeling and mental assimilation, and the like, Shields proceeded to demonstrate how the Church's sacraments, in their matter and form, corresponded splendidly to principles that in his day were being described as peculiarly modern. "In the light of the body of scientific truth which we have been considering," he began, "it would seem that the vitality of the Church's teachings, judged by human standards and apart from the supernatural influence of Divine Grace, depends in no small measure upon the way the Church, in her organic teaching, utilizes the chief epochs of feeling in human life for implanting and nourishing into life the germs of the great spiritual truths of which she is the divinely appointed Guardian and Teacher." The sacraments, Shields explained, provided an excellent example of how the Church taught and sanctified. They served principally to infuse the soul with divine grace in order to build up the supernatural virtues and to conform the recipient more closely to his divine model. In this alone they were redolent of modern pedagogical principles, in that the inward, invisible grace they conferred was signified by outward, visible signs.[76]

But, Shields went on to argue, the sacraments served an additional purpose—as "educational agencies" through which the Church "implants in the souls of her children in each of the great epochs of human feeling the germs of the divine truths that will guide them safely through this world of darkness to the portals of eternal life." In educating her flock in this way, the Church demonstrates that she had long recognized the modern principle that a lesson's presentation ought to correspond to the state of the development of the child's mind. Thus at that moment around the child's seventh or eighth year when "the great, puzzling, outer world begins to reach his intelligence and to fill it with questioning wonder," the Church leads him into the confessional "and with loving kindness helps him to read his riddles." "From the tenth to the twelfth year," Shields wrote, "the dawn of emotions and passions whose meaning is still obscure to the child begins to trouble the quiet of his soul." And again the Church extends supernatural assistance; for it is at this age that she "leads him to the Communion rail and in the midst of flowers, bridal wreaths, lights and music, accompanied by all the joy that breathes in her ritual," she teaches him that "love is the key to the world of emotion and passion that is stirring the depths of his soul." The Church, through Holy Communion, impresses upon him in an unforgettable way that a life permeated with love for God and for one's fellowman, a life centered on self-sacrifice and dedicated to truth and justice, leads to true happiness and joy—and that one rooted in selfishness leads to "wretchedness here and to eternal misery hereafter."[77] For Shields, the Church's wise ordering of its sacramental system serves to stir the soul in just the right way at just the right moment. At the same time, it seeks a proper balance between feeling and intellect. "The Church," Shields wrote in *Philosophy of Education*, "through all the forms of her organic teaching, aims at cultivating feeling, but she does not allow her teaching activity to culminate in feeling, which she values chiefly as a means to an end; she employs it to move to action and to form character and she never leaves it without the stamp and the guidance of intellect." The Church takes feeling and imparts to it a definite direction, that it might animate the soul in the pursuit of right conduct.[78]

Thus Shields could conclude that modern educational principles were in fact deeply rooted in the constant practice of the Church, and far from forcing Catholics onto the defensive they should themselves be considered a source of pride. "It is a source of great joy to the fervent Christian," Shields wrote elsewhere, "to find that every great fundamental principle of education which the development of modern science has yielded up is to be found in its most perfect embodiment in the pages of the Gospel and in the organic teaching activities of the Church." Indeed, Shields explained, here was another excellent argument in favor of the divine foundation of the Catholic Church. The natural talents and intelligence of her faithful could not account for the embodiment of these principles in the Church's teaching activity for the simple reason that their discovery within the disciplines of psychology and biology were of relatively recent origin, whereas the Church appears to have had recourse to them from the earliest times. Indeed, "the Church in the Apostolic times, the

Church of the Fathers that found expression for its doctrines in the terms of Platonic philosophy, the Church in the darkest days of the eighth century, the Church of the Schoolmen, the Church that created the Medieval cathedral, and the Church of to-day, was ever obedient to these unchanging principles of education."[79]

Shields went on, however, to castigate the Protestant reformers and their descendants for having abandoned the sound pedagogical wisdom of the Apostolic See, from which they were so miserably separated. Here as elsewhere Catholics demonstrated their lack of correspondence with the irenic and ecumenical spirit of the Progressive Era. It was a thoroughgoing indictment:

They suppressed feeling from their public worship as an unworthy accompaniment of revealed truth; they accused the Church of idolatry because of the way she employed sensory phenomena for the conveying of spiritual truth; they extinguished the lights on her altars; they banished the incense from her sanctuaries; they broke the stained glass of her windows and the images of her saints; they suppressed the sacraments and the ritual. Ignorant of the laws of imitation, they would have neither guardian angels nor patron saints. Not knowing the vital necessity of expression, they held that faith without works was sufficient for salvation. With the Saviour's warning ringing in their ears, "The letter killeth, it is the spirit that giveth life," they accepted the rigid standard of the written word in lieu of the living voice of the teacher. And as a result, revealed truths, one by one, were extinguished from their midst, leaving the descendants of confessors and of martyrs wandering in exterior darkness where, like the Children of Israel, they were compelled to make bricks without straw, where they sought to teach supernatural truth, while violating the fundamental laws of the mind.[80]

Despite this overall confidence in the basic principles underlying the Catholic educational inheritance, not all Catholic discussion on education shared this tone of self-congratulation. These great principles, in many cases, were not being translated into practice. The pages of the *Catholic Educational Review*, for example, reveal a general lack of satisfaction with prevailing methods of catechism instruction. Teachers were having students memorize definitions and formulas before their minds were fully prepared to absorb what was being taught them. This was not a new problem; as Father Lambert Nolle pointed out, this unease regarding the teaching of the catechism dated back at least a hundred years. But the overwhelming burdens under which the clergy had labored had made any systematic reform out of the question.

The time had come, however, to examine the matter more closely. An especially important stimulus to further investigation of new methods in teaching came from the Sacred Congregation of the Sacraments in Rome, which, under the direction of Pope Pius X, issued a decree lowering the age at which a Catholic child could receive his first Communion from ten to seven—the moment at which ecclesiastical authority presumed that he had reached the age of reason. A special urgency was suddenly attached to the proper instruction of young children in the faith. In the Catholic Educational Review Father Nolle called on his fellow Catholics to seize the opportunity to discard the "formalism and rationalism" into which the old method had ossified, in favor of supplying the children with "the sweet and nourishing milk of Divine revelation." The old method, he complained, consisted of filling little minds with "highly technical but perfectly useless formulas." Such an approach could lead not merely to unsatisfactory results, he said, but even to plainly negative ones; it could, for example, impress upon children the notion that the catechism is not something to be understood, or it might even leave them with a general distaste for religion itself. Moreover, while seven was a fair enough approximation of the point at which the child began the mature exercise of his powers of reason, the line was a fine one, and it certainly varied from child to child. Methods had thus to be devised to fill children who may in fact not yet have reached the age of reason with an all-consuming desire to receive the Eucharist and to draw deeply from this copious font of grace. The memorization of formulas and definitions was not likely to have such an effect on any children, let alone those whose reasoning faculties remained partially undeveloped.[81]

Francis Kerze adopted the term "didactic materialism" to describe this defective state of Catholic catechesis. It is "a delusion all too prevalent among us," he said, that mechanical memorization constitutes true religious education, one that moves and stimulates both mind and heart. "Mere verbal memorizing has not yet produced a single Christian. A definition of contrition has not as yet made a single convert." In order to create a lasting impression on the child's mind, then, and in order to prevent his accumulated knowledge from growing desiccated and sterile, the child had to be led to a true love for his faith. To do so, Kerze explained, certain principles ought to be observed—principles with which Dewey would doubtless have agreed. "Learning is dependent upon interest and education," he reminded his readers. "Correlate with the life of the pupil." "Never tell a pupil what he may wisely be led to see for himself." An approach guided by such principles, he predicted, could foster in children both sound learning and an earnest affection for their faith more effectively than could the method then in use.[82]

More than once did such Catholic writers remind their readers that religious education as currently practiced was in fact "at variance with the historic practice of the Church." The Church, indeed, had always appreciated the didactic role of her liturgy, her churches, her art, and her music. "We could almost construct our catechisms from the frescoes found in the Roman catacombs of the second century," Kerze pointed out. "What of the *Biblia Pauperum* in the Middle Ages, what of the Christian art, as expressed on the walls of our medieval cathedrals, in the very liturgical system of the Church?"[83] As long as Catholics were not "hasty in lauding the 'new education'" or "one-sided in the adoption of every supposedly accepted result of modern pedagogical research," their use of methods taken from secular sources (even if once the patrimony of the Church herself) could yield splendid results.[84]

It was common for Catholic educational theorists to point out that the pedagogy employed by Christ himself, in method if not in content, was not much different from those that were gaining currency during the Progressive Era. First, Christ adapted his message, supernatural and sublime, to the capacities of his listeners and issued his revelation in a gradual and systematic way. The more difficult and detailed the teaching, the greater the divine preparation. One of the Church's holiest mysteries, a teaching that has prompted breathtaking art and music as well as endless theological debate and refinement, is the doctrine of the Real Presence of Jesus Christ in the Eucharist—that in Holy Communion the communicant receives, as the Council of Trent put it, the body, blood, soul, and divinity of the Lord. Of this unfathomable mystery, as Saint Thomas Aquinas expressed it in his "Tantum Ergo," "*Praestet fides supplementum sensuum defectui*"—"faith for all defects supplying where the feeble senses fail." Thus Christ, in imparting a teaching so hard to understand, foreshadowed the spiritual nourishment that the Church would transmit to her flock through this heavenly bread by performing the multiplication of the loaves and fishes—a miraculous deed, to be sure, but one easier for witnesses to grasp and one that would only later be appreciated for its value as a pedagogical device. That such gradualism was characteristic of the divine method of imparting the truths of revelation was readily apparent in the use of Old Testament figures and events as "types" for the unfolding of the New Covenant, and in John the Baptist's preparation among the Jewish people for the message of Christ.[85] Christ also "took some familiar thing in the natural or social order and attached His lesson to it," thereby adapting his message to the minds of the people and rendering it more easily comprehensible.[86]

The *Catholic Educational Review* anticipated the objection that since the method of simple memorization then in use appeared to have worked so well in the past, nothing but a lust for innovation could justify significant change. While the standard question-and-answer format had indeed sustained the faith of generations of exemplary Catholics, the present generation faced such ubiquitous threats to their faith that educational method had to rise to the challenge. A nun from Delaware, Ohio, explained that many adults, never having come into contact with some of the less agreeable elements of modern society, were loath even to believe that such things existed. But the fact was that children "do meet all kinds of people, hear all manner of topics freely discussed without either faith or reverence; they hear virtue sneered at and behold indulgence in vice held up as liberty; they are told that God is a myth, that religion is a fairy tale." Contemporary popes noted, with a vigor mingled with sadness and frustration, that Catholics were living through especially wicked times—a period in which the Vatican found itself subjected to ceaseless humiliations, Christ was being more and more visibly dethroned from his position as King of Nations, and unscrupulous men, in public and in secret, were actively seeking to undermine the Church. These factors, combined with the moral degradation that the popes insisted always accompanied a falling away from the law of Christ, placed a special burden on the younger generations to resist the spirit of the age and to defend their spiritual patrimony. Could it be any wonder, then, that children "whose only knowledge of religion consists in the memorized answers to the questions of the catechism find themselves totally unprepared for their surroundings and fall victims to the prevalent unbelief if not to the prevalent vices?"[87]

There was some movement in this direction in catechetical studies. Already in 1908 Father James A. Burns could observe:

Here and there throughout the country the effort is being made to bring the methods of catechetical instruction into accord with sound psychological principles. In a number of our best schools, catechism is now being taught by employing the same means as prevail in the teaching of the other common branches. In these schools direct religious instruction is accompanied by object lessons, blackboard and chart illustrations, songs, and devotional exercises. In a word, the senses, the imagination, the emotions, the will and the affections are all appealed to as well as the intelligence, in the effort to bring down the religious truths that are taught from the region of the abstract and metaphysical, and to render them easily assimilated for the mind of the child.[88]

Of all major Catholic educators and theorists it was Thomas Edward Shields, the first head of Catholic University's education department, who was most responsible for this trend in Catholic education and who has been seen as most sympathetic to the cause of Progressive education. And in some ways his views on educational method did indeed reflect those of John Dewey. Shields's first and most important book, *The Psychology of Education* (1906), emphasized a number of standard Progressive ideas. The importance of activity, the conformity of the curriculum to the development of the child's mind, the development of a center of correlation among the various subjects taught—all these and more were relatively familiar themes by the time Shields's early work began to appear.[89] He developed an important textbook series for the study of religion that moved away from the traditional emphasis on memorization to an approach that he believed was more likely to be naturally assimilated by the child's mind and truly incorporated into everyday thought and activity. The catechism, Shields explained, was a relative novelty in Catholic pedagogy, dating back only to the sixteenth century, when it emerged to compete with Luther's catechisms. Even then they were intended to be tools for teachers and theologians, not students. It was only by a twist of fate that the catechism should have come to be viewed not only as the student's principal instrument in religious education but also as the traditional method of imparting such education. A related concern for Shields was the erection of the Sisters College to train sisters in the various teaching orders in the new kind of instruction he was advocating. Merely distributing his textbooks to American dioceses was worse than useless if teachers were not properly trained in the method that Shields had intended to accompany them. In the meantime, and at great personal expense, Shields joined fellow Catholic University educator Edward Pace in launching the *Catholic Educational Review*, a scholarly periodical that sought to create a forum within which Catholic educational principles could be discussed.

Shields's method, in fact, while attracting a surprising amount of clerical and lay Catholic support, also received its share of criticism in his day. In a celebrated debate, Father Peter Yorke, a respected theologian, called it "nothing less than revolutionary."[90] And by the standards of traditional catechetical instruction, the Shields method *was* unusual. But the Catholic University educator was surely correct to dismiss this sort of criticism as a misguided if well-intentioned effort to protect the Church from the kind of rash innovation that seemed to be wreaking such havoc in the world at large. For Shields was not, as his detractors would have it, utterly discounting the importance of memorization. As Edward Pace explained, "Doctor Shields does not object to the cultivation of memory. What he does object to is the use of the memory in such a way as to make the mind a mere record of answers which may or may not be understood."[91] In the environment of the Church of the early twentieth century, however, the cautious reaction that Shields at times received was not difficult to understand and probably was to be expected. It reflected on the part of some Catholics, at a time when heresy seemed to be insinuating its way into the Church's very bosom—a heresy whose hallmark was an excessive attachment to the modern—an inability to distinguish on the one hand between doctrinal novelty that challenged the Church at its heart, and on the other an innovation, based on new information, intended to help the Church better perform her traditional functions.[92] Pope Pius X, for his part—along with Shields's many American supporters—had no difficulty distinguishing between the two. "Far, far from the clergy be the love of novelty!" the pope had declared in his encyclical against Modernism; he was here concerned not about newness per se but about the abandonment of Scholasticism in favor of more modern approaches to theology and philosophy.[93] For at the same time, the pope, a notorious foe of ill-considered innovation, was an enthusiastic supporter of Shields's Sisters College, even sending a personal financial contribution of his own. The Apostolic Delegate went so far as to describe Shields's work as the most important of the century for the Church.[94]

In fact it was Shields himself, who warned his fellow Catholics of the need to "discriminate real advance from mere innovation," who best demonstrates the limited extent to which Catholics embraced modern trends in education.[95] For all his differences with his opponents—of whom there were, in fact, relatively few strong ones—together they constituted the broad front against Progressivism that united Catholic intellectuals of the period. They shared the suspicion that they were being asked to abandon their posture of distinctiveness in the name of the centralized democratic state that was being forged both institutionally and ideologically during the Progressive Era. Whatever diversity of opinion existed regarding practical educational questions was subordinated to this overriding concern. For while John Dewey and other Progressive educators were aiming to employ the educational process as a means of weaning Americans away from too pronounced an attachment to particular sects in favor of a conception of citizenship thought to be more consonant with the demands of an emergent social democracy, Shields was one with his critics in emphasizing the crucial importance for Catholics to maintain and strengthen this kind of attachment. It is for this reason that the only book-length study of Shields's life and work noted that it was only from "a superficial standpoint" that the Catholic University educator's theories "might appear to have much in common with that of John Dewey and the other men of his time," and why the most recent student of Shields's work took special notice of how his philosophy, at its root, seemed to run counter to Progressive currents.[96] Shields intended his contributions to Church education to strengthen and deepen children's Catholic faith and to prepare their minds for the reception of absolute truth. The new pedagogy "was to serve the primary purpose of Christian education, the transformation of man to a child of God."[97] To allow for greater initiative on the part of the student on the one hand, and yet on the other to guide him inexorably to assent to an external dogma, had been far from the intention of John Dewey and his colleagues. Shields insisted that Catholics' readiness to adopt salutary innovations from the secular world did not reflect a readiness to surrender their distinctiveness or to become assimilated to values foreign to their faith: "The willingness of our Catholic teachers to look for help beyond their own order, or even outside the Catholic Church and her institutions, must not be taken as evidence of the surrender of principle, nor must it be taken to mean an abandonment of anything which these teachers consider essential; nor does it mean an express desire on the part of our schools or of our teaching communities to coalesce with non-Catholic systems of education."[98]

The Diocese of Cleveland was the first to implement the Shields method systematically and on a large scale, complete with a slate of teachers who had received the appropriate training. Cleveland's superintendent, Rev. Dr. William A. Kane, exulted that with regard to religion, the children "are familiar with a great part of the Old and New Testaments and can answer readily, not in the language of dry formulae, but in their own words, questions of Christian doctrine that come under the assignment. They have a better understanding of the material than those children who have only studied the catechism." He went on:

In music, I have found that the children of the third grade master in ten minutes exercises for which those of the eighth grade require an hour.

The teachers were delighted with the Series. In the beginning they were doubtful. The books seemed very difficult and the method was strange. Now the teachers confess that the results are far superior to any-thing of the past.

He concluded: "I am convinced that nothing in the educational field will contribute more to the honor and glory of God and the salvation of souls than the Catholic Education Series properly handled in our schools."[99]

Dr. Kane also vouched for an incident recorded by one of his teachers involving a third-grade child:

Last Thursday during the noon recreation, I noticed a number of high school girls grouped around a little child from the third grade. She was amusing the girls by telling them the story of Zan and Bobo [a story from Shields's *Third Reader*]. Finally, coming to that part of the story where Zan's pride leads her to wish to be like God, the little girl told this part of the story with a great deal of indignation, shaking her head over the dreadfulness of Zan's pride. The girls were much amused by the child's earnestness and thought it a good chance to draw her out.

"Well, Marie, why was that so bad in Zan? If she were good, could-n't she be like God?"

"Of course not," promptly answered Marie. "She couldn't possibly be good enough to be God."

"But Sister over there—she's good. Couldn't she be God?"

"No, she couldn't. Even the Pope couldn't be good enough. Besides, there can be only one God and He is so good that nobody could ever be nearly that good."

At this point, the Sister joined the group and she said:

"Tell me, Marie, who is next to God?" When asking the question, she had in mind the Blessed Virgin, but the child's answer took her breath away:

"Why, the Son of God as man."

"Where does the Son of God live?"

"He lives in Heaven and in the little tabernacle in the Church."

"But the tabernacle is such a little house."

"Yes, I know," she hastened to assure us, "but He doesn't mind that because He takes the form of a tiny white Host. It isn't a Host, though (and she kept shaking her head to emphasize the fact) but it looks like one. It really is Our Lord."

"Why did Jesus take that form?"

"Because He loved us and wanted to be with us."

"Marie, perhaps you can tell these girls how much Jesus loves little children?"

She then told the story of Christ blessing the little children and she dwelt with such fondness on the description of the little girl on His lap [a picture illustrating the story in *Religion—First Book*] that I thought it a good chance to test her further.

"That is a beautiful story, Marie. Wouldn't you love to have been that little girl on the knee of Jesus?"

"Yes indeed," she answered, and then, after a moment's thought, "But you know, Sister, we can get much closer than that little girl."

"How, Marie?"

"Why, in Holy Communion. He comes right into our hearts, and that's closer than being on His knee."

With that, Marie ran off to join her playmates. The older girls, impressed when the teacher told them that any child in the class could have answered as well as Marie, asked:

"What catechism do they study, Sister?"

"They have not had any catechism; religion comes into all their work."[100]

Religion, indeed, was the "center of correlation" for the various disciplines under the Shields method, but it was not only in religious education that Shields's system enjoyed success. The only biography of Shields includes as an appendix quite an arresting example of its effectiveness. It is another testimony from Cleveland's superintendent of Catholic schools, about a history test given in January 1919 to a fourth-grade child. The superintendent begins by noting that the report that follows is a stenographic one to which no corrections in language have been made in the process of transcription. Furthermore, the child had done no special preparation for the talk, unaware until that day that she was to make it. The little girl was asked to speak to high-school students on the subject of the famous mid-fifth-century confrontation between Pope Leo the Great and Attila the Hun. She did so at very great length, beginning with background on Attila, the terror of the Roman population when it was learned he was contemplating an invasion, and finally the confrontation itself. She spoke with an eloquence and an attention to detail so unlike a child of her age that the reader really must read it for himself. Further evidence that it was not merely a memorized speech is that she spoke on the subject on several other occasions over the ensuing months and used her own (and different) words each time.[101]

Shields received praise from around the country. A nun in Texas wrote to say: "We find our second-grade pupils better readers—better students in every way—than the present fourth-grade pupils" who had not had the benefit of the Shields method.[102] Noting the success achieved in Cleveland, the Diocese of Pittsburgh adopted Shields's book series and reported similar results. Pittsburgh's superintendent of Catholic schools, Dr. Ralph M. Hayes, whose career would include serving as bishop in Montana and later in Iowa, and for a time occupying the position of rector of the North American College in Rome, noted that the Shields method had "given the greatest satisfaction."

Community supervisors write to me in this strain: "The majority of our first-grade teachers are more than satisfied, they are enthusiastic. The subject matter . . . could not be improved. The method, its arrangement and presentation, all appeal to the children. . . . They are encouraged to think and to express their thoughts by word and action and song and art work. They are always ready to respond, so ready, indeed, that at times it is difficult to curb their enthusiasm . . . !" You know that the Second Book is not an easy one, yet I have seen Polish and Slavic children who came to school almost entirely ignorant of the English language, after one year's training in the Method, handle that Second Reader with ease and even with an understanding that no one can doubt.[103]

In addition to the standard curriculum, Shields insisted on the central importance of art and music, disciplines that he believed stirred the soul and helped to form good character. Naturally, as part of his music course he emphasized Gregorian chant. One of Shields's collaborators later recalled: "In 1920 Doctor Shields had the long-awaited joy of hearing ten thousand little children succeeding each other for three days, filling the huge Cathedral of St. Patrick in New York with their young voices. It was on the occasion of the International Congress of Gregorian Chant at which Dom Mocquereau himself was present. Here were the first fruits of our music series."[104] Gregorian chant, a stunning musical inheritance of Roman Catholicism that had been a support to piety and worship since before Pope Gregory the Great's late-sixth-century codification, was such a beautiful aspect of Catholic worship that Shields was committed to having children trained in it, that they might draw as abundantly as possible from the spiritual riches of the holy Sacrifice. It was typical of Shields's entire approach, in that he would never have dreamed of dumbing down the Church's liturgical music for the sake of the children; for the sake of the children he sought to elevate them to the sublime heights of the Church's hallowed chant.

Thus Shields's method was intended to bring children to a love for their Catholic faith; it was not socialization or democracy that was at stake in the educational process as it was for Dewey. Progressive education, moreover, would have banished religious training to the exclusive purview of the Sunday school, at the parents' discretion. Shields, however, insisted that the most complete education integrated Catholic thought even into otherwise nonreligious subject matter; the child's whole experience ought to be infused with the Catholic faith. Catholic parents should not tolerate any artificial separation. Shields's approach to education was one in which not only religion but all subjects, including history, literature, geography, science, and music, inasmuch as they would all be centered in God, would participate in a single unity. "The unitary character of life and the inseparable relations of nature and grace demand that the natural and supernatural unfold in the child's consciousness simultaneously and in their true relations. The natural and supernatural in the virtues which she must inculcate must function as one indivisible vital entity. The supernatural must ever strengthen and invigorate the natural."[105]

Pace was of the same mind on this matter. He believed he could point to recent advances in psychology to support his claim

> that the reception the mind gives to any idea is determined not simply by the nature of that idea, but also by the nature of the ideas that are already in the mind. If the new idea is altogether strange or foreign to those that have been acquired, it is not welcomed but intruded upon the mind, it will have little or no effect upon the mental development, it will remain a solitary, unassimilated thought, and will quickly perish for want of support.[106]

This was an example of what Pace meant when he suggested that the findings of a sound psychology could shed useful light for Catholics in education and elsewhere. Thus if religious instruction were to take root in the mind and soul, if it were to bear real fruit rather than remain an unassimilated adjunct of thought, it would have to be presented systematically and as an integral part of the curriculum.

In addition to the argument from psychological effectiveness, Pace offered the additional consideration that by excluding religious instruction altogether from the standard curriculum and relegating it to Sundays alone, or to some other time outside of normal class hours, the likely outcome would not only be that such instruction would seem utterly extraneous to what the students were learning in school but, worse still, students would also be likely to interpret this relegation as an indication that religious knowledge was of secondary importance. If it were truly central to a good education, would it not be included as part of their regular course of study?[107] It is, furthermore, rather significant and indeed quite indicative of the tone of militancy and intellectual unity that characterized the Catholic Church in the United States during the Progressive Era that Pace and Shields, carelessly described by some historians as "Progressives," should have rejected so decisively the compromise settlement advocated by the small minority of Americanists a generation earlier—namely, that specifically religious instruction be provided after school hours.

What is important to recognize, then, is that Catholic educational theorists did not partake of the often revolutionary philosophies attached to those methods of modern pedagogy that they accepted. One Catholic writer, for example, noted that Johann Herbart had been successful "not on account of his peculiar philosophic system, but in spite of it."[108] Time and again exponents of the new education called it more than a mere method; it was, they said, a way of life. For the Catholic educator, on the other hand, it *was* simply a method, and worth consideration only insofar as it assisted in accomplishing the ultimate end of education.[109] If a Catholic educator suggested an approach to education that took into account the state of the child's developing mind, or that emphasized learning by doing, or a host of other modern principles, he did so not because he believed truth and authority to be immanent in humanity, or because he entertained Romantic notions of the inherent goodness of the child, or because he saw the inculcation of a social ethic as the primary end of education. It might be said that Catholics used Progressive principles in education for decidedly non-Progressive purposes—a classic example of the cautious and selective assimilation that characterized the entire Catholic intellectual enterprise during the Progressive Era.

Moreover, while John Dewey was more aware than anyone of the revolutionary nature and implications of his philosophy of education, it is difficult to find any such radicalism in the educational practice of even those Catholics who were most sympathetic to Progressive methods. The Catholic response to Progressive education was a textbook example of Pope Leo XIII's counsel that Catholics ought to appropriate for their own use those elements of modern thought that could reap clear benefits for the Church while discarding those that were thought incompatible with

Catholic faith and practice. Hence Catholics, far from obstinately resist-ing all intercourse with modern thought and resting comfortably in the assurance that, being in possession of the fullness of the truth, they had no need to be instructed by an often hostile outside world, were eager to use what the social sciences could offer in order to convey their religion with greater effectiveness and permanence. One searches in vain for radicalism in the issues of the *Catholic Educational Review*—which was edited by Thomas Edward Shields and Edward Pace, thought to be the most Pro-gressive Catholic educational theorists—that were published during the Progressive Era.

It is only at a very superficial level, then, that the work of Edward Pace, Thomas Edward Shields, and other Catholic pedagogues can be referred to uncritically as Progressive. To be sure, they had recourse to so-called modern methods in education and they studied seriously the conclusions of psychology. They believed, furthermore, that one of the baneful conse-quences of the secularization of education was that religious instruction had become isolated from the rest of the curriculum and therefore from advances in other disciplines that could enrich religious education. But here, as elsewhere, the Catholic perspective, based as it was on natural law, was teleological. To what *end* was the child being educated? For that matter, for what end had the child been created? These questions, more than discussions of method and psychology, were what was fundamentally at stake in the debate over Progressive education, and the willingness of Catholics to make use of secular learning in teaching their faith—a strat-egy that the Church had used at least since the second century with Saint Justin Martyr's *Dialogue with Trypho*—should not obscure the important chasm separating Catholic from Progressive educators.

The educational question bore a striking parallel to the issues raised with regard to Catholic versus Progressive sociology. The budding disci-pline of sociology looked to improve the lot of humankind, but without recourse to a systematic philosophy of man. From the Catholic point of view, the Progressive emphasis was on procedure rather than substance, the study of the improvement of the human condition without a philo-sophically rigorous definition either of improvement or of man himself. Sociology's prescriptions for social amelioration might point to *how* man could make his society wealthier, or its members more equal, but modern sociologists left unanswered the more fundamental questions of *what* man *ought* to do, what his goals for himself and for society ought to be. Like-wise with education: there could be no objection to advances in educa-tional theory in themselves, just as there could be none to legitimate developments in sociological thought; but insofar as either one substituted materialism for a philosophy mindful of man's spiritual soul—whether through an explicit repudiation of extrasensory phenomena or implicitly through the evolutionist bias that permeated modern thought—it could not be tolerated by the Church.

In both cases the emergence of a nonsectarian national creed as a central feature of the intellectual milieu of the Progressive Era is clear. And in both cases the Catholic Church in America declined to be absorbed into any such amalgamation. "Professor Dewey assures us that the public schools are developing a new and higher form of religion that is devoid of all denominational content," scoffed the putative Progressive Thomas Edward Shields. The result of such an effort, he warned, would be to undermine all religion.[110] Willing as he was to use new methods to improve religious education, Shields nevertheless perceived the ideological underpinnings of the Progressive education movement as a whole and rejected them.

At the very time, then, that education was taking a studied and deliberate stand on the ethics of social democracy, which raised flexibility and toleration to the level of absolutes, Catholics were growing more insistent than ever on the unique and irreplaceable nature of specifically Catholic education. The first principle of the Church's approach to education was that the individual possessed a soul made in the image and likeness of God that was destined to live forever. They had no intention, obviously, to impose Catholic education on every school system throughout the country. What they did not refrain from doing, however, was warning their fellow countrymen of the consequences of supplanting the Church's philosophy of education with one based on naturalistic humanitarianism and an ill-defined quest for social comity through syncretism. For as Michael J. Larkin put it, "It is this [former] system of education that has built up civilization and it is *this system alone* that can conserve it."[111]

5 / ECONOMICS
AND THE SOCIAL QUESTION

EW ISSUES CREATED MORE APPREHENSION in the minds of Americans or were discussed more vigorously during the Progressive Era than that of the condition of labor. Disputes between capital and labor had been especially violent and chaotic in the late nineteenth century, and as the new century dawned the situation was far from resolved. "In the solution of this question," wrote a solemn Father (later Monsignor) John A. Ryan, one of the most distinguished pro-labor Catholic thinkers, "is involved to a great degree the future of religion, of morality, of true civilization."[1]

Historians of American Catholicism, in their treatment of the Progressive Era, have tended to conflate the Catholic response to labor unrest and poverty with that of secular Progressives. And indeed the two sides agreed on the need to ameliorate the lot of the worker and to insist that business observe what they considered a minimal level of "social consciousness." The way they reached their conclusions, however, differed considerably. A distinctly moral perspective grew less and less pronounced over the course of the Progressive Era, giving way to a growing attachment to scientism among American intellectuals, who were increasingly anxious to defend their position "on the basis of science rather than moralism."[2] As Jeffrey Lustig has observed, it was "the language of objective fact and inductive method . . . that dominated their work, clothing and eventually hiding the religious element."[3] "Many came to view political reform not in terms of good against evil," explains historian Edward Purcell, "but in terms of knowledge, efficiency, and scientific planning against ignorance, error, and economic waste."[4] On one level, then, the social question had to do with improving the lot of the ordinary worker. Yet on a more subtle level the matter revealed a widening chasm between the metaphysics of the Catholic Church and the technocratic, pragmatic outlook of much of the American intellectual elite.

Furthermore, the arguments that Catholics tended to use when search-ing for the causes of strife between labor and capital reveal a hostility to modernity in general that is more or less absent from the standard Pro-gressive critique. For the most part, Catholic commentators viewed the social question not as an isolated problem but as part of a larger disease plaguing the West. Consequently, in addressing the issue they used argu-ments that Progressives would have found at best unhelpful—for instance, attributing the precarious condition of labor in the modern world in part to some of the social and ideological consequences of the Protestant Reformation. While they made certain suggestions and policy proposals and often promoted them with vigor, Catholics warned that patchwork solutions that failed to acknowledge larger trends had little chance of proving to be lasting remedies.

Both aspects of the Catholic argument—its natural-law approach and the sharp criticism of modernity—evoke the larger division between Catholic and Progressive thought that informs this study. Once again, what separated Catholic intellectuals from their Progressive counter-parts, even in an area such as economics and labor in which they enjoyed significant agreement in matters of policy, was the Catholic insistence on natural law on the one hand and the Progressives' distaste for metaphys-ical systems and their inclination toward a more "scientific" approach on the other. This is not to say, of course, that there was no moral element to the Progressive outlook; indeed, political debate during this period was often carried on in an intensely moralistic idiom. Progressivism was in this sense mildly schizophrenic, the center of a conflict between "a liber-alism centered in humanitarian and moral passion and one based in an ethos of scientific analysis."[5] The point to be emphasized here is not, therefore, that Catholics introduced moral arguments into the discussion of labor, for even the most hardened Pragmatist tended to speak in terms of moral categories; and it would be difficult, furthermore, to deny that the Social Gospel theologians were animated by moral concerns. What is important is the way both sides thought and reasoned. In his famous study of the social thought of the Progressive Era, Morton White identi-fied its defining principle as a "revolt against formalism," a rejection of a priori deductive systems in favor of empirical and historicist approaches to the various branches of the study of society.[6] This new approach to the social sciences is one of the most important developments in the intel-lectual life of the Progressive Era, and in maintaining a deductive, natu-ral-law approach to problems of economics and labor, Catholics were implicitly—and often explicitly—challenging the new epistemology.

"That common ground existed at all is surprising," writes historian John McGreevy, "since Catholics and liberals now worked from starkly different philosophical premises."[7]

Yet there was common ground. Monsignor Ryan, who played an important role in integrating Catholic thought into mainstream reform circles, was the chief intellectual influence behind the surprisingly radical Bishops' Program of Social Reconstruction, adopted in 1919, following the end of World War I. This important document, which falls just outside the period of the present study, called not only for a living wage but also for government-funded housing, a variety of legal benefits for labor unions, control of "monopolies," an attack on middlemen (in the distribution process), comprehensive social insurance, and still other proposals besides.[8] It was favorably received in Progressive circles. The *New Republic* noted with satisfaction that "if this sort of thing goes on unchecked, we shall soon arrive at a pass where the real stand-patter will be quite unable to find a spiritual fold." A contributor to *The Nation* spoke hopefully of a possible new "kinship" between Catholics and reformers.[9]

The point to be emphasized here, however, is that the policy agreements between people like Monsignor Ryan and secular Progressives in general, real and important as they were, have tended to obscure the serious and profound philosophical differences between the two sides that we have seen thus far. Beneath the surface, those differences can be seen to continue even in matters of economics and labor, where the two sides enjoyed such considerable common ground. Despite basic agreement in the conclusions they reached, the Catholic natural-law approach revealed a philosophical outlook and worldview that was largely alien to Progressives and that helps to account for the divergence and mutual ill will that characterized Catholic and Progressive confrontations in other social sciences, where their respective conclusions were not, as in economics, happily coincident. Moreover, the anathemas they hurled at modernity were themselves anathema to a Progressive—who, if not an unqualified supporter of the modern age, certainly preferred it and the intellectual and philosophical trends associated with it to the period of the High Middle Ages, to which Catholics appealed. As a recent study of Christian social thought put it, "American Catholic intellectuals exhibited a strongly European and medievalist inclination, channeling European and neomedievalist religious ideas directly into the mainstream of American cultural and intellectual history."[10] The Vatican's emphasis on the centrality of Scholastic theology and philosophy, which grew more insistent under Pope Saint Pius X, "decisively forced Catholic Progressivism into the ambit of neomedievalism and thus ensured that American Catholics would engage American modernity from a potentially more creative critical location than that occupied by their liberal Protestant counterparts."[11] None of this meant that Catholics were unwilling to work with prominent Progressive figures for the improvement of society; in fact, they welcomed such opportunities for cooperation. What it did mean was that whatever they were able to accomplish together, Catholics and Progressives were both the products and the inhabitants of different intellectual worlds.

Before proceeding to the American scene, we must examine, albeit briefly, a central figure in this question: Pope Leo XIII. It was this pontiff's celebrated and influential encyclical *Rerum Novarum* (1891), which was solemnly commemorated in later encyclicals by two subsequent popes—in Pius XI's *Quadragesimo Anno* and John Paul II's *Centesimus Annus*—that set the stage for Catholic commentary for the next century. The encyclical was, if not especially detailed, still such an exhaustive and authoritative statement of Church teaching on the "social question" that Father John A. Ryan could observe that subsequent papal writings on the matter, by Leo XIII himself and by his successor, Pius X, were really only a series of footnotes to it.[12]

Leo XIII was a somewhat enigmatic figure, to be sure, and it is not easy to assign him to a particular ideological category. What is certain, however, is that some historians have exaggerated the differences between this pope and his predecessor, Pius IX, who is remembered especially for his insistence at the First Vatican Council on the doctrine of papal infallibility and for his notorious *Syllabus of Errors* (1864). Yet the idea of a systematic attack on modern errors appears in fact to have originated with the future Leo XIII himself, when he was still bishop of Perugia.[13] Others have found in *Rerum Novarum* the beginning of a Catholic liberalism that would culminate in the positive disposition toward religious and other modern liberties that emerged from the Second Vatican Council.[14] A reading of Leo's encyclicals *Immortale Dei* and *Libertas*, however, reveals that the venerable pontiff had no intention of compromising or altering traditional Catholic teaching in these areas.[15] His efforts to reconcile Catholics with the French Third Republic, sometimes cited as an example of his liberalism, seem to have been driven less by intense conviction than by a realism that recognized the futility of opposing the inevitable.

But a change of tone, though not nearly as extreme as some historians have claimed, was indeed evident in Leo's pontificate. Pius IX, the longest-reigning pope in Church history, had concentrated his energy on positioning the Church firmly against what he called "the particular errors of our age." Leo also condemned modern errors, forcefully and repeatedly. But he wanted to engage the world with vigor, and to demonstrate that the Church had more than condemnations for the modern errors he deplored—it had an inspiring and intellectually rigorous alternative. To counter rationalism, Kantianism, and other modern "isms," he issued his encyclical *Aeterni Patris* (1879), which launched a systematic campaign to revive the study of Saint Thomas Aquinas within Catholic seminaries and among Catholic scholars.[16] It is not a coincidence that the same pontiff who issued this encyclical should also have written *Rerum Novarum*, for just as Leo had countered what he considered the errors of naturalistic and materialistic philosophies with the sure foundation of traditional Thomism, he answered the anarchy into which labor and capital had descended with *Rerum Novarum*, a thoroughly Thomistic document.[17] The encyclical is an attack on certain modern ideas, to be sure, particularly in its condemnation of socialism and its criticism of certain aspects of modern capitalism; at the same time, however, it is a positive expression and vindication of what a just social order based on Catholic principles should look like. Leo XIII had, therefore, registered a truly extraordinary achievement: he had synthesized the teachings of Aquinas with modern developments, thereby constructing an edifice of Catholic social thought that proceeded deductively from the truths of man's existence and purpose all the way through the justice of private property and finally to an outline of a Christian solution to the social question. During the Progressive Era, American Catholics drew not only on the teachings of this revered pontiff but also on the method he used, deducing principles of social life from immutable truths about man.

There were, of course, differences of opinion as to how these broad principles ought to translate into policy. One of the most respected treatments of the subject was John Ryan's *A Living Wage*, the thesis of which will be described below, but which in general argued for a moral obligation incumbent upon employers to provide their workers with a wage that allowed both them and their families to live in reasonable comfort.[18] But a reviewer for the *Catholic University Bulletin* in 1907 objected that Ryan, in his understandable zeal to vindicate the laborer's right to a living wage, overlooked the fact that, both realistically speaking and as a matter of justice, the economic value of the work done must play a key role in an employer's determination of wage rates. Ryan's discussion of the need for a proper family wage for heads of households suffered from a similar shortcoming, the reviewer pointed out. It is true that every man, when he comes to have his own family, has both the duty and the right to support it decently. But since his remuneration must be a function of the value of his work in the eyes of his employer, his status as head of household is irrelevant to the terms of his wage contract. "As an individual or as head of a family, the laborer produces the same amount of work; how then could the employer as such be obliged in strict justice to take into account a condition which is of no advantage to him?"[19] Ryan attempted to answer these arguments in a cordial, if spirited, reply in the *Bulletin* early the following year.[20] Such disagreements, although relatively rare, appear on occasion in Catholic periodicals of the time.

But what is of particular importance for the present discussion, as a work of intellectual history, are the broad philosophical and intellectual trends at work, not the various policy disagreements that inevitably ensued from efforts to see Catholic principles vindicated in civil law. Leo XIII himself cautioned that *Rerum Novarum* not be considered an endorsement of this or that particular program; much still remained to be said on both a theoretical and a practical level, and he thought Catholics ought to be free, taking Catholic principles for granted, to discuss the best way to bring Church teaching to bear on current problems. "If I were to pronounce on any single matter of a prevailing economic problem," the pope wrote, "I should be interfering with the freedom of men to work out their own affairs. Certain cases must be solved in the domain of facts, case by case as they occur. . . . Men must realize in deeds those things, the principles of which have been placed beyond dispute. . . . These things one must leave to the solution of time and experience."[21]

For all its agreement with non-Catholic Progressives, there emerges in Catholic commentary on the social question a self-conscious distinctiveness. In an intellectual environment dominated by positivism and Pragmatism, both of which saw in empirical data the only scientifically meaningful source of revelation, as it were, Catholics appealed to what they called the immutable demands of natural law. Ryan, it is true, seems to have been influenced by the German Historical School, which rejected "economic laws" not derived from observation and experience; but at the same time his primary argument was a moral one. That economics had effectively ceased to be a moral science was a complaint of a number of Catholics;[22] and into a discipline devoted, so to speak, to *is*, Ryan introduced a moral *ought*.[23] At the very time, then, that Progressive thought was beginning to exalt the value-free political thinker, whose "scientific" methodology was presented as evidence of his posture of disinterestedness and strict impartiality, John Ryan, perhaps the most important Catholic

commentator on the social question, was leading his coreligionists in precisely the opposite direction.

In a recent study of American Catholicism, historian Charles Morris
makes this relatively unappreciated distinction. Speaking of New Dealers
in a way that could easily apply to the Progressives of earlier decades, Morris observes that even if they "and [John] Ryan reached very much the
same conclusions regarding economic policy, they arrived at them by
entirely different routes." Secular economic planners, he explains,

> were technocrats, with an instrumentalist faith that modern theoret-
> ical and technical advances, like punch card machines, gave them the
> tools to manage the economy to everyone's benefit. Ryan's approach,
> in stark contrast, was almost entirely deductive. *The Living Wage* and
> *Distributive Justice*, although they were taught in Catholic economics
> classes, are actually works of ethics. They proceeded by elaborating
> the teachings of the Church fathers, St. Thomas Aquinas, and the
> popes to establish basic natural law principles and then derive second-
> and third-level economic conclusions. There is scarcely a number in
> either book and not a single formula or graph . . . .
>
> It surely would have puzzled secular economists to watch Ryan or
> the encyclicals take such pains, for example, to derive the right of
> private property from St. Thomas—why should anyone care what a
> thirteenth-century monk thought about forms of property holding?
> But to Ryan, the popes, and virtually all the writers in *Commonweal*,
> *America*, *Catholic World*, and even the *Catholic Worker*, it was a mat-
> ter of first importance.[24]

It is of considerable significance that Saint Thomas Aquinas and the
Scholastics should have rejected the theory of the state held, for example,
by Saint Augustine—namely, that the state came into existence as a result
of original sin. Aquinas denied that the state was merely a necessary evil,
arguing instead that even had man not fallen from his original state, government would still be both necessary and just. It is significant that this
came to be the dominant view within the Church, since a philosophy that
placed the origins of the state in the consequences of human iniquity was
much less likely to emphasize the state's positive role of securing the common good. At the same time, the state's power was not unlimited. As John
Ryan explained, "The State has a right to do only those things which are
conducive to the attainment of its end, namely, the common welfare."[25]
Elsewhere he laid down specific restrictions on state activity: "Now the

family cannot rightly discharge its functions unless the parents have full control over the rearing and education of the children, subject only to such State supervision as is needed to prevent grave neglect of their welfare. Hence it follows that, generally speaking, and with due allowance for particular conditions, the State exceeds its authority when it provides for the material wants of the child, removes him from parental influence, or specifies the school that he must attend."[26] But while it could not transgress these boundaries, the state did have a positive obligation to regulate social life such that society's various groups would work in concert for the common good. A favorite quotation of Catholic commentators was that of Pope Leo XIII, who declared in Rerum Novarum: "Whenever the general interest or any particular class suffers, or is threatened with harm, which can in no other way be met or prevented, the public authority must step in to deal with it."[27]

Hans Kelsen, one of the most distinguished positivists of the twentieth century, observed correctly that "there is no natural-law doctrine of any importance which has not an essentially religious character."[28] And indeed, the Catholic natural-law approach to the labor question began with a religious premise: that man was created by God with a purpose, to spend eternity in enjoyment of the beatific vision. One Catholic writer after another began his analysis of economic issues by reminding his readers that the Church's *primary* role was not to agitate for legislation or to secure anyone's material welfare. The Church was founded to sanctify souls and to lead men to heaven. But earthly welfare and temporal justice, they insisted with equal fervor, were not easily separable from man's ultimate end. The cause of justice for the workingman was inseparably linked to the Church's responsibility for his eternal well-being. As John Ryan explained, men are "more susceptible to religious influence [and] can know and serve God better when they are contented and comfortable than when they are impoverished and miserable."[29] Thus the insistence on the need for a living wage that could support a working family in reasonable comfort, and indeed the entire corpus of Catholic thought on the matter, not only accorded with eternal principles of justice but also led to an environment in which the greatest number of people would be able to save their souls.

The patristic consensus, Catholic writers explained, held that the ownership of property was lawful and in conformity with the demands of man's nature; at the same time, it condemned as positively un-Christian an enjoyment of riches in utter disregard of the needs of the poor.[30] As Leo XIII explained in one of his own defenses of property, every man has, very simply, a right to marry, and it is evident that as head of his household he has a responsibility to provide for those under his care. "Now, in no other way can a father effect this except by the ownership of productive property, which he can transmit to his children by inheritance."[31]

Leo spoke of a "natural right" of association, a right he extended to a host of private organizations, including labor unions. This right he derived from the very nature of the state—which, since it exists for the sake of securing the common good and for harmonizing antagonistic interests and classes, may not deny the workingman the right to organize peacefully in defense of his just interests. "For, to enter into a 'society' of this kind is the natural right of man," he wrote, "and the State has for its office to protect natural rights, not to destroy them."[32]

John Ryan, some of whose work had its share of facts and figures, made the pope's approach his own, deducing his economic views from principles he held to be axiomatic truths. Thus in his early book A Living Wage (1906), for example, and in more concise form in Distributive Justice (1916), Ryan founded his pro-labor stance on the distinctly Scholastic conception of the world as teleological, created for a purpose and within which everything tended toward its natural end. For Ryan, the basis for the rights of labor to a "living wage," a wage that allows a worker or a family to live in reasonable comfort, derived ultimately from the fact that God created the world for the sustenance of all men. Thus while this act need not imply that all men are entitled to an equal share of temporal goods, it at least suggests, since no social class is any more or less important to God than any other, that all men have equally a right to some share of earthly bounty as an inheritance from this divine gift. Related to this principle was the empirical fact that it is through labor that man acquires this share of nature's goods. The Bible offered a physical as well as a moral commandment when it observed that man shall earn his bread through the sweat of his brow. From this fact, finally, came Ryan's third principle: that "the men who are in present control of the opportunities of the earth are obliged to permit reasonable access to these opportunities by persons who are willing to work. In other words, possessors must so administer the common bounty of nature that non-owners will not find it unreasonably difficult to get a livelihood." Should a man who is willing to work be denied this right, he is "no longer treated as the moral and juridical equal of his fellows," but rather is "regarded as inherently inferior to them, as a mere instrument to their convenience; and those who exclude him are virtually taking the position that their rights to the common gifts of the Creator are inherently superior to his birthright."[33]

That the worker is entitled to a wage that is to some degree higher than one of bare subsistence, one indeed that affords him a modest degree of comfort, Ryan based on the fact that "human life and the human person possess intrinsic worth; because personality is sacred."[34] Ryan was critical of those who would found the case for a living wage on what he considered grounds inferior to these. Thus Sidney and Beatrice Webb, for example, British socialists who advocated a national minimum wage for the purpose of checking the industrial evil of "parasitism" (that is, the existence of businesses "in which the wages paid are too low to maintain the workers in industrial efficiency, and to enable them to reproduce and rear a sufficient number to take their places") came up for censure in *A Living Wage*:

> Admitting the premises, this conclusion is obviously correct, but it is only partially satisfactory to anyone who regards the laborer primarily as a being endowed with a personality and rights of his own. Like every other person, he exists primarily for himself, not for society; and he has rights that are derived from his own essential and intrinsic worth, and whose primary end is his own welfare. Society exists for the individual, not the individual for society, and when there is question of fundamental rights and interests the good of the individual, that is, of all the individuals, should be the supreme consideration.

"Social welfare when taken as an ideal of effort entirely apart from the welfare of the particular individuals of whom society is composed," Ryan went on to conclude, frequently ends up "an empty abstraction."[35] No social considerations, in Ryan's judgment, could substitute for an ethics of labor and capital based on the sacredness of the human person as a creation of God unlike all other creatures. Unlike the brutes, he is endowed with a spiritual soul and is hence capable of perfecting himself indefinitely with the help of divine grace. For the soul to reach this potential—and it was with the hope that he would indeed reach this full potential that mankind was created in the first place—he must have the opportunity to become "intellectually wiser, morally better, and spiritually nearer to God." If a laborer "is deprived of these opportunities he cannot realize the potentialities of his nature nor attain the divinely appointed end of his nature. He remains on the plane of the lower animals."[36]

The argument for a family wage grew out of the Church's traditional conception of the family, and not the individual, as the fundamental building block of society, the sacred cell of human development whose form and whose internal division of labor was established by God himself. That the careless application of the term "Progressive" to Father Ryan has tended to conceal as much as it has revealed is illustrated yet again in his description of the family. Christ, he wrote in the *Catholic Encyclopedia*, "placed the Christian family itself upon the plane of the supernatural. The family is holy inasmuch as it is to cooperate with God by procreating children who are destined to be the adopted children of God, and by instructing them for His kingdom." The functions to be performed respectively by husband and wife

are determined by their different natures, and by their relation to the primary end of the family, namely, the procreation of children. Being the provider of the family, and the superior of the wife both in physical strength and in those mental and moral qualities which are appropriate to the exercise of authority, the husband is naturally the family's head, even "the head of the wife," in the language of St. Paul. This does not mean that the wife is the husband's slave, his servant, or his subject. She is his equal, both as a human being and as a member of the conjugal society, save only that when a disagreement arises in matters pertaining to domestic government she is, as a rule, to yield. To claim for her completely equal authority with the husband is to treat woman as man's equal in a matter in which nature has made them unequal. On the other hand, the care and management of the details of the household belong naturally to the wife because she is better fitted for those tasks than the husband.

"Inasmuch as the average man will not put forth his full productive energies except under the stimulus of its responsibilities," Ryan argued, "the family is indispensable from the purely economic viewpoint."[37] In general, the family is of divine institution, the husband is its head and provider, and hence the common good demands that society's building blocks not be denied the wages that will allow them to flourish.

Ryan's fundamentally teleological outlook was evident throughout his arguments for the rights of labor. Again and again he spoke of the ends and natures of things. To the objection that labor unions impeded freedom of contract, for example, he shot back that the Catholic teaching on liberty had nothing in common with either license or anarchy, and did not entitle men simply to do as they pleased. Liberty in the Catholic sense, according to this line of argument, applies only to those actions that conform to man's proper end; Edmund Burke stated this position very simply in his *Reflections on the Revolution in France* when he said that we should not congratulate ourselves on having liberated men to do what they please until we discover what exactly it shall please them to do. If natural law is to be taken seriously, liberty cannot be divorced from truth or from the common good. Now a liberty that insisted on the dissolution of labor unions on the grounds that they impaired the freedom of the individual laborer to bargain on his own terms would therefore be a false liberty, for it would undermine the conditions that Ryan thought led to prosperity for workers, thereby bringing great harm upon the household. The household, in turn, was that smallest of political societies ordained by God, the very font of Christian society whose centrality was permanently inscribed in the natural law.

Catholic opposition to socialism—which was, for all practical purposes, unanimous—was also rooted, for the most part, in these very natural-law considerations. For some of the reasons already enumerated, the Catholic could not join the socialist in condemning the institutions of private property or the wage system as intrinsically wicked.[38] These institutions, like everything in this vale of tears, were open to abuses for which the Church did not hesitate to prescribe a corrective, but they conformed well to man's nature and the divine order. Socialists often appealed to the example of Christ and of various early Christian communities, but Catholic commentators were quick to point out that Christ nowhere enjoined his followers to adopt poverty as a universally binding commandment. His instruction to the young man to sell all his goods if he wished to be perfect the Church called an evangelical counsel or a "counsel of perfection," a supererogatory work not only not necessary for salvation but also positively harmful to the common good if implemented by force. Socialism, in trying to impose on an entire society a system that Christ had urged only on those to whom he had given a special grace, made demands on society and on human nature that could lead only to antagonism and confusion in the state.[39]

Natural-law arguments did not utterly exhaust the Catholic arsenal. Some Catholic writers combined natural-law arguments with arguments from utility or efficiency—e.g., that socialism could not deliver what it promised, that it invited economic chaos, and so on. Others pointed out what they saw as a not incidental link between socialism and materialism—and, what they considered the same thing, the connection between socialism and atheism.[40] It was not without reason that the Church feared socialist prejudice against religion, and Catholicism in particular; socialists in general made little effort to conceal their contempt for the very idea of the supernatural. The hundreds of articles on the link between socialism and atheism notwithstanding, Catholics were more than prepared to refute socialists on their own terms. A considerable minority of Catholics warned that to dismiss socialism simply as an atheistic system—even if true—was unwise; it might, for example, be perceived as an evasion of the economic issues at stake.[41] Such arguments in themselves proved nothing, since it was at least possible to conceive of a form of socialism that did not reject revealed religion. The most common strategy among Catholic intellectuals in countering socialism remained, therefore, the appeal to natural law.

Following the lead of Leo XIII, Catholics thus advocated a kind of *via media* between two modern systems, both of which, they believed, were derived from a materialistic, disintegrative liberalism. Although even John Ryan insisted that state intervention be admitted only as a last resort,[42] a consensus existed to the effect that a just and lasting solution to the present chaos had to avoid the individualistic laissez-faire approach of the capitalists as much as the "state despotism" of their socialist counterparts.[43] They took their stand not from utilitarian considerations, much less from any fascination with efficiency or fixation with empirical data. "Political economy in all its branches has been reduced to quite an exact science," the Jesuit Richard Tierney observed. But "mere knowledge cannot of its nature cure social ills." Political economy "lacks to a vast extent the higher saving spirit of Christ, the one thing necessary above all others. . . . Revealed religion alone can stem the tide, not bare, cold political economy."[44] Catholics used their share of charts and graphs, but for what they saw as the barrenness of empirical political science they substituted a systematic philosophy that considered who man was and how he prospered, both materially and spiritually.

Catholics thus offered both general principles and concrete suggestions toward a just resolution of the social question; and yet one senses in their writing a certain unease, a sense that more was at stake in the issue than the mere resolution of an industrial dispute, albeit a significant one. It is impossible to escape the tone of triumphalism that underlay all this commentary. Time and again Catholic essayists portrayed the labor question as yet another case in which the Church found herself doing battle with the errors of the modern world, a proud world that was suffering the consequences of neglecting Church teaching. Only with this in mind can the Catholic outlook on economic matters be properly assessed and appreciated. As Hilaire Belloc put it in John Burke's *Catholic World*, "Well, in this matter as in every other important social affair, the Catholic Church is on one side and its enemies upon the other."[45] Indeed, the literature of Catholic economic commentary during the Progressive period is replete with testimonies to the salutary consequences that accrue to states that fashion laws in conformity with Church teaching. Many Catholics took the opportunity afforded by the conflict between capital and labor to remind their fellow Americans of the perennial wisdom of the Church's position—and of the consequences of neglecting it. Surveying the economic scene, Father Edward Murphy maintained that "most of our modern fiascoes are the outcome of the opposite of her doctrine."[46] Since the Church was a divinely ordained institution, established by Christ himself for the sanctification of the world, to follow its counsel in social life was the only sure way to assure social tranquillity without neglecting the claims of justice. Joseph Husslein cited a priest colleague as having observed that what the working classes were suffering from in England was "suppressed Catholicism." The same was true, Father Husslein explained, in the United States. "Suppressed Catholicism is at the heart of the labor movement. Suppressed Catholicism is at the center of the great social unrest. Suppressed Catholicism is the spirit struggling for liberation beneath the crackling, breaking bursting shell of an unnatural and un-Christian social order. It is the pre-Reformation spirit of social freedom, which the Church alone can prevent from degenerating into lawlessness or injustice once it has achieved its liberation."[47]

Joseph Husslein was only the most insistent of a considerable number of Catholic intellectuals who, in their search for historical examples of approaches to capital and workers that conformed to Church teaching, settled upon what he called "the greatest labor movement in history," that of the medieval guilds. He was by no means alone; the fascination that the guilds held for many nineteenth- and twentieth-century socialists is well known. In the late nineteenth and early twentieth centuries, the popes themselves had encouraged a resurrection of the guilds, albeit in modified form.[48] In *Rerum Novarum*, Leo XIII recalled the "excellent results" brought about "by the artificers' guilds of olden times." They were, he said, "the means of affording not only many advantages to the workman, but in no small degree of promoting the advancement of art, as numerous monuments remain to bear witness. Such unions should be suited to the requirements of this our age."[49] Pius X reminded Catholics that "the social question and social science did not arise only yesterday" and that the Church had a long history of working to alleviate the conditions of the worker and to raise him to the level of dignity to which manual labor was entitled. He thus called on the Church to "take up again, with the help of the true workers for a social restoration, the organisms which the Revolution shattered, and to adapt them, in the same Christian spirit that inspired them, to the new environment arising from the material devel-opment of today's society. Indeed, the true friends of the people are nei-ther revolutionaries nor innovators; they are traditionalists."[50]

American Catholic commentary of the early twentieth century is replete with paeans to the virtues of the guilds, which were seen both as the bulwarks of stable and just social and economic relations and as fine examples of the medieval world's incarnation of the religious spirit within all aspects of life. Guilds in a given town or city were organized by trade, and every craftsman, if he wanted to pursue his craft there, had to belong to the appropriate guild. Ideally, their purpose was to regulate a town's economic life for the benefit of consumer and craftsman alike. They deter-mined prices and maximum hours, and adjudicated disputes. The guilds, moreover, were intended to temper the spirit of avarice through regula-tions that, for example, prevented a master or a workman from acquiring raw materials at an unusually low price, thereby giving him an advantage over his fellows; instead, other members of the guild were to be entitled also to make purchases at the low rate.[51] The guilds also served as self-policing regulatory agencies, ensuring the quality of the goods sold by their members. A town's reputation often rested on that of its guilds—that is, on the probity of the guilds' craftsmen and the quality of their product. The government thus had an interest in chartering guilds in order to attract settlement and economic activity within its jurisdiction; for the same reason, the leaders of the guilds had an incentive to maintain high standards. Anticipating the modern fraternal association, the guilds boasted a system of mutual aid, which included assistance in time of sick-ness, old age, or some other unanticipated misfortune, as well as provi-sions for proper burial rites for those who could not afford them.[52] In con-trast to the situation that obtained in their own day, some Catholic labor advocates suggested that the guild system had been relatively free from so-called class warfare.[53] "What is best in modern developments of social thought and action," *America* magazine proclaimed, "had often been anticipated in a far more perfect way by the guilds of the Middle Ages."[54]

And unlike modern labor unions, which the popes feared were operated by "secret societies" antagonistic to Catholicism, the guilds were explic-itly Catholic both in the economic principles they observed and in the religious dimension they shared.[55] Each guild had its own patron saint and faithfully observed the feast days of the Church. Each had its own church or chapel, which through the efforts of ordinary men it strove to make the most beautiful in a given area. Father Richard Tierney observed with pride: "It may seem strange to us to hear that simple, busy work-a-day men were strongly instrumental in building up the religious art and literature of the Middle Ages. But truth is often stranger than fiction. These guilds and societies that grew up within them or beside them were responsible for a vast deal of the art and literature that to-day is the marvel of travelers and students."[56]

It was not nostalgia for days past so much as an alienation from (or at least a guarded suspicion of) the modern world and its growing independence from the Church in matters both moral and political that drove much Catholic thought; and the track record of the guilds—whose Catholic imprint it was difficult to gainsay—gave many Catholic commentators a bludgeon with which to beat that modern world. Thus Joseph Husslein, voicing a common sentiment, remarked: "It is with a sense of relief, therefore, that we turn back to those earlier and better days, and with Lowell dare to say: 'I am not ashamed to confess to a singular sympathy with the Middle Ages.'"[57] Father Edward Murphy joined Husslein in defending the medieval period:

If it is complained that in medieval times, when the Church, preceptor of equity, was regent, poverty also reigned, it may be answered that old Europe, emerging from the grimy depths of barbarism, should not have been expected to look utterly ideal; that the serf was at least sure of his food and lodging, and raised his family without deadly fear of an awaiting wolf to snatch it up; and that, if the Continent succeeded in progressing from savagery to civilization under ecclesiastical regime, very logically it might have ascended from culture to social perfection had it remained spiritually true to the traditions which raised it from the mud. Catholicism gave humanity wings; modern spirit, locomotives. We have indeed gone fast without the Church, but our traveling has been in a circle, leaving us still on earth with the creeping things.[58]

Husslein put the matter succinctly: "Than her [that is, the Church], labor has never known and can never find a more sincere and constant friend."[59]

Catholic writers were not making the ridiculous argument sometimes attributed to them that what was needed was a simple return to the Middle Ages—whatever that may mean. They aimed, first, to demonstrate the good that could result from an application of Catholic principles to the social order, and, second, to point out the consequences of alien doctrines. In the material realm, they believed, the matter was obvious. The less fortunate had clearly not benefited from the destruction of the monasteries, which had supported the poor, and, following behind that, the destruction of the guilds, which had been "the strength and protection of the laborer."[60] In *Rerum Novarum*, Leo XIII himself had noted the void that remained after the destruction of the guilds. "Some opportune remedy must be found quickly for the misery and wretchedness pressing so unjustly on the majority of the working class: for the ancient working-men's guilds were abolished in the last century, and no other protective organization took their place."[61]

Much of the enthusiasm for the guilds was clearly intended as part of a larger polemic against the entire political order of the West in the period following the Reformation and especially after the French Revolution. In the name of what Catholic commentators would call a "false liberty," Western philosophers and political leaders had dismantled the corporate order on which the "true liberty" of the Middle Ages had rested, one that had been composed not of a mere aggregate of individuals but of the liberties, accumulated through custom and recognized in law, of independent associations that derived their existence from a natural right of human beings to associate peacefully, rather than from the indulgence of the monarch. The unfortunate condition of modern laborers, according to this line of argument, had much to do with the destruction of the authority of the independent associations—guild, monastery, town, village—that constituted the peculiar political texture of the Middle Ages and that in those times had provided the ordinary laborer with security, camaraderie, and real identity. In place of these very concrete institutions now stood the large and often distant and formidable structures of the corporation and the modern state. No longer was the laborer a part of a true community of workmen, his identity forged by his association with trade, guild, and religion. He had been reduced to a mere employee, a miserable adjunct to be hired or dismissed at will. This critique was not without some truth. But it does not seem to have occurred to Catholic writers and scholars that the enormous wealth that modern industrial society had made possible was precisely what allowed a laboring class as large as that seen in modern times to survive at all. In previous ages, without direct access to the tools of their profession—primitive "means of production," as it were—men faced certain impoverishment or even starvation. The number of people who, not in possession of the necessary tools, could sell their labor to others was small. Whatever misfortunes the laboring classes suffered, it at least needed to be acknowledged somewhere within the Catholic polemic that the very system so often criticized as the source of their oppression was at the same time the force that made it possible for so many workers to survive and reproduce at all.[62] Whether the admiration American Catholics had for medieval social and economic relations was founded in an entirely fair assessment of the modern period is less important, however, than the fact that they should have been so insistent on the defects of modern conditions and on the idea that a more harmonious system, under the direction of the Church, had once existed and flourished. This kind of polemic revealed, once again, the unease with the modern world as well as the triumphant exceptionalism that characterized American Catholic intellectuals of the Progressive Era. They were not merely another set of economic observers or social critics; they were the inheritors of a treasury of divine wisdom that they sought to spread with an apostolic zeal. The guilds thus recalled a great moment in Catholic history and provided empirical verification that through the ages it was the Church that had been labor's true friend and protector.

John Ryan, who was perhaps the most skeptical of the utility of discussing the guilds in the modern context, nevertheless insisted on the moral superiority of the guild system to modern capitalism and portrayed it as such in his lectures.[63] Still, in Ryan's mind discussion of the guilds served at least one practical purpose. The modern era, he believed, needed to recognize "the political and social principle that underlay the guild organization of industry"—the idea that various groups exist in society and deserve the recognition and protection from the state that is their due. The objection that various state proposals for the protection of labor constituted "class legislation" was, to Ryan, nonsensical. Of course it was class legislation; but this claim in itself could constitute an objection only to those who insisted on viewing the individual as a social atom rather than as a member of a natural, spontaneously occurring group. As the guilds demonstrated, social harmony was possible, and perhaps alone possible, in a corporative order.[64]

It is true, of course, that a number of socialists and Progressives were themselves impressed and intrigued with the tradition of the guilds, an interest that can doubtless be attributed at least in part to the more general revival of interest in medievalism that characterized the early twentieth century.[65] Joseph Husslein was aware of the similarity of his outlook with that of the so-called guild socialists, but he hastened to point out that any such similarity was attributable to the influence, whether people were conscious of it or not, that the ideals of Christendom had had on secular society.[66]

The destruction of the guilds was attributed in part to social principles emanating from the Protestant Reformation, but the Catholic criticism of the consequences of the Reformation did not end there. James J. Walsh, the prolific historian whose highly successful book *The Thirteenth: Greatest of Centuries* (1906) made him one of the best-known and most admired Catholic writers of the Progressive Era, wrote a series of essays on charitable activity before and after the Reformation.[67] What demanded explanation, he said, was the plain fact that such activity declined precipitously in the wake of Luther's revolt. The Catholic Church, he argued, with its monasteries and missionary priests, had helped children, the poor, the aged, and the insane to an extent that was not fully appreciated. Luther himself, he noted, after a 1511 trip to Florence, spoke in glowing terms of the city's hospitals, noting that patients received high-quality care, in clean surroundings and with good food.[68]

Walsh attributed the drop-off in such charitable work in large part to the central tenet of Lutheran theology: the all-sufficiency for man's salvation of the act of faith and the utter worthlessness of good works from a soteriological point of view. If good works suddenly counted for absolutely nothing on the ledger of a man's salvation, fewer good works would be done. It was especially revealing, he noted, that the Protestant social consciousness should have been awakened on any considerable scale only in the modern era, with "the gradual dissolution of Protestantism as a dogmatic religion" and its evolution into a brand of mere naturalistic humanitarianism. For today, said Walsh, the typical Protestant, whose religion has been evacuated of supernatural content, embraces that doctrine—namely, the idea that "it makes little difference what a man believes provided he lives an upright life and does good to others"—that Luther would have condemned as Pelagian. "In a single word," Walsh concluded, "the movement that led to the ruin of our hospitals and of nursing was the so-called Reformation."[69]

To many Catholics the economic consequences of the Protestant Reformation went much deeper than the confiscation of the monastic lands and other depredations at the hands of secular rulers. They accused the Reformation of having introduced in germ the intellectual premises and social foundations on which economic liberalism would ultimately be built. The *Catholic World* published an article by Hilaire Belloc early in 1912 in which the celebrated British distributist, surveying the state of Western civilization, concluded that "it was the Reformation, and no mere physical cause, which produced, stage by stage, that detestable arrangement of temporal affairs under which the mass of free Christian men are disinherited of capital and of land, the means of production concentrated in the hands of a few, and human life upon its material side degraded to a limit which antiquity never knew and which mankind today will certainly not long tolerate."[70] Even the relatively irenic John Ryan indicted the Reformation on this charge.[71] They issued this attack on Protestantism, Joseph Husslein explained, not to promote gratuitous discord or ill will, but simply so that the "new reconstruction" might be "based upon more sound and lasting foundations."[72]

Catholic commentators especially deplored a trend that had been at work since the Reformation and was accelerated by the French Revolution, and that was contained at least implicitly in nearly all modern political philosophy: the derogation and eventual destruction of the various intermediate bodies that during the medieval period had stood between the individual and the state.[73] Marx observed that Hobbes had been "the father of us all," and in this respect he was correct: post-Renaissance political philosophy followed almost exclusively the Hobbesian model in which the state was composed of mere individuals. In an age of centralization, there was little room either in theory or in practice for the corporate bodies that had once commanded the allegiance of Europeans. In the previous age, John Ryan explained, the individual "was primarily regarded, not as one of a multitude of equally powerful atoms, but as a member of a certain class. Accordingly the different classes received from the civil authority recognition and privileges . . . which were more or less adapted to safeguard their peculiar welfare."[74]

Leo XIII was consciously seeking, in *Rerum Novarum* and in his Catholic Social Action program, to revive this corporative idea of life that the Enlightenment and the French Revolution had destroyed.[75] Pope Leo noted on several occasions that in writing his celebrated encyclical he had been especially influenced by the work of Wilhelm Emmanuel, Baron von Ketteler (1811–1877), Bishop of Mainz. Von Ketteler, a German nobleman and prelate, had observed in *Die Arbeiterfrage und das Christenthum* (*Christianity and the Labor Question*) that the current economic order would ultimately "bring about the dissolution of all that unites men organically, spiritually, intellectually, morally, and socially." "The working class are to be reduced to atoms and then mechanically reassembled," he went on. "This is the fundamental generative principle of modern political economy." What Catholics must confront, therefore, was "this pulverization method, this chemical solution of humanity into individuals, into grains of dust equal in value, into particles which a puff of wind may scatter in all directions."[76]

With his traditional sources of protection now destroyed, the laborer found himself alone and bereft of protection in the face of organized capital. A Jesuit summed up the consequences:

The baron, prince, ruler, seized monastic and other religious lands and possessions; the stronger among the people took hold of what they could get of power and legalized plunder, and the weaker went to the wall. There was no Hildebrand nor Boniface to stand between the Sovereign and baronial magnates and the people in Protestant communities; there were no monasteries left to relieve the needs of the people by alms or employment; and the merchants', trades', crafts' and workmen's Guilds, which, cooperating with the Church in greater or less degree, upheld popular rights, were, when shorn of ecclesiastical support, suppressed, confiscated or corrupted, and finally annihilated by the French Revolution, in the name of Fraternity.[77]

"The free craftsman of the Middle Ages," Husslein added, "who could lift up his head as a man and a Christian, without envy of lord or king, had now become the merest slave of the machine and an instrument of wealth. And all this, thanks to the Reformation!"[78]

The modern labor union, while a far cry from the medieval guilds, still seemed to many Catholics to be an example of the kind of independent institution that needed to be revived and protected. Criticism of the labor union per se, John Ryan believed, and not simply of those acts of violence that all reasonable men deplored, derived from an atomistic conception of the individual that had no place in Catholic thought and that only fueled the war against the corporative idea. Again he warned his coreligionists not to oppose the labor union on the basis of the "specious" claim that the individual laborer should be free to agree to the conditions under which he will work. "This unreasonable extreme of liberty," Ryan said, "is no part of either Catholic theory or practice."[79]

Over and against this denunciation of the Reformation as responsible for the alleged excesses of the Industrial Revolution, it might be objected that, in fact, the reformers intended no such thing. For one thing, neither Luther nor Calvin was especially sympathetic to the free market. Although it is significant that Calvin approved of usury, Luther vigorously rejected the practice; it was the sixteenth-century Spanish Scholastics, building on the work of their predecessors, who were increasingly prepared to argue its lawfulness.[80] Richard Tawney's characterization of Luther was by and large accurate: "Confronted with the complexities of foreign trade and financial organizations, he is like a savage introduced to a dynamo or a steam engine. He is too frightened and angry even to feel curiosity. Attempts to explain the mechanism merely enrage him; he can only repeat that there is a devil in it, and that good Christians will not meddle with the mystery of iniquity."[81]

Yet for all the force of this objection, as far as Progressive Era Catholics were concerned, the economic opinions of the reformers did not matter very much. Once the Pandora's box of individualism had been thrown open, there was no telling what the consequences might be for civil society, and those Protestants who had so impiously dared to peek inside had to be held accountable for whatever managed to escape. Individualism, it seemed, proceeded with a momentum of its own, and there was no way to confine the individualism of Protestant thought to the religious sphere. "This false individualism in religion," wrote Joseph Husslein, "soon had its parallel in the false economic individualism on which the Protestant prosperity was founded."[82]

Moreover, for our purposes it is not so important whether the reformers were themselves economic liberals, or whether their religious views and political philosophy happened to lend support to economic liberalism, or any such controversy. The matter at hand is the simple fact of the unease with modernity that characterized the Catholic perspective on the social question. Very few Catholic thinkers in any of the social sciences even tried to argue that the problems they perceived in contemporary America were simply the result of (or, for that matter, could be solved by) this or that public-policy measure, though such things could do some good. They were convinced that the question struck much deeper than most Progressives were prepared to admit.

The problem possessed a profoundly religious aspect. "Only in proportion as men shall once more return to the unity of the one faith of Christ, or at least acknowledge the principles which it has ever guarded through the ages, is any solution of the labor problem possible," wrote Joseph Husslein. "Without this precaution," he warned, "organization itself will but degenerate into a tyranny of godless Labor to replace the old despotism of individualistic Capital."[83] John Ryan pointed out that "the social question is primarily moral and religious, not merely economic," and that "all the strivings of men to solve the question will be in vain if they leave out the Church."[84]

Indeed, Ryan insisted that "the social question is for us in great part a religious question." A just resolution of the social question would conduce to the spread of the Gospel. And yet the Church's efforts in the economic arena promised still more than this. Ryan pointed out that a peculiar lethargy paralyzed the modern mind and made it view religion as a matter of indifference. The majority of non-Catholic Americans remained outside the Church because she was never presented in a way that would seem attractive to them; and the "spirit of indifferentism" prevented them from feeling compelled to make a closer investigation on their own. How would the Church ever reach such souls? "How are these people to be aroused to a sense of the importance of religion, and the obligation of seeking out the true religion?" Surely not through "cold and rigid argumentation" but by "such a presentation as will touch their ideals and sympathies." One of the best ways of accomplishing this task, Ryan was convinced, was by drawing special attention to Catholic social teaching, and demonstrating that the Church had a remedy for the most vexing problems of modern times. The corpus of Catholic social teaching was a treasure of which the Church could rightly boast, and in an increasingly secular age it should be harnessed in order to reach men of goodwill who might otherwise remain aloof from her entreaties. "In this way," he concluded, "we shall have their attention [and] win their sympathy, and their native yearning for religious truth will do the rest."[85]

By a happy coincidence, then, some Catholics' arguments in favor of protecting the laborer and securing what they considered a more just distribution of property harmonized well with the Progressive milieu. The usual story of the period, however, which fails to note these clear differences between Catholic and non-Catholic thinkers, overlooks the most intellectually significant aspect of the Catholic contribution to the discussion of the proper relations of capital and labor, state and economy. Concealed beneath all the apparent agreement was a philosophical chasm that set Catholic thinkers apart from virtually all their Progressive counterparts. Walter Rauschenbusch was not alone among representatives of the American left when he puzzled over American Catholicism, which he saw as constituting "a complexity of the most ancient and modern elements, a mixture of reactionary and progressive forces."[86]

The tone of Catholic exceptionalism that characterized much Catholic writing on this issue also could not have been more removed from mainstream Progressive thought. That some Catholics sensed that they were speaking a different language from their contemporaries is more than evident. Thus Father Joseph Husslein observed that "if all the world were Catholic we could appeal to it in a language intelligible to all." As things stood, however, there was "no power to restrain the passions of men or to overrule their prejudices. There can be no greater social work than that which consists in bringing men back once more into the one true Fold."[87] Polemics arguing the wisdom of the Church and the need for a religious outlook on economic matters could not be especially welcome to the more or less technocratic regime that the Progressives were trying to erect—a regime that looked with confidence to the value-free certainty provided by science. ("The Creed," *America* magazine once observed to the contrary, "is the only possible salvation for industrialism."[88]) And placing the political and economic condition of the modern worker in the context of world-historical developments, as Catholics did, stretched beyond the somewhat more limited time horizon that generally characterized the Pragmatic temper of mind—a mind that, in any case, was not likely on balance to be entirely critical of the drift of civilization over the past several centuries.

Catholics did not neglect to make common cause with like-minded non-Catholics, and they gladly pointed to the writings of top Progressive thinkers when they coincided with their own. John Ryan, for example, in his entry on poverty in the *Catholic Encyclopedia*, recommended such works as Robert Hunter's *Poverty* and Edward T. Devine's *Misery and Its Causes* in his concluding bibliography. But they were forthright in insisting that Catholics alone could fully appreciate the magnitude of the present crisis—that the world was suffering the consequences in the economic arena that it must suffer in any area of life in which it disregarded the font of divine wisdom. Yet again, it seemed to them, it had fallen to the Church to condemn and correct the errors of a world deceived into thinking it could long prosper severed from divine authority and natural law. Beneath a veneer of real agreement between Catholics and their Progressive counterparts lay the same exceptionalism and the same challenge to the drift of American intellectual life that rears its head in so many other areas. Such differences did not preclude Catholic involvement in common causes with non-Catholics of goodwill, but they do suggest that the distinctive Catholic posture we have identified was present even in areas in which its presence may not have been immediately obvious.

6 / AGAINST SYNCRETISM

THE THEMES DISCUSSED THUS FAR have long been recognized as among the principal intellectual trends of the Progressive Era. The development of a secularized social science, Progressive innovations in educational practice, and a heightened interest in political economy as a result of ongoing labor-capital disputes—all these movements, undergirded in large part by a heavy dose of Pragmatist philosophy, made the Progressive Era one of the most intellectually innovative periods of American history. Accordingly, they have received ample treatment in standard historical studies of the late-nineteenth- and early-twentieth-century United States.

What is only gradually coming to be recognized as a movement of potentially equal importance to any of these developments is a growing syncretism, a desire among intellectuals for a shared ethical code that could rise above sectarian differences and bind the nation together under a single set of beliefs. The intellectual currents of the Progressive Era— Pragmatism, toleration, Social Gospel theology, and the like—logically converged in a contemporaneous (and sometimes only implicit) movement for a uniform, nondogmatic national creed, what historian Eldon Eisenach has called "the religion of the American way of life." All these trends, their promoters insisted, represented the wave of the future, an approach to religion, to human conduct, and to individual dignity that spurned the alienating dogmas of the past in favor of a naturalistic, humanitarian creed more in line with the outlook of modern man and the demands of the democratic ethos. It is not always easy for the historian to pinpoint the temporal priority of intellectual trends that are so intertwined. In the case of the Progressive Era, the ideas of Pragmatism, Progressive education, and a creedless ethical code appear to have interacted synergistically, with each affecting and being affected by the others.

But while Eisenach performed the valuable service of chronicling the interest that many Progressive social scientists demonstrated in the development of such a nonsectarian national creed, he did not examine the explicit efforts at work during that period to draw up such a creed and to introduce it into everyday life. To record and analyze this movement with anything like comprehensive treatment is the task of another historian; we must be satisfied here with enough of an overview of the basic philosophy and goals of its proponents to make possible a clearer understanding of the precarious intellectual relationship that American Catholicism enjoyed as a dogmatic institution in an increasingly creedless nation. And indeed it was a conflict that American Catholics were not slow to perceive. The Zeitgeist was expressed in one Catholic periodical this way: "You may hold any faith or religion you please, but then you must not belong to any specific sect or be bound by any dogma."[1]

When *Everybody's Magazine* organized a competition to answer the question "What is a Christian," for example, *America* magazine pounced. What answer had *Everybody's* reached? That if a man "is perfectly moral he need not believe anything about Christ to be a Christian."[2] It is not easy to see a possible reconciliation between this view, which was growing more and more prevalent at the time, and that of Father Henry Woods, also writing in *America*: "We, on the contrary, holding the true and only Christian religion, know that one who, however he may rule his actions by Christian precepts, refuses to bend his intellect and will to the obedience of faith, is as much an infidel as if, instead of Christian, he had chosen Moslem, Buddhist, or Confucian morals."[3]

The project of establishing a nonsectarian creed drew deeply from the intellectual and philosophical springs of Progressive thought. Although it did not correspond perfectly to philosophical Pragmatism, the two ideas had much in common. John Dewey may have been a relativist, but he was not a nihilist. It was not creeds in themselves to which Pragmatists objected; it was the pretensions of creeds to absolute truth and universality. Moreover, from a metaphysical and epistemological point of view Pragmatists rejected religious dogma and its claim to validity in and of itself, apart from any correspondence or lack thereof to the individual's own experience. Thus an ethic that was divorced from supernatural religion, that made less ambitious claims for itself than had the Christian moral tradition, and that at the same time could provide the social comity that any society needed could well receive the approbation of the Pragmatist.

From the point of view of the Progressives themselves, the most important religious conflict during the Progressive Era, although it has gone virtually unrecorded, was not between Catholics and Protestants but

between the Modernists and the traditionalists in each camp. If the project of a national creed were to enjoy any success, it would have to be safe
from assault by traditionalists who insisted on the importance of specific
religious dogmas. The sociologist Albion Small in particular emphasized
the importance of the victory of theological Modernism in order for this
great ethical enterprise to succeed.[4] The new vision outlined by Small
"precludes not only officially promulgated (church) creeds, but also the
imposition of creeds based on the experience and interpretations of one
people upon those whose 'experience and interpretations may have been
of a different order.'"[5]

American Catholics were well aware of the movement afoot among secular intellectuals of their day to establish a kind of religion of humanity,
free from "superstition" and dogma. Part of this impetus toward a creedless
faith sprang, they recognized, from the Social Gospel theology that had
overtaken much of American Protestantism. Thus Dudley Wooten could
observe that "Christianity, as represented by the ablest of its Protestant
advocates, is today in this country little more than a sentiment, a system
of social service, of ethical philosophy, of philanthropic enterprise. . . . Its
professions of humanitarian service and sacrifice are no longer illumined
by the radiance of faith in the mysteries of the Godhead or in the authority and authenticity of revealed truth. Its sacred symbols have been trans-
muted into mere types of earthly virtues."[6] They observed contemporaneous Protestant efforts toward Christian unity with bemused indifference; it
was a movement "with which Catholics can have nothing to do," for their
participation would not only increase the already rampant religious indifferentism then prevailing in the world but would also seem to suggest that
there was some alternate route to Christian unity apart from the individual reconciliation of Protestant believers with the Holy See.[7]

All such efforts toward Christian unity, it was understood, were tainted
by an implicit—and sometimes explicit—desire to retreat from the dogmatic differences that separated the various Christian bodies and to recast
Christianity as a primarily ethical system concerned exclusively with
men's relations to each other. And indeed a common feature of Social
Gospel theology was a disdain for creeds and theological formulas. Walter
Rauschenbusch, perhaps the most influential of these divines, in fact
argued that it had been only through later accretions to the original, undefiled Gospel message that Christianity had developed into a dogmatic system in the first place. In his seminal *Christianity and the Social Crisis*
(1907), Rauschenbusch claimed that the Christian faith had originally
been completely nondogmatic and that a later dogmatic superstructure, as

it were, was merely the unfortunate result of the influence of the Greek intellectual tradition.[8] Belief in the immortality of the soul was also a later addition, having no foundation in the Old Testament or in the authentic teaching of Christ. Rauschenbusch also joined a trend current in his day to identify the purpose of religious belief or moral endeavor with the regeneration of society rather than with the working out of individual salvation. "The Kingdom of God is a collective conception involving the whole social life of man," he wrote. "It is not a matter of saving human atoms, but of saving the social organism. It is not a matter of getting individuals into heaven, but of transforming the life on earth into harmony with heaven." Indeed "in its original purity" Christianity insisted simply on "right relations to men as the expression of religion."[9] Thus Christianity had to be emancipated from the Roman encrustations, wholly extrinsic to its fundamental nature, that over the course of centuries had become attached to the primitive faith. Only such a nondogmatic Christian religion could properly address the urgent problems facing industrial society in the early twentieth century.

Catholics, of course, were prepared to make no such concessions, and a Jesuit writer for *America* summed up his Church's perspective on the matter when he explained that "Catholics can not possibly regard that as a correct conception of God's Kingdom which directly or by implication excludes from it dogmas as objects of our faith, rites as forms of divine worship, sacraments as means of sanctification, a church organization, and hierarchy as teaching and administrative power."[10] Catholic thinkers met the Social Gospel threat in a direct, straightforward manner. But the fascination with new ideas and approaches to God, religion, and ethics was not confined to the ranks of Social Gospel theologians, and Catholics knew it. Again, Immanuel Kant was a chief villain. Kant, Father Edmund Shanahan argued, was the font of the modern movement in religion "to turn it away from the service of God to the service of man." The Königsberg philosopher reduced the meaning of faith, which in its Catholic understanding had referred to an assent to divinely revealed truth, to the mere acceptance of and adherence to a code of ethics.[11] What American Catholics were facing, therefore, was not simply a movement among high-profile Protestant clergymen to evacuate the Christian faith of its supernatural dimension and to redirect it to earthly concerns. It was a much broader trend at work among a much wider range of American intellectuals, the culmination of a tendency toward a kind of religious naturalism that had been in evidence since the eighteenth century. Decades after the ravages visited upon orthodox Christianity by Darwin's theory of evolution, and with the contemporaneous impetus provided by critical biblical scholarship and the overall philosophical ethos of the Progressive Era, the time seemed to many thinkers to have come for a new Christianity, a new religion, a new foundation for the brotherhood of man.

One of the first issues of *America* magazine, in fact, featured a lengthy commentary on this new development in religion. The new movement, it said, seemed to hold that "the God of the Christians is not big enough, nor liberal enough, nor wise enough to deal with the Twentieth Century conditions, and so they have to create one of their own who will make man free, give to him unlimited liberty, endow him with great wealth, confer on him a vast amount of power that will enable him to rule the spiritual as well as the material world, a God who will deify man and make him cease to be a subject being."[12] The belief that traditional notions of God had outlived their usefulness and indeed were no longer believable was fairly well established among a good number of American intellectuals, and a portion of that number considered it important to seek something to replace an institution that, whatever else they may have thought of it, they agreed had served as a bulwark of morality and social order.

Harvard University president Charles Eliot provides an especially high-profile example of this intellectual quest. Eliot was particularly outspoken in his advocacy of a new religious creed, free of the oppressive dogmas of the past, to which modern man could give his wholehearted allegiance. He outlined the basis of his new religion—which he insisted was in essence that of Jesus Christ—in an important article that originally appeared in the *Harvard Theological Quarterly* and that would be reprinted in full in many American newspapers. The new religion would abandon such outmoded mythologies as the Fall, the Redemption, a heavenly paradise, and the divinity of Christ. In place of the personal God of traditional Christianity he would substitute a "sleepless, active energy and will" that is recognized "chiefly in the wonderful energies of sound, light, and electricity." This new Christianity, moreover, "will not be based on authority either spiritual or temporal," these also being accretions from the Church's dogmatic and authoritarian past.[13]

As Eliot saw it, it was liberal Protestantism that best exemplified the "renewed Christianity" he sought. Unlike the Catholic Church and the more authoritarian of the Reformed elements, he argued, these churches have "definitely abandoned the official creeds and dogmas of the past, all ecclesiasticism, and almost all symbolism and ritualism. Their membership, modest in number and little disposed to proselytism, consists exclusively of persons who propose to be free, simple, and candid in their religious

thought, and in all expressions of that thought." Eliot was confident that the
new idea he was outlining would prove to be "the religion of the future."[14]

American Catholics were less sure. "President Eliot is back from his
voyage of exploration into the future," *America* magazine announced dryly
in 1909.[15] His creed, the magazine insisted, was laughable. He all but
denied sin—"a fact as plain as potatoes," G. K. Chesterton had said—as
well as Revelation and man's need for a Redeemer. His religion was the
"worship of humanity."[16] Worst of all was its plain self-contradiction, for
"having exploited to the utmost Christ's authority to enjoin service of our
neighbor, and refused to recognize His authority in any other point," Eliot
went on to undermine all authority in religion—including, perhaps
unwittingly, his own—with his insistence that it had no part to play in the
religion of the future. And for all the saccharine promises Eliot attached
to the adoption of this new religion, *America* remained firmly persuaded
that "if Dr. Eliot's doctrines are ever taken seriously, the world will be little better than hell."[17]

A lesser proposal emerged from the pen of Lake Forest College's Professor Henry W. Wright, and received no more sympathetic a response from
America. His was yet another effort to make of religion a vehicle for social,
rather than individual, perfection—"apparently oblivious," Father
Edward Murphy noted, "that Christianity has always aimed at both." Professor Wright's religion was one in which modern man, having at last
come of age, would no longer beseech God for supernatural help but
would use the tools of modern science to satisfy his needs. "Modern man,"
he said, "secures his own natural existence and well-being not by bargain-
ing for divine protection against natural ills but by gaining mastery over
natural forces through his own experimental science, inventive skill and
technical proficiency. He does not rely upon divine Providence to protect
him from a shipwreck at sea; he makes a compass, constructs a steamship,
invents the wireless telegraph." The monastic life, likewise, he expressly
condemned and repudiated. "With regard, secondly, to the spiritual goods
whose acquisition spiritual religion pretends to ensure, modern man has
learned that these are attained not by individuals who withdraw from
worldly pursuits and devote themselves to supernatural concerns, but by
those who avail themselves most successfully of the spiritual resources of
their fellow men, as these are developed through personal association and
cooperation." It was, in effect, a religion of human self-sufficiency—
which struck the ear of a Catholic critic as the classic example of modern
impiety. Man had indeed registered some truly extraordinary technologi-
cal achievements in the modern era, but the prideful self-confidence

instilled by his increasing mastery over nature led to a lust for domination that both willfully excluded God from his moral calculus and had promoted the mindless barbarism of World War I.[18]

The Catholic contempt for modern ideas about God was so great that commentators could not restrain themselves from bitter sarcasm. "The Christianity of Thomas Aquinas and Christopher Columbus is too slow for an age of steam engines," wrote one. "If we must be religious, at least let the smart brand of the twentieth century glitter on our beliefs."[19] "We trust Dr. Eliot is not exhausted by his efforts," said another. "Next year would be dull indeed without another new religion."[20]

In place of the modern thirst for innovation and for man-centered philosophy and religion, Edward Murphy suggested the possibility of conforming minds and hearts to the old religion, rather than insisting that the old religion conform to our "advanced" minds and hearts.[21] A writer for the *Catholic World* agreed, and issued a vigorous condemnation of the very spirit of the Progressive Era when he declared: "Social consciousness, civic welfare, economic justice, service to humanity, universal democracy, the brotherhood of man, the gospel of service—these are the pet phrases of the new deliverance; but in all the cant and jargon of this current philosophy, the mind and soul are called to contemplate no higher source of authority, no more reliable test of fundamental truth, than the subjective standards erected by human reason and to be enforced by human agencies."[22] It was this above all to which Catholics objected: no longer was man to conform himself to an external standard; from now on, all ideals, all rules of conduct, were in some way to emerge from within his own breast. As the organ of the Paulist Fathers put it, "It is not a 'new religion,' a 'new Christianity' that we need, but a new efflorescence of faith and hope and love in the age-old Church of Christ." A man-made religion or moral code, it went on, like all things human, by its very nature is subject to perpetual change. Only a faith and a moral tradition built on manifestly divine foundations could hold steady amid rapid change, "meeting every emergency with a divinely begotten wisdom and prudence."[23]

This counsel had polemical value among Catholics and conservative Protestants, but it held little water outside Christian circles. A logical consequence of the new, nondenominational creed was an increasing tendency to attempt to establish the foundations of morality on grounds independent of revealed religion. Some such efforts were plainly quixotic. In 1918, Father Paul Blakely noted in *America* that an organization called the National Institution for Moral Instruction had awarded $5,000 to William J. Hutchins, a professor at Oberlin College, for his code of morals.

The Hutchins moral code scarcely merits so much as a historical footnote, but the Catholic response to it serves to reflect the widespread awareness within the American Church of syncretistic tendencies at work in the United States and within the Western world as a whole during the early twentieth century. To Blakely, the very idea of proposing such a code seemed absurd. "Now a certain code of morality, fairly well known to all civilized nations, was promulgated on Mount Sinai some centuries ago. As its Author is Almighty God, I have no doubt whatever that the Mount Sinai code is as superior to the code of Oberlin as Almighty God is to Dr. Hutchins." "Furthermore," he continued, "since Almighty God, an infinitely wise law-giver, legislated in that code for all times and for all peoples, I refuse to believe that we need a new code in 1918."

The Hutchins code embodied all the characteristics that most alarmed Catholics about Progressivism. Not surprisingly, it was completely naturalistic; as Paul Blakely put it, if Professor Hutchins had ever heard of God as a moral teacher "he has no mind to communicate that knowledge to his fellows." It began, oddly enough, with an exhortation "to be physically fit" and ended by declaring loyalty to humanity to be the highest law. In fidelity to the Progressive outlook, moreover, in Blakely's words the code "substitut[ed] for the Divinity that vague abstraction 'humanity.'" Apart from this cursory description, Blakely's polemic against it sheds little light on its actual content. But while perhaps unhelpful from a journalistic standpoint, his article and its tone speak volumes about the brusque dismissal that pretenders could expect to receive at the hands of a Catholic population and intellectual cadre that were certain of being in possession of the truth.[24]

The so-called ethical culture movement was perhaps the classic example of the effort to establish a new ethical code. Taking the motto "deed, not creed," Felix Adler founded the Ethical Culture Society in the United States in 1876. Adler, born in Germany in 1851, had come to the United States with his family in 1857, making his home in New York City. When he returned to his native Germany for graduate study—as did many promising American intellectuals of the late nineteenth century—he began to take an interest in philosophy. Kant, especially, held him spellbound. It was from Kant that Adler absorbed the conviction that God's existence could not be rationally demonstrated, as well as the belief that morality could be grounded on something other than theology—ethics, that is, was fully "autonomous." The combination of these beliefs ultimately gave rise to the movement for which Adler is known. Since by its very nature no religious creed could in Adler's view be demonstrated as true with any real certainty, and since morality did not strictly require religious sanction, ethical culture would seek to construct a moral system that avoided religious and dogmatic controversy and embraced the rationally apprehended moral principles on which all men of goodwill could agree. Thus on May 15, 1876, at New York City's Standard Hall, Adler announced: "Diversity in the creed, unanimity in the deed. . . . This is the common ground where we may all grasp hands . . . united in mankind's common cause."[25]

Adler went on to found the *International Journal of Ethics* in 1890, which would feature the writing of top American philosophers—including, naturally, William James and John Dewey. (The journal continues to be published to this day by the University of Chicago under the truncated title of *Ethics*.) He went on in 1902 to become professor of political and social ethics at Columbia University, where he taught until his death in 1933, all the while continuing to lead the ethical culture movement he had founded a quarter century earlier.[26]

Ethical culture was, certainly, a reaction against the cold materialism and determinism that had visited such devastation on religion during the nineteenth century. Having concluded that the religious cause was dead, this movement attempted to construct at least some basis on which to encourage moral behavior with its supernatural sanction thought to be gone forever.[27] Surveying modern industrial society, Adler was concerned that the misfortune he witnessed all around him, and that rightly or wrongly he attributed to the capitalist system as such, was being opposed by no reigning ethical system—and that in fact no existing ethical system was adequate to the task. Although in some respects he always considered himself a follower of Kant and remained quite indebted to Kant's position that ethics was at root a rational science, Kantian ethics was in his mind too individualistic to be able to contribute to a problem that was social and collective in nature. Likewise, the various Christian denominations were tied to tired theologies whose central concern was individual sin. This latter criticism, though commonly held, was of course rather peculiar, since the Christian recognition that only the individual can properly be considered a moral agent obviously in no way implies that Christian moral theology has nothing to say about social ills. Nevertheless, Adler considered the development of an alternative to these systems to be not simply an important intellectual exercise but actually essential to the establishment of some kind of harmonious economic and social life in the modern world.[28]

One leader of the movement, Alfred Martin, insisted on his belief in

God but insisted more strongly still on the virtue of the broad toleration that the ethical society extended to its members in matters of belief, requiring as it did no religious test of any kind for membership. Instead, he wrote in the *New York Evening Post*, membership was based "solely on the human desire to live the moral life, a basis, and indeed the only possible basis, which all men, whatever their religious opinions, can unite upon."[29] On another occasion he predicted that there was "no future for any religious movement bearing a sectarian name, and making fellowship conditional on the acceptance of any theological creed, however brief."[30]

The project that Adler initiated was doomed to failure, Catholic periodicals agreed. The reason was straightforward: "Obligation implies law and law implies the binding of the human conscience. Such a binding force implies a law-giver whose authority reaches the conscience. But there is no such law-giver apart from a Personal God, and consequently the existence of moral obligation cannot be taught apart from religion."[31] It was one thing to persuade the intellect of the rightness and duty of moral conduct. It was quite another, especially among sons of Adam and inheritors of the baneful consequences of his primordial disobedience, to reach the human will, to train people to act on the basis of what they knew to be right. Saint Paul himself had observed with some consternation that he found his own will doing what he knew to be evil and omitting what he knew to be good. For this reason, only the supernatural could guarantee the possibility of consistent right conduct. "It may be galling to the devotees of the modern spirit to base their morality on God and religion," said an essayist in the *American Catholic Quarterly Review*. "But until they do so it shall possess neither stability nor fruition."[32] As another scholar of religion put it, "Ethics must either perfect itself in religion, or disintegrate itself into Hedonism."[33] Still another Catholic observer reminded the faithful that Aristotle himself, who of course wrote a great ethical treatise, conceded regretfully that it would do nothing to encourage men to do good or shun evil.[34] In short, the Catholic consensus on the question was that the morality that Ethical Culture sought to advance could not enforce itself. It demanded a force outside itself in order to bind its precepts on man's recalcitrant will. Moral education and the cultivation of a sense of duty within individuals were themselves beyond reproach, but something greater than both of these was necessary in order to restrain desire and avarice in cases in which moral action did not correspond with the individual's material interest.

For similar reasons, the growing effort to introduce this type of nonreligious, or "creedless," moral instruction into the schools met with a forceful and unanimous Catholic opposition. *America* magazine proudly published a statement to this effect by Philadelphia's Archbishop Patrick Ryan:

> One of the most fatal and demoralizing superstitions of this country is this attempted separation of morality from doctrinal teaching. Doctrines are as the granite foundation to the whole edifice of Christian ethics, and with them that edifice must stand or crumble into ruins. What underlies the value of holy childhood but the doctrine that the child has an immortal soul? Abolish this, look at the child only in the light of its utility to the State, and soon infanticide will commence again, and deformed children will be put to death, when men shall have lost the tendencies which Christianity has produced and fostered. In the name of our Christian civilization, I, a Bishop of the Christian Church, lift up my voice to warn you that the popular modern system of teaching morality without the doctrines that motivate it, whether that system be called Christian ethics or moral instruction or unsectarian teaching, is sapping the very foundation of Christianity and Christian civilization.[35]

Sometimes this attempt to undermine religious dogma could be concealed behind a religious gloss. Thus Father Timothy Brosnahan reminded his readers of Horace Mann's efforts during the nineteenth century to modify religious instruction to cater to a kind of lowest common denominator, so that no particular Christian tradition could object. By means of Mann's program, which attempted to "teach a religion which, because it was no one's religion, was supposed to be acceptable to everybody," the modern system of "agnostic schools" was reached.[36] For his part, Charles Eliot had his own suggestion for religious instruction: a manual that "would contain no dogma, creed or ritual, and no church history" but would "set forth the fundamental religious ideas which ought to be conveyed to every American child and adolescent in the schools of the future. Such teaching would counteract materialism, promote reverence for God and human nature, and strengthen the foundations of a peace-loving democracy."[37] Albion Small could not have put it better.

Coming under particular attack from the Catholic press was the Ethical Culture School in New York, which was the educational component of the entire ethical culture enterprise. These educational experiments sought to apply the principles of ethical culture to the moral training of the rising generation. Not through fear or promises of eternal blessedness would young people now be exhorted to lead lives of virtue, but through a rational assessment of the demands of duty. The alarming tendency away from moral education in the schools was thus to be countered by a new kind of moral education founded on naturalistic and Kantian principles, not by agitation for more religious instruction.

One of the main shortcomings of this kind of moral training, according to Catholic commentators, was that it simply did not work. As in their analysis of modern educational methods in general, Catholics conceded that their opponents possessed some virtues worthy of imitation. The ethical culture schools, for example, sought to excite the children to great deeds through the use of biographies of great men, by encouraging moral reflection in the students, and the like. But, as a nun from the Teachers College at the Catholic University explained, "the entire scheme rests upon no solid foundation because the substantial informing principle of morality is wanting." In place of a divine Lawgiver, the human conscience in the new dispensation was said to originate exclusively from within man's mind itself.[38]

In their attempt to form "useful and progressive members of society," ethical culture teachers turned the children's attention away from the kind of dogmatic formation and absolute truth emphasized in Catholic education and toward society itself. "Society has been idealized," a Catholic critic complained, "so that the teachers may now say, 'Humanity and God—they are the same thing.'" Benevolence and social service were fine virtues to inculcate, but in keeping with the spirit of the age they had been evacuated of their proper motive. Society could never satisfactorily function as "an end in itself of human action."[39]

The proponents of ethical culture, particularly in education, sought to replace the traditional supernatural sanctions of right conduct, which they believed had actually harmed mankind and dulled man's natural moral faculties, with a purely rationalistic basis for moral action. "Right for right's sake," they would say—and the Kantian overtones of this statement were no coincidence. Ethical culture was at root an effort to apply a somewhat expanded version of the Kantian categorical imperative to everyday moral reflection. From such a point of view, it was to be expected that the Catholic Church's exhortations to virtue through the dual promise of everlasting blessedness in heaven or eternal punishment in hell would seem crude and vulgar—at the very least, a far inferior approach to one that emphasized the nobility of the purely disinterested act of virtue. This, however, was a misconception, the *Catholic Educational Review* explained. It was true that the Church made her faithful aware of the prospect of eternal damnation, but the point of this emphasis must be borne in mind. "A moral code must be able to restrain the weak man in temptation as well as to stimulate the noble nature to virtue," it explained simply, "and the fear of punishment restrains where a higher motive sometimes fails. Once saved from falling, he will advance to virtue by the higher motive." Fear of the Lord, after all, is the beginning of wisdom. But the principal motivation in the life of the Catholic, especially one striving to grow in grace and sanctification, was the love of God—a positive, not a negative, precept. What the Church uses to reach beginners to the spiritual life cannot with justice be confused with this highest of motivations that it holds out to all its faithful, especially those whose spiritual lives are more mature.[40]

Why, on the other hand, should the child trained in the new secular ethic obey its commands? One representative of the ethical culture movement pointed to the Kantian *ought*: "The 'ought' is an 'ought' which exists. It is because the 'ought' is an 'ought' that 'is' that it is capable at the same time of being the object of religious veneration and of scientific wonder and curiosity."[41] How this rather stern commandment would be translated into terms children could comprehend and assimilate was not clear. A Catholic writer imagined the teacher of ethical culture "printing the word Ought in great letters on the blackboard and training the children reverently to salute the word as they are accustomed to salute the national flag."[42]

Indeed, the principal difficulty that critics noted regarding moral teaching that grounded itself on something other than Catholic dogma was that it had to rely on a mind trained to look at all times to this universal "ought," when it was precisely the reasoning faculty that became most clouded amid the throes of temptation. In order to tame the passions and subject them to the reason, therefore, something more than the categorical imperative was necessary, something more than an a priori precept of the moral conscience.[43] In a famous passage summing up the Church's position, Cardinal John Henry Newman had observed: "Quarry the granite rock with a razor, or moor the vessel with a thread of silk; then may you hope with such keen and delicate instruments as human knowledge and human reason to contend against those giants, the passion and the pride of man." Sister Mary Ruth of Wisconsin's Sisters of St. Dominic put it this way:

> Even perceiving adequately the dignity of human nature, and even sensitive to the feelings of reverence and awe in the contemplation of the high principles of truth and justice and magnanimity, yet what

will stand one in the hour of moral crisis when the question arises, Why ought I do right even at my own cost? The *only satisfactory answer*, the only answer of driving power is the answer that the Catholic Church teaches her children, "I owe this service to God, my Creator."[44]

Thus in a society and an age tending more and more toward secular creeds, man-centered morality, toleration, pluralism, and emancipation from the dogmas of the past, Catholics clung to their Church's traditional exclusivity, insisting with one voice that the *only* satisfactory answer to moral chaos was that provided by the Catholic Church. It was the ultimate case of Catholic resistance to the Progressive Zeitgeist. As Progressives were promoting a nonsectarian creed—indeed, a humanistic religion of sorts—on the national level, and on the individual level encouraging an experiential approach to creedal systems, Catholics continued to insist on the universal and exclusive validity, for the nation and for individuals, of a creed based on the teachings of Christ.

EPILOGUE / INTO THE FUTURE

P ROGRESSIVE INTELLECTUALS EMERGED from World War I, in the
words of F. Scott Fitzgerald, "to find all gods dead, all wars fought,
all faiths in man shaken."[1] Some of the Progressive spirit lived on,
it is true; but many Progressives were chastened, their hopes of founding
a new civilization based on science, democracy, and coordinated intelligence seemingly misplaced. Indeed, a small industry has developed among
historians around the question of where, after the war had ended, all the
Progressives had gone.[2]

Catholic intellectuals, on the other hand, in large part because they had
stood aloof from and even rejected much of the Progressive project, not
only did not suffer a similar decline in the postwar years but in fact flourished in an impressive philosophical and literary renascence that spanned
the next several decades. As one historian notes, "In an intellectual world
at first unaccustomed to disillusionment and the uncertainty of all values,
but eventually forced to make uncertainty a way of existence, the Catholic
was driven by a desire to proclaim and affirm."[3] Although as intrigued by
the possibilities of social science as were the Progressives themselves,
Catholic thinkers never seriously entertained the notion that the new disciplines could actually fulfill the saccharine promises of secular redemption that some Progressives had attached to them. While the barbarism of
the Great War profoundly challenged the Progressive confidence in the
Enlightenment conception of man as essentially good and his nature mal-
leable under social direction, to the Church this was merely another
episode, albeit an especially bloody and barbaric one, in the lengthy catalogue of human folly and sin.

When Catholics perceived at least an implicit hostility toward the
Church in one area of Progressive intellectual endeavor after another, they
were not simply imagining things. This is not to suggest that the Progressives aimed their critiques (both explicit and implicit) at Catholics alone.

As I noted in the introduction, a diverse array of American thinkers felt alienated by and stood aloof from the intellectual mainstream of the early twentieth century. But when Pragmatists criticized Scholasticism and denounced dogma as an obstacle not only to the discovery of truth but also to democracy itself; when Progressive educators encouraged experimentation and socialization as guiding pedagogical principles and looked with suspicion on Catholic schooling; and when a whole series of American intellectuals claimed that the comity and order of American democracy demanded that creedal systems be replaced by a nondogmatic moral system that could bind the consciences of all alike, Catholics could hardly be blamed for perceiving a growing hostility to their entire outlook.

As the foregoing discussion has made clear, though, Catholics, while anxious to preserve their faith undefiled and convinced of its relevance in a wide array of disciplines, never retreated into utter isolation. They were prepared to accept good and useful things that the modern world had to offer. Still, they had to reject the very spirit of the Progressive Era, as well as many of its central principles. Here Eldon Eisenach's discussion of the nonsectarian national creed that the Progressives sought to establish has proven especially useful, for it helps to explain why Catholics found it difficult to assimilate themselves more readily to their intellectual environment. They were not content to be merely one sect among many or to submerge what they considered the Church's unique message into the syncretistic blend that Albion Small and other Progressives envisioned for philosophy, education, sociology, and even morality itself.

Moreover, it was precisely this partial isolation, this refusal to be assimilated to the spirit of the age, that would prove a source of vibrancy and life for American Catholicism in the ensuing decades. Many intellectuals sensed that something was awry in the modern world, and the very fact that in an age of toleration and subjectivism the Catholic Church presumed to call herself the exclusive font of salvation, and to insist on the existence and attainability of absolute truth, held out a certain romantic attraction. (This was certainly the perspective of the great historian and convert Christopher Dawson, about whom more below.) Far from retreating into a triumphalist isolationism, American Catholics, convinced that they possessed a moral and philosophical tradition that could reinvigorate true intellectual life and rescue their country from a creeping nihilism, found themselves with a critical and exhilarating mission of evangelization.

It was an exciting time for Catholicism on both sides of the Atlantic. Hilaire Belloc remarked that "the more powerful, the more acute, and the more sensitive minds of our time are clearly inclining toward the Catholic side."⁴ "Despite the defeat of Al Smith," writes historian Charles Morris, "American Catholics achieved an extraordinary ideological self-confidence by the 1930s, much to the envy of Protestant ministers."⁵ Converts, often of considerable intellectual standing, played an especially important role in this Catholic revival, and it is interesting to consider what attracted such figures to the Church. Although Pope Pius X found himself the subject of ceaseless ridicule at the hands of many European intellectuals for the vigor with which he battled Modernism, for others this otherwise gentle man's obstinacy seemed to be the mark of a true man of God. In fact it was only after the issuance of *Lamentabili Sane* (1907), the list of condemned errors of the Modernists, that many of the Church's great converts made their way into her fold. In England, for instance, the great historian Christopher Dawson entered the Church in 1914, the former Anglican Ronald Knox in 1917, and G. K. Chesterton in 1922. Dawson vigorously defended Pope Pius IX's *Syllabus of Errors* as an antidote to modern secular liberalism, which denied "the subordination of human society to divine law."⁶ Thus the Church's uncompromising stance itself ultimately compelled many to enter her fold. As for the United States, Peter Huff notes that the American Church "witnessed such a steady stream of notable literary conversions that the statistics tended to support Calvert Alexander's hypothesis of something suggesting a cultural trend." The pre–Vatican II Catholic Church in the United States was, he argues, "a highly imaginative world of myth, meaning, and ritual, based upon the classical vision of Catholicism's cultural mission."⁷

The Catholic revival of 1920–1960, which built on intellectual foundations that Catholics had laid during the Progressive Era, was multifaceted. Surveying this cultural phenomenon, William Halsey describes pre–Vatican II American Catholicism as constituting a full-fledged "countersociety." His partial listing of Catholic organizations is impressive:

In chronological order from 1900 to 1950, Catholics organized: The National Catholic Educational Association (1904), Catholic Press Association (1911), Catholic Writers Guild of America (1919), American Catholic Historical Association (1919), Catholic Library Association (1921), American Catholic Philosophical Association (1926), Catholic Association for International Peace (1926), Catholic Anthropological Association (1928), Catholic Book Club (1928), Catholic Poetry Society of America (1931), Catholic Biblical Association of America (1936), Catholic Art Association (1937), Catholic Theatre Conference (1937), American Catholic

Sociological Society (1938), Catholic Renascence Society (1940), Catholic Economic Association (1941), Catholic Commission on Intellectual and Cultural Affairs (1946), and the American Catholic Psychological Association (1947).[8]

And yet, Halsey goes on to argue, although Catholics established an extraordinary array of parallel associations, they did so not because they cherished separateness or exclusion per se. What at times was an institutional isolation did not indicate a lack of concern with the nation as a whole; on the contrary, Catholic spokesmen contended that it was precisely through cultivating a robust Catholic culture that they could truly serve their country. Catholic culture, Halsey writes, "was an attempt to save middle-class culture from its own decadence. While isolating themselves from disillusionment, these agencies were busy affirming values which were either under attack, forgotten, or going through the disquieting process of transformation."[9]

A distinct note of urgency is perceptible in this great Catholic enterprise as it unfolded from the Progressive Era through the eve of the Second Vatican Council. Thus the great historian and Catholic convert Christopher Dawson spoke freely of a titanic struggle that had the world in its grip. The Church's adversaries, he wrote, were themselves appropriating the language of religion in setting forth their programs. He foresaw a conflict not "between religion and secular civilization, but rather between the God religious and the social religious—in other words, between the worship of God and the cult of the state or of the race or of humanity."[10] "For the first time in the world's history," he went on, "the Kingdom of Antichrist has acquired political form and social substance and stands over against the Christian Church as a *counter-church* with its own dogmas and its own moral standards, ruled by a centralized hierarchy and inspired by an intense will to world conquest." This was certainly a reference to communism and fascism, but Dawson also meant to include in his warning the growth and spread of liberal, naturalistic humanitarianism.[11] This was not something peculiar to Dawson; the thoughts of this eminent historian were fairly typical of Catholic thinkers in the decades before Vatican II. The two broad features that contributed to the Catholic intellectual milieu at this time, both of which were plainly evident in the Catholic discourse of the Progressive Era, were, first, a remarkable confidence that the Church had much to contribute to combating the errors and ills of modern society, and second, the conviction that the Church was locked in a great struggle over which vision—the secular or the religious—was to inspire the civilization of the twentieth century and beyond. And the balance of Catholic opinion perceived the attempt to suppress or to syncretize creeds as a tactic of the secularists.

Within such an environment, Catholic solidarity appeared more urgent than ever. Sociologist Joseph Varacalli has borrowed the term "plausibility structure" from Peter Berger to describe the social and intellectual milieu that is necessary to give a religion a certain public coherence and to serve as a constant reinforcement to the faith of its adherents.[12] Thus Berger observed:

There is a further aspect . . . that is extremely important for the reality-maintaining task of religion. This aspect refers to the social-structural prerequisites of any religious . . . reality maintaining process. This may be formulated as follows: worlds are socially constructed and socially maintained. Their continuing reality, both objective (as common taken-for-granted facticity) and subjective (as facticity imposing itself on individual consciousness), depends on *specific* social processes, namely those processes that ongoingly reconstruct and maintain the particular worlds in question. Conversely, the interruption of these social processes threatens the (objective and subjective) reality of the worlds in question. Thus each world requires a social "base" for its continuing existence as a world that is real to actual human beings. This "base" may be called its plausibility structure.[13]

Varacalli himself put it this way:

By the Church's plausibility structure is meant the series of interlocking social institutions (e.g., parishes, seminaries, educational organizations, mass media outlets, professional and voluntary associations) that, in toto, are theoretically capable of producing a Catholic environment generating and making "real" among its inhabitants authentic Catholic thought and behavior. At its very best, this "Catholic ghetto"—as it has been referred to by its Catholic detractors—does not shield away all non-Catholic influence but allows for the formation of authentic Catholic identity and character development capable of engaging in a critical dialogue with the outside world.[14]

Berger believed that American society, because fundamentally pluralist, was inherently antagonistic to the construction of the kind of plausibility structure he described. In medieval Europe all of society in effect served as a plausibility structure because every institution with which the individual came into contact supported and validated his religious faith. It was foolish, Berger believed, to expect this kind of public unanimity of the American public order. Varacalli, however, makes a persuasive case that the Church itself is capable of maintaining a reinforcing structure for its faithful even when the surrounding culture is indifferent or hostile. Individuals, he says, "can be and are successfully socialized by what Charles Horton Cooley termed 'primary groups,' by what Emile Durkheim called 'intermediate institutions,' and by what a 'later' Peter L. Berger and Richard J. Neuhaus label 'mediating structures' *regardless* of the state of affairs of the other society . . . *so long as the internal integrity and coherence of the plausibility structure is maintained.*" Building upon the foundation established during the Progressive Era, the Catholic Church in the United States, according to Varacalli, "was a vital and distinctive sub-cultural reality" in the period from 1917 until the Second Vatican Council; its "plausibility structure was functioning well."[15]

Monsignor George Kelly, who has written extensively about—and taken part in—the struggles and disagreements among Catholics along the ideological spectrum since the close of the council, lists five principal features of the healthy "plausibility structure" of the preconciliar Church in the United States:

1. The overwhelming majority of the Catholic people had been effectively reached by the Church's manifold structures. They were practicing Catholics.
2. The Church through its supported family life and school systems became the instrument of Americanization and upward social mobility.
3. The leaders of the Church—bishops, priests, religious, lay apostles—won the loyalty of the vast numbers of Catholics in major matters involving Church doctrine and Church policy.
4. Catholic parishes for the most part were important local communities. Sometimes they were solely ethnic, most often neighborhood centers for Catholics, and occasionally social communities that related successfully to indigenous non-Catholics and to custodians of municipal affairs.
5. The institutional Church also presided over the emergence of a Catholic elite—mainly through its colleges, seminaries, and lay apostolic movements for social justice, international peace, family life, and spiritual perfection. These movements owed their exis-

tence to the impetus given them by the Holy See from Leo XIII onward. Even the loyal opposition (typified by John Courtney Murray and Dorothy Day) proposed new approaches and new accommodations within the framework of the Church structure.[16]

Thus the Church was absolutely certain about its identity, and this certainty was reflected in the various Church structures with which the faithful came into contact. A fundamental unity was perceptible in the decades that preceded the council. The Catholic population was composed of "soldiers for Christ," whose task it was to Christianize the social order and convert their fellow citizens to what they believed to be the true faith. If Catholicism really was as universal and as universally necessary to the salvation of souls as it claimed to be, no other posture made sense. This very outlook formed the basis at a fundamental level for what it meant to be Catholic; this confrontational posture, in effect, rendered the entire Catholic package plausible.

When this posture was effectively abandoned following Vatican II, the plausibility structure of the Church in the United States was, in Varacalli's view, a principal casualty, bound up as it was with that posture. Elsewhere Varacalli has argued that in the years following Vatican II, the abandonment of the effort to establish a Catholic sociology—in other words, the abandonment among Catholic sociologists of the overall intellectual project begun by Catholics during the Progressive Era—represents and symbolizes the disintegration of the once-flourishing Catholic plausibility structure. Standard, orthodox Catholic doctrine and catechesis, he suggests, "cannot hope to compete against the antagonistic messages of, for instance, the secular mass media if what is learned through orthodox catechetical instruction in a Catholic high school or in an orthodox department of theology in a Catholic college is opposed, either explicitly or implicitly, in a secular-oriented sociology (or, for that matter, psychology, art, or English literature) course of that same institution."[17]

What Varacalli means by a "Catholic sociology," and what its actual practitioners in the decades leading up to Vatican II meant by it, was not an approach to sociological knowledge that would be radically separate from, and utterly without influence by, secular branches of sociology. Still less was it conceived of as a willfully tendentious brand of study, anxious to vindicate Catholic principles at all costs. The Catholic sociologist sought to undertake research that would be at once dispassionate and identifiably Catholic. By its very nature, he argued, sociology cannot escape value judgments. The decision as to which topics are worthy of investigation itself implies a value judgment. Likewise, the act of deciding on what social phenomena constitute problems in need of remedy cannot be value-free. The disintegration of the traditional family structure, to some a disaster with terrible social consequences, may to others actually be welcome in that it represents the breakdown of an antiquated institution that has institutionalized abuse and done much to frustrate individual self-realization. The function of the Catholic sociologist, therefore, can be explained as follows:

a) to provide objective social research
b) in assisting the Catholic Church in the tasks of 1) understanding how surrounding social forces affect the Faith and 2) reconstructing the social order along Christian principles
c) by applying, where appropriate, Catholic principles and a Catholic sensibility to the existing body of sound social scientific theory, concepts, and methods
d) through a thorough public intellectual exchange.[18]

In the years following Vatican II, however, the leadership of the American Catholic Sociological Society began to retreat from, and even to repudiate, this vision of the role of the Catholic within the discipline of sociology. The Catholic sociological enterprise envisioned by its pioneers had never fully materialized; although intellectually respectable in the immediate pre–Vatican II period, it still remained inchoate and perhaps even a little confused. The precise role and function of a Catholic sociology was a matter of ongoing debate during the interwar and postwar years. That the project was worth attempting was generally accepted. What was happening now was something entirely different. Now it was being suggested that the entire enterprise had been ill considered from the start and ought to be abandoned.[19]

To be sure, there is a certain sense in which Vatican II lent encouragement to Catholic forays into the social sciences. Gaudium et Spes observed that there "should be no false opposition between professional and social activities on the one part, and religious life on the other. . . . In the exercise of all their earthly activities . . . [Christians] can thereby gather their humane, domestic, professional, social, and technical enterprises into one vital synthesis with religious values, under whose supreme direction all things are harmonized unto God's glory."[20] The council likewise emphasized the importance of the role of the laity in the life of the Church and in spreading the Catholic faith in the course of their social and professional activity, although this point was merely an outgrowth of the exhortations issued by Popes Pius XI and XII urging Catholic laity to engage in "Catholic Action."

In practice, however, these are not the themes of the council that have received the greatest emphasis. Instead, the council has frequently been invoked in order to put a stop to such activity. In the wake of the council, Catholics were being encouraged to take a more optimistic view of the modern world and its potential openness to the Gospel message. Dialogue, adaptation, and *aggiornamento* were the conciliar catchwords; the uncompromising yet strangely effective strategy that American Catholic intellectuals had been pursuing suddenly seemed out of date. The kinds of enterprises in which Catholics engaged during the Progressive Era, and which flourished through the 1950s, were now generally looked upon as retrograde examples of Catholic triumphalism, which ran counter to the spirit of a council whose documents appeared to show such friendship with the secular world. Whether this is an accurate interpretation of Vatican II is not at issue here; the fact is simply that this, more often than not, is what the council has come to mean in the minds of a considerable number of cardinals, bishops, priests, and religious. Historian Patricia Byrne, speaking of the lives of female religious, summed up this change in praxis, this more irenic relationship with the world that began to dominate Catholic life in all its aspects, by observing that "when Vatican II spelled the end of the separation of Church and world, the convent-world dichotomy came to an end as well."[21]

The abandonment of a distinctly Catholic outlook in the social sciences was, of course, only a small part of the collapse of the plausibility structure that Varacalli describes. By the 1950s some of the Catholic distinctiveness that we have seen had begun to give way more generally, doubtless under the pressures of the Cold War and the apparent need to create a broad front against the threat of Communism. It was a relatively irenic decade in American politics as a whole, and arguably the high point of the "vital center" moderation that Arthur Schlesinger Jr. advocated. Historian Arnold Sparr, for his part, contends that by the 1950s voices could be heard suggesting that the time may have come for American Catholic thinkers to abandon their traditional sense of distinctiveness and come to terms with pluralism.[22] Still, it cannot be emphasized enough that Catholic identity remained sufficiently strong even then that Paul Blanshard could identify it as a "problem" for American secularism.[23]

But it was only in the aftermath of the Second Vatican Council (1962–1965) that a clearly noticeable and deliberate retreat from American Catholicism's often confrontational posture began to occur. Pope John XXIII spoke highly of the Church that his predecessor Pius XII had bequeathed to him. At the same time, he proposed a program of *aggiorna-mento*, by which the Church would "update" various of her practices and begin to come to terms with the modern world and modern ideologies. He would bring into being a Catholic Church that would respond to moral or doctrinal error not with condemnation and discipline but with the clear light of the truth—in his judgment, error's best refutation. Ideological, philosophical, and theological errors of the day, the pope observed at the opening of the council, had in the past been condemned by the Church "with the greatest severity," but in our own day "the Spouse of Christ prefers to make use of the medicine of mercy rather than that of severity. She considers that she meets the needs of the present day by demonstrating the validity of her teaching rather than by condemnations."[24]

Vatican II continues, even today, to be a source of bitter controversy and ill will across the spectrum of Catholic opinion. Although much of this debate concerns the wisdom of certain conciliar initiatives (ecumenism chief among them), division within the Church over the council is also traceable to a certain ambiguity in the conciliar texts themselves, which in general lack the precision and brevity of the decrees of previous councils. Thus in matters ranging from liturgy to religious liberty to ecumenism, a stunning amount of ink has been spilled over the question of what the council really meant with regard to this or that issue. It would likely come as a surprise to most Catholics to learn, for instance, that *Sacrosanctum Concilium*, the conciliar document on the liturgy, calls for Gregorian chant, which since the council has all but vanished from Catholic life, to have "pride of place," or that "the Latin language is to be preserved in the Latin rites."[25] The difficulty of interpretation lay in the conciliar documents' liberal use of qualifying phrases, as well as numerous clear cases in which some parts of the text appear to undermine other ones. Oscar Cullmann, one of the most distinguished Protestant observers at the council, noted this: "On far too many occasions," he said, the conciliar texts "juxtapose opposing viewpoints without establishing any genuine internal link between them."[26] Thus the very ambivalence and even ambiguity of some of the council documents has only increased the frustration of those attempting to discern their actual intention, since Catholics along a wide ideological range can each with some justice claim to be supporting the letter of the council. Cardinal Joseph Ratzinger, prefect of the Congregation for the Doctrine of the Faith since 1981 and, to a lesser extent, Pope John Paul II himself, have set forth an interpretation of Vatican II that, while conceding the extraordinary novelty of some of its pronouncements, attempts to view it within the context of the church's entire tradition. Catholic liberals, in turn, have accused such figures of obstructionism and of having betrayed the spirit of the council. Traditionalists, for their part, have suggested that certain of the council's initiatives, primarily pastoral in character and thus qualitatively different from irreformable dogmatic decrees, ought in retrospect to be rethought or abandoned altogether.

The problem of conciliar interpretation notwithstanding, it can hardly be denied that the surprising optimism of such important Vatican II documents as the Pastoral Constitution on the Church in the Modern World (*Gaudium et Spes*), represents a dramatic change from the lucid and pithy condemnations of Pius IX's *Syllabus of Errors*, and even from the opinion of a pope as recent as Pius XII, whose own view of the modern world, repeated throughout his pontificate, was summed up in the 1950 letter *Evangeli Praecones*: "Venerable brethren, you are well aware that almost the whole human race is today allowing itself to be driven into two opposing camps, for Christ or against Christ. The human race is involved today in a supreme crisis, which will issue in its salvation by Christ, or in its destruction." While of course far from suggesting that mankind had achieved perfection, *Gaudium et Spes* approaches the secular world in a spirit of congratulation and praise, confident that an especially auspicious moment for the spread of the Gospel had arrived.[27]

Whatever else one might say about the preconciliar Catholic Church, it was precisely the clarity of the Vatican's pronouncements and, in an increasingly ecumenical age, the curiously militant posture it consistently adopted, that had provided the basis for the profound self-confidence and sense of mission that characterized Progressive Era Catholicism in the United States. Along these lines, it is quite remarkable to note what the Vatican had to say about the ecumenical movement, the quest for Christian unity that continued to grow stronger in certain Protestant circles, a mere thirteen years before the convocation of the Second Vatican Council. In 1949 the Holy Office issued an official instruction on the ecumenical movement and how Catholic bishops were to proceed in relation to it. They should be on guard, the instruction warned, lest "on the false pretext that more attention should be paid to the points on which we agree than to those on which we differ, a dangerous indifferentism be encouraged." Care must be taken lest "in the so-called 'irenic' spirit of to-day, through comparative study and the vain desire for a progressively closer mutual approach among the various professions of faith, Catholic doctrine—either in its dogmas or in the truths which are connected with them—be so conformed or in a way adapted to the doctrines of dissident sects, that the purity of Catholic doctrine be impaired, or its genuine and certain meaning be obscured." The document continues in this vein:

> With regard specially to mixed assemblies and conferences of Catholics with non-Catholics, which in recent times have begun to be held in many places to promote "union" in the faith, there is need of quite peculiar vigilance and control on the part of Ordinaries. For if on the one hand these meetings afford the desired opportunity to spread among non-Catholics the knowledge of Catholic doctrine which is generally not sufficiently known to them, on the other hand they easily involve no slight danger of indifferentism for Catholics. In cases where there seems to be some hope of good results, the Ordinary shall see that the thing is properly managed, designating for these meetings priests who are as well qualified as possible to explain and defend Catholic doctrine properly and appropriately. The faithful, however, should not attend these meetings unless they have obtained special permission from Ecclesiastical Authority, and this shall be given only to those who are known to be well instructed and strong in their faith. Where there is no apparent hope of good results, or where the affair involves special dangers on other grounds, the faithful are to be prudently kept away from the meetings, and the meetings themselves are soon to be ended or gradually suppressed.

The document closes by reminding the bishops that "nothing more effectively paves the way for the erring to find the truth and to embrace the Church than the faith of Catholics, when it is confirmed by the example of upright living."

The Holy Office was only elaborating on the position of Pope Pius XI, who had devoted his seminal 1928 encyclical *Mortalium Animos* to surveying the state of the ecumenical movement and concluding that it was an enterprise that could in no way earn the support of Catholics. To partake in such proceedings would implicitly compromise the position of the Catholic Church by seeming to imply that the unity of all Christians could be accomplished in some other way than the return of the erring to the one fold and one shepherd. This was the kind of language that had formed the backbone of the preconciliar Catholic plausibility structure; it had given Catholics around the world a feeling of distinctiveness and a sense of mission.

In the decades following Vatican II, such language all but disappeared. In a widely quoted statement in 1968, Cardinal Franz König made what to Progressive Era Catholics would no doubt have seemed the astonishing claim that in the kind of dialogue he envisioned with the world, the Catholic "is not considered as possessing all the truth, but as someone who has faith and is looking for that truth with others, both believers and non-believers."[28] More recently, in the January 20, 2000, issue of *L'Osservatore Romano*, Bishop (now Cardinal) Walter Kasper, who was appointed secretary of the Pontifical Council for the Promotion of Christian Unity by Pope John Paul II in 1998, called the traditional paradigm into question more explicitly still. Until Vatican II, he explained, the Church "understood the re-establishing of Christian unity exclusively in terms of 'return of our separated brothers to the true Church of Christ . . . from which they have at one time unhappily separated themselves.'" This understanding "is no longer applicable to the Catholic Church after Vatican II. . . . The old concept of the ecumenism of return has today been replaced by that of a common journey which directs Christians toward the goal of ecclesial communion understood as unity in reconciled diversity."[29] The Balamand Statement drawn up between representatives of the Catholic and Orthodox Churches in 1993 expressly forbade proselytization between the two groups. Representatives of the Catholic Church's Pontifical Council for the Promotion of Christian Unity proclaimed that Catholics and Orthodox constituted "sister churches . . . jointly responsible for the People of God." This was quite a novel teaching, and indeed neither side even attempted to conceal the novelty of the concept of "sister churches." It was, however, yet another example of Rome's apparent retreat in the postconciliar milieu from the kinds of exclusive claims that for so long had seemed to form the essential backbone of Catholic teaching.

It may seem peculiar, even in an epilogue, to devote such attention in a study of this kind to the various approaches to ecumenism that the Church adopted from the Progressive Era through the present day. There is a reason—a fairly critical one—why the discussion is not out of place. It accentuates in stark relief the change in posture that the Vatican adopted with the Second Vatican Council and into the postconciliar period. The kind of vitality that the American Catholic world experienced in the early twentieth century would probably not have been possible without the certain trumpets of Rome. Ubiquitous throughout American Catholic writing in this period is an obvious confidence in the judgment of the Holy See and an immense respect for the swiftness and, yes, harshness with which ecclesiastical authority could move against potential disruption or incipient heresy. American Catholic thinkers of the Progressive Era were only adopting the tone of their Roman hierarchy when they embarked on their ambitious and confident intellectual enterprise. The preconciliar popes went out of their way to portray Catholicism as something unique and irreplaceable and resisted every development, ecumenism chief among them, that seemed to call this uniqueness into question. This was precisely the message that Catholics of the Progressive Era expressed with such frequency. At a time when intellectual fashion was looking especially askance at the dogmatic nature of the Catholic position, American Catholics clung to that position all the more tenaciously, clearly inspired by the similar attitude of their hierarchy in Rome. Such an enterprise would have been difficult if not impossible to carry out, and perhaps even unthinkable to begin with, amid the confusion and chaos that has beset the Catholic Church since Vatican II. Despite Pope John Paul II's reputation for conservatism, his disciplinary regime has in fact been relatively lax, particularly in comparison with those of his preconciliar predecessors and especially Pope Saint Pius X, the last pope to be canonized, whose battle against theological Modernism has earned him the opprobrium of so many unsympathetic historians.

At the council and especially in the years that followed, key churchmen claiming to speak for the Church at large radically reconfigured both the Church's conception of herself and of the Protestant and other non-Catholic religious confessions that stand outside her visible confines. In the year 2000 the Congregation for the Doctrine of the Faith (formerly the Holy Office) issued an immediately controversial document titled *Dominus Iesus*, which purported to correct a series of liberal errors regarding the uniqueness of the Catholic Church and the centrality of Christ in human salvation. Most notable about this document was less its actual contents, which in fact were nowhere near as uncompromising as its opponents suggested, than its reception by spokesmen for non-Catholic denominations. The outrage and indignation of representatives of the Anglican and other Protestant communions, as well as the anger of Jewish groups, made headlines for days after the document's release. Had the Vatican been engaged in good-faith dialogue with the various Protestant groups all this time, a simple clarification of the necessity of the Catholic faith for salvation could hardly have come as a surprise to any of the participants in the ecumenical venture. That a fairly simple restatement of the Church's view of its unique spiritual mandate should have come as such a shock and even a cause for offense among non-Catholics suggests that Catholic spokesmen at ecumenical meetings over the past several decades have been intimating that Christian unity could in fact imply something distinct from the straightforward conversion of non-Catholics to Roman Catholicism.

The purposely irenic posture that the Church has chosen to assume vis-à-vis other religions, and in particular the noticeable retreat that some of her key spokesmen have beaten from the kinds of exclusive claims she used to make have affected the texture and tone of Catholic intellectual life in the United States as much as the confidence and ecclesiastical discipline did, in a radically different way, earlier in the century. This new tone has, again, tended to undermine the plausibility structure that the Church in America had erected during the preconciliar period. That structure had been characterized by an explosion of Catholic organizations, such as the ones Halsey lists above, dedicated to disseminating and cultivating a distinctively Catholic perspective in a wide range of areas. It also featured a clergy and hierarchy, to say nothing of periodicals, lay associations, and the like, whose outlook toward non-Catholic religions and the world at large, while one of goodwill, was nevertheless characterized by an intense commitment to the absolute uniqueness of the Catholic faith. Catholicism was, simply put, the true religion, faithful adherence to which offered the promise of an eternity with God. In the temporal sphere, the Catholic faith was believed to be the strongest source of social comity and moral order, of stimulus to the arts and sciences, and indeed of all the fruits and blessings of civilization. And it was with sincere and profound determination that Catholic leaders and organizations worked to disseminate this faith.

During the Progressive Era, as this study has shown, one Catholic writer after another looked with dread upon the modern world and the direction in which it was heading. That dread was countered by a conviction that was at least as strong and certain: that the Catholic Church had the answers to the problems that vexed both society and the human soul. To the anxieties ushered in by Darwinism she offered a teleological philosophy of life and the universe, reinserting the purpose into the cosmic order that Darwin had so violently removed. It was the Hebrews, in the Church's Old Testament, who even more than the Greeks bequeathed to Western civilization an abiding concern for the study of history, for the Hebrews' own faith was based upon a series of discrete, unique, and unrepeatable historical events. The ancients, as well as civilizations of Near and Far East, posited a universe of eternally recurring cycles, ultimately meaningless because they tended toward no particular goal or purpose and were destined forever to repeat themselves in one form or another. The

Hebrews, on the other hand, and the Catholics who followed them, insisted that the world did have meaning, that history was linear rather than cyclical, and that far from a meaningless agglomeration of divine whim, the universe, befitting the good God who had created it, was orderly and intelligible.[30] By an interesting happenstance it was this very point, on which such early fathers as Clement of Alexandria, Origen, and Augustine had elaborated so eloquently, that in the modern age the Church was once again so eager to convey.

This, of course, was not all. To the confusion and restlessness that seemed to be the product of relativism, the Church offered a philosophical defense of absolute values. To a world undergoing radical and seemingly ceaseless change, the Church responded with the piety and reverence of the traditional Latin Mass, which in its dignity and stately reserve, and in its reservation of sacred tasks to the priest alone, served to remind man that some things were not to be touched by him. Above all, the Church insisted on the importance, uniqueness, and purpose that lay behind human life, confident that her message could cover the spiritual nakedness that she believed modernity had inflicted upon the masses.

Thus she made war upon philosophical trends, Pragmatism chief among them, that had gained such currency in the Progressive Era and that threatened to undermine the very confidence in the purposefulness and intelligibility of the universe that the Church believed the world so desperately needed. She substituted the philosophical categories and overall approach of Saint Thomas Aquinas, not in the spirit of a curious medieval artifact but as a living edifice of thought that had much to say to modern man. As we have seen, the Church in the United States did not retreat into an intellectual "ghetto" in the sense of rejecting everything modern or secular. There was quite a widespread agreement among Catholic scholars that with good and sober judgment the Church could selectively appropriate particular aspects of modern thought that might prove useful to her. Thus while refusing to yield on the philosophy and purpose of education, Catholics were more than willing to study the findings of modern psychology as they related to the learning process, and indeed in Edward Pace and Thomas Edward Shields they offered pioneers of their own. Underlying this intellectual project, meanwhile, was the desire to convert America to Catholicism, a goal repeated and referred to countless times throughout Catholic periodical literature in the Progressive Era and beyond. In 1941, the Catholic historian Theodore Maynard could casually observe in his history of American Catholicism: "Never can a truly Catholic zeal be content merely to hold what it has; it must boldly push out to conquest."[31]

This is precisely the spirit that has, by comparison, grown relatively dormant within the Church, and especially in the United States, since the close of Vatican II. As one might expect, along with this fairly obvious decline in evangelical zeal has come a precipitous decline in the practice of the faith among lay Catholics. This trend manifested itself in many ways among a certain segment of American Catholic intellectuals, but it began with what Monsignor George Kelly describes as the first fallout of Vatican II: "the rise of Catholic masochism." This was the curious phenomenon by which a number of Catholics of note recalled the days of the preconciliar Church in order to ridicule it and render it absurd and contemptible. Such a phenomenon, Kelly says, "might have been an expected by-product, although the volume and intensity of abuse against the Catholic body by its own surprised everyone."[32] The remarkable unity and obvious self-confidence of the American Church of the early twentieth century thus became a thing of the past as Catholic spokesmen made a point of ridiculing the Church of their youth, generally to the applause of fashionable opinion within the secular world. Garry Wills, the *National Review* writer whose own transition from conservatism to liberalism occurred during these years, was fairly typical in describing the faith of his youth as having consisted of nothing more profound than

prayers offered, heads ducked in unison, crossings, chants, christenings, grace at meals; beads, incense, candles, nuns in the classroom alternately too sweet and too severe, priests garbed black on the street and brilliant at the altar; churches lit and darkened, clothed and stripped, to the rhythm of liturgical recurrences; the crib in the winter, purple February and lilies in the spring; confession as intimidation and comfort and so forth.[33]

Of course, Wills appears to be describing a religion fairly rich in symbol and meaning, and perhaps cannot himself be held altogether blameless for having failed to perceive the inner core of mystery and belief whose external expressions he catalogues. But as Kelly points out, the immediate postconciliar years were scarcely a time of sober reflection and cool reason. An exasperated Pope Paul VI himself observed in 1968: "The Church is in a disturbed period of self-criticism, or what would better be called self-demolition. It is an acute and complicated upheaval which nobody would have expected after the Council. It is almost as if the Church were attacking herself." Seven years later he exclaimed, "Enough of internal dissent within the Church! Enough of a disintegrating interpretation of pluralism! Enough of Catholics attacking each other at the price of their own necessary unity! Enough of disobedience described as freedom!"[34]

That the Catholic Church in the United States, and indeed throughout the West at large, has been in a state of crisis since 1965 is subject to relatively simple empirical verification. It is reflected in rapidly falling attendance at Mass, an ongoing crisis in priestly vocations, and in the failure of American Catholics, according to most polls, to differ in any significant way from their non-Catholic fellow citizens in their opinions on a whole host of important moral issues. That the current situation represents a dramatic break with the situation that obtained during the years immediately before the council is not difficult to demonstrate. Consider what is easily one of the Church's most demanding and controversial teachings: the intrinsic immorality of artificial contraception. A survey conducted in 1952 found that while more than half the Catholics questioned considered contraception sinful, only 14 percent of Protestants and 10 percent of Jews agreed. Eleven years later, Chicago priest Andrew Greeley, who has since become notorious for his regular public dissent from papal statements, concluded that in this matter "most Catholics keep the Church's law (at least most of the time)."[35] Allan Carlson, a Lutheran scholar of the family, further observes that the so-called baby boom, erroneously attributed to various secular factors, was "largely a Roman Catholic event." Thus while the fertility rates for non-Catholics in 1951–1955 and 1961–1965 were 3.15 and 3.14, respectively, the figures for Catholics were 3.54 and 4.25. A survey conducted from 1952 to 1955 revealed that only 10 percent of Catholics under forty were having four or more children; the Protestant figure was a comparable 9 percent. In 1957–1959, though, the Catholic figure had more than doubled, to 22 percent, while the Protestant figure was unchanged. Pertinent research also reveals that "this 'Catholic fertility' event was tied to more frequent attendance at Mass, and to prior attendance of the mothers at Catholic parochial schools, colleges, and universities. Pope Pius XII and the whole 'teaching church' gave much more frequent attention in these years to the nature of the Christian family as a sign of obedience to God's will."[36] This fairly dramatic testimony indicates that the spirit of distinctiveness that this book has identified as among the fundamental characteristics of the Catholic intellectual milieu also had its counterpart in the lives of ordinary faithful.

To be sure, a number of discrete factors converged to bring about the unhappy situation within the Catholic Church today, and it would be facile to attribute this catastrophic decline exclusively to the change of orientation just described. At the same time, it is difficult to escape the conclusion that the quite numerous changes made to the texture of Catholic life—a texture that had marked Catholics and had served to remind them of the uniqueness and special importance of their religion— must have played some role in eroding the feeling of exceptionalism that had existed throughout the Catholic population before the council and that certainly existed among the Catholic intellectuals treated in this study. These changes range from items as seemingly minor as the elimination of the requirement that the faithful abstain from meat on Fridays to a radical liturgical reorientation whose effect was to move the Church away from the ritual and order of centuries past to the more familiar, less mysterious, and more community-based worship of the revised rite of Mass. In all of these ways the Catholic lifestyle was made, by degrees, to conform more and more to that of the secular world. By contrast, when Catholic immigrants began making their way to the United States in large numbers by the 1840s and 1850s, the American hierarchy was anxious to guard the Catholic faith with a special vigilance, all too aware that the pressures of assimilation in a country whose anti-Catholic prejudice had more than once expressed itself in violence would inevitably take their toll on a people already disoriented by their new surroundings. An argument can be made that this kind of guidance and pastoral solicitude on the part of the bishops is in fact even more appropriate to current circumstances, at a time when the consensus of previous generations has given way to a moral pluralism that nineteenth-century opinion could scarcely have imagined. Yet it is precisely now that the visibility of the American Catholic hierarchy on issues of importance appears to have reached an all-time low. The triumphalist Church of the Progressive Era, eager to convert America to Catholicism, appears to be in full-fledged retreat, with many bishops apparently even embarrassed by the zeal of their preconciliar predecessors.

But during the Progressive Era this new orientation was still decades away, and intellectually worlds away. At that time, Catholics remained a self-consciously distinct group, aware of their solemn charge to safeguard the purity of their doctrine, and mindful of Pope Leo XIII's warnings, in the encyclical *Longinqua Oceani* (1895) and the apostolic letter *Testem Benevolentiae* (1899) that, encouraging as were the growth and vitality of the Church in the United States, Catholics would always have to be on guard against the kind of religious indifferentism that a pluralistic religious system inevitably encouraged. They were, moreover, one of the only groups in the United States who offered a serious, systematic response to the intellectual innovations of the Progressive Era. While their secular counterparts looked confidently to the future, Catholic intellectuals, feeling uneasy about what they saw ahead, urged their countrymen to be mindful of the wisdom of the past. "Why our scholars should shriek 'On, on!' when 'Back, back!' would be so plainly the more sensible cry," one Catholic proposed, "the great fault of the day—immoderate pride of progress—answers."[37] No doubt they received the grudging admiration of some of their anti-Catholic countrymen for the apparent obstinacy of the positions they adopted. There was still a price to pay for resisting the spirit of the age, and insisting in the midst of an agnostic intellectual milieu that man at his best could come to know a truth outside himself, and by following that truth could both sanctify his soul and regenerate the world around him. But it was this strategy that sustained American Catholicism in a hostile environment, and that kept it mindful of its unique mission, in the words of Pius X's personal motto, "to restore all things in Christ."

NOTES

I. THE STAGE IS SET

1. Thomas J. Gerrard, "Modern Theories and Moral Disaster," *Catholic World* 95 (July 1912): 433–45.
2. See, for example, T. Jackson Lears, *No Place of Grace: Antimodernism and the Transformation of American Culture, 1880–1920* (New York: Pantheon, 1981).
3. Patrick W. Carey, *The Roman Catholics* (Westport, Conn.: Greenwood, 1993), 50.
4. Twelve Southerners, *I'll Take My Stand: The South and the Agrarian Tradition* (1930; reprint, Baton Rouge: Louisiana State University Press, 1977); Peter Huff, *Allen Tate and the Catholic Revival: Trace of the Fugitive Gods* (New York: Paulist, 1996).
5. Pius IX, "Syllabus of Errors," in Henry Denzinger, *The Sources of Catholic Dogma*, trans. Roy J. Deferrari, 442 (Powers Lake, Md.: Marion House, 1955).
6. Ibid., 436.
7. John Tracy Ellis, "The Formation of the American Priest: An Historical Perspective," in John Tracy Ellis, ed., *The Catholic Priest in the United States: Historical Investigations*, 61 (Collegeville, Minn.: St. John's University Press, 1971).
8. Morton G. White, *Social Thought in America: The Revolt Against Formalism* (New York: Viking, 1952), 203–19.
9. Albion Small, "The Bonds of Nationality," *American Journal of Sociology* 20 (1915): 678.
10. Eldon J. Eisenach, *The Lost Promise of Progressivism* (Lawrence: University Press of Kansas, 1994), 60.
11. Ibid., 7. Emphasis added.
12. "Father Blakely States the Issue," *New Republic* 7 (July 29, 1916): 320.
13. An interesting if unsympathetic treatment of how conservative Protestants reacted to the Social Gospel is Stewart G. Cole, *The History of Fundamentalism* (New York: Harper and Row, 1931).
14. For a discussion of the influence of the eighteenth-century Zeitgeist on Catholic worship, see Aidan Nichols, O.P., *Looking at the Liturgy: A Critical*

View of Its Contemporary Form (San Francisco: Ignatius Press, 1996), 21–24, 26–35.

15. "American Catholics and the Propagation of the Faith," *American Ecclesiastical Review* 20 (March 1899): 225.

16. Dudley G. Wooten, "The Propaganda of Paganism, II," *Catholic World* 106 (November 1917): 165.

17. See, for example, K. K., "Catholic Protest in Vienna," *America* 5 (April 15, 1911): 15; M. J. O'Connor, S.J., "A Challenge to German Critics," *America* 5 (April 22, 1911): 30; Editor, "Pius X: Man, Pope, and Priest," *America* 11 (August 29, 1914): 465–66.

18. "Editorial Announcement," *America* 1 (April 17, 1909): 5–6. See also Carey, *The Roman Catholics*, 342.

19. A modest sample of contemporary writing on the two encyclopedias includes three articles by T. J. Campbell, S.J.: "The 'Encyclopedia Britannica,'" *America* 5 (July 8, 1911): 293–94; "The 'Encyclopedia Britannica,' II," *America* 5 (July 29, 1911): 365–66; and "The 'Encyclopedia Britannica,' III," *America* 5 (August 12, 1911): 413–14; also see " 'The Encyclopedia Britannica,'" *America* 5 (August 26, 1911): 470; Walter Dwight, S.J., review of *The Catholic Encyclopedia, America* 5 (September 9, 1911): 522–23; "The Editor of the Encyclopedia Britannica Replies," *America* 6 (October 28, 1911): 62; "The 'Encyclopedia' and 'The Tablet,'" *America* 6 (November 4, 1911): 86; review of *The Catholic Encyclopedia, American Catholic Quarterly Review* 37 (January 1912): 186–88.

20. J. Harding Fisher, S.J., "An Attitude and a Fact," *America* 11 (September 26, 1914): 569.

21. Edward A. Pace, "Education," *Catholic Encyclopedia*, 2d ed., 1913.

22. James A. Nuechterlein, "The Dream of Scientific Liberalism: The *New Republic* and American Progressive Thought, 1914–1920," *Review of Politics* 42 (1980): 175.

23. "Father Blakely States the Issue," 320.

24. Jacques Maritain, *Moral Philosophy: An Historical and Critical Survey of the Great Systems* (New York: Scribner's, 1964), 417.

25. Arnold Sparr, *To Promote, Defend, and Redeem: The Catholic Literary Revival and the Cultural Transformation of American Catholicism* (New York: Greenwood, 1990); William M. Halsey, *The Survival of American Innocence: Catholicism in an Era of Disillusionment, 1920–1940* (Notre Dame, Ind.: University of Notre Dame Press, 1980).

26. R. Scott Appleby, *"Church and Age Unite!": The Modernist Impulse in American Catholicism* (Notre Dame, Ind.: University of Notre Dame Press, 1992). This book will say relatively little about Modernism itself, for two principal reasons. First, Scott Appleby's study of this relatively short-lived intellectual phenomenon is reasonably comprehensive and, given the state of the manuscript collections and other relevant primary materials, is unlikely to be superseded anytime soon. More important, this project seeks to explore sustained Catholic efforts

to interact with their Progressive milieu, and after the papal condemnation in 1907 open Modernism essentially vanished. The Catholics writing in the mainstream journals were anti-Modernists in good standing with the Church.

27. Robert D. Cross, *The Emergence of Liberal Catholicism in America* (Cambridge: Harvard University Press, 1958); Thomas T. McAvoy, C.S.C., *The Great Crisis in American Catholic History, 1895–1900* (Chicago: Henry Regnery, 1957).

28. Theodore Maynard, *The Story of American Catholicism*, vol. 2 (New York: Macmillan, 1941; reprint, Garden City, N.Y.: Image Books, 1960), 2:150.

29. Charles R. Morris, *American Catholic: The Saints and Sinners Who Built America's Most Powerful Church* (New York: Random House, 1997), 44.

30. Ibid., 75.

31. Marvin R. O'Connell, *John Ireland and the American Catholic Church* (St. Paul: Minnesota Historical Society Press, 1988), 295 ff.

32. Ibid., 301.

33. Gerald P. Fogarty, S.J., "The Catholic Hierarchy in the United States Between the Third Plenary Council and the Condemnation of Americanism," *U.S. Catholic Historian* 11 (Summer 1993): 28.

34. Ibid., 27; O'Connell, *John Ireland and the American Catholic Church*, 328–30.

35. Some commentators have mistakenly suggested that Americanism was a position that held that the American separation of Church and state was the ideal relation between the two institutions, and a system according to which the Church should organize itself around the world. In fact, this proposition was condemned not in Pope Leo's 1899 apostolic letter on Americanism but in *Longinqua Oceani*, his 1895 encyclical on Catholicism in the United States. There the pope warned: "Yet . . . it would be very erroneous to draw the conclusion that in America is to be sought the type of the most desirable status of the Church, or that it would be universally lawful or expedient for State and Church to be, as in America, dissevered and divorced. The fact that Catholicity with you is in good condition, nay, is even enjoying a prosperous growth, is by all means to be attributed to the fecundity with which God has endowed His Church, in virtue of which unless men or circumstances interfere, she spontaneously expands and propagates herself; but she would bring forth more abundant fruits if, in addition to liberty, she enjoyed the favor of the laws and the patronage of the public authority." Leo XIII, *Longinqua Oceani* (1895).

36. The scholarly literature on Americanism, including biographies of a number of the key figures, is considerable. For a thorough and useful overview, see Philip Gleason, "The New Americanism in Catholic Historiography," *U.S. Catholic Historian* 11 (Summer 1993): 1–18. In short, the principal works on Americanism, and especially Thomas McAvoy's book *The Great Crisis in American Catholic History*, had generally argued—as had the Americanists themselves—that the errors contained under the designation of Americanism had not actually been held by anyone in the United States. This is the "phantom heresy" position. More recently, historians have begun to suggest that some of the lead-

ing Americanists did in fact hold some of the positions condemned in Leo XIII's letter. The most systematic study along these lines is Margaret Mary Reher, "The Church and the Kingdom of God in America: The Ecclesiology of the Americanists" (Ph.D. diss., Fordham University, 1972); see also David P. Killen, "Americanism Revisited: John Spalding and *Testem Benevolentiae*," *Harvard Theological Review* 66 (October 1973): 413–54. Historians have also begun to draw connections between Americanism and the heresy of Modernism— –again, a contention fiercely denied by previous historians and by the Ameri- canists themselves. The overwhelming majority of scholarship on the subject maintains that the two positions were absolutely distinct, and while not a great deal has been written to revise that judgment, one especially well-known study now argues for a connection: Margaret M. Reher, "Americanism and Mod- ernism: Continuity or Discontinuity?" *U.S. Catholic Historian* 1 (Summer 1981): 87–103. What appears to have happened in this most recent generation of Catholic historical scholarship, and what Gleason himself seems to suggest without explicitly saying so, is that liberal scholars sympathetic to pluralism, democracy, and liberalism in general have sought antecedents of their position in the Americanist camp. My own judgment, which admittedly is not that of a specialist in this area, is that certain trends in the thought of Archbishop Ire- land and his colleagues are indeed problematic from a traditional point of view, but the relatively few figures who held them do not appear to have thought out all their implications. The purported connection between Americanism and Modernism, moreover, appears to lack substance.

37. Maynard, *Story of American Catholicism*, 2:144–45.

38. McAvoy, *Great Crisis*, 344–45.

39. Morris, *American Catholic*, 133.

40. McAvoy, *Great Crisis*, 17. It is with some trepidation that I use the word "nonessential" in this context. The word is accurate in the sense that from the perspective of traditional Catholic theology, while a Catholic who pertina- ciously denied a central dogma of the Church—original sin or the Virgin Birth, for example—would be liable to severe judgment, a man of goodwill who believed that contingent circumstances called for adaptation of the Church in its external manifestations to new conditions, such as those obtaining in Amer- ica, while perhaps naïve, unwise, or frankly mistaken, is unlikely to be consid- ered to have called down upon himself a similar judgment. It is the difference between opposing a teaching central to the *depositum fidei* and debating a mat- ter of prudential judgment.

However, too great a deprecation of "nonessentials" fails to reckon with the role played by practices that while not in themselves "essential" to the Catholic faith, having been hallowed by tradition and popular piety, have helped to con- vert the truly essential features of Catholicism into living realities in the lives of the faithful. Less abstrusely, we can take the example of the Rosary, or a mul- titude of other devotions. However holy these things may be and however central to the spiritual lives of the faithful, they are, strictly speaking, not "essential" to the Catholic faith. But it was precisely by suppressing such alleged "nonessentials" that the Reformation in England was able gradually to diminish the Catholic faith that those devotions had nourished among the population. Thus see, for example, Eamon Duffy, *The Stripping of the Altars: Traditional Religion in England, c. 1400–c. 1580* (New Haven, Conn.: Yale University Press, 1992). Likewise, while the form of the liturgy is not, strictly speaking, an article of faith, it is what in practice transmits the teaching of that faith to generation after generation of faithful, and hence to treat it carelessly is to invite confusion and disorder. It has been argued that the Greek Orthodox Church, lacking the visible center of unity that the Catholic Church possesses in the person of the pope, nevertheless maintained the dogmatic aspects of the Christian faith in their integrity precisely because of their reverence for its traditional liturgy. Cf. Alfons Maria Cardinal Stickler, "Erinnerungen und Erfahrungen eines Konzilsperitus der Liturgiekommission," in Franz Breid, ed., *Die heilige Liturgie*, 166 (Steyr, Austria: Ennsthaler Verlag, 1997).

    This digression, then, is meant to indicate that when I refer to some of the issues dividing American prelates as "nonessential" I do so with the mind of the historian, aware that certain of the "external" aspects of Catholicism, while not inseparably bound up with the essentials of the faith, are not for that reason to be disparaged or dismissed as unimportant.

41. McAvoy, *Great Crisis*, 362.
42. James Hennesey, S.J., *American Catholics: A History of the Roman Catholic Community in the United States* (New York: Oxford University Press, 1981), 216.
43. John Ireland, "Three and a Half Years of Pius X," *North American Review* 184 (1907): 35–45; John Ireland, "The Dogmatic Authority of the Papacy," *North American Review* 187 (1908): 486–87.
44. Reher, "Americanism and Modernism," 89.
45. McAvoy, *Great Crisis*, 35–36.
46. Thomas T. McAvoy, C.S.C., *A History of the Catholic Church in the United States* (Notre Dame, Ind.: University of Notre Dame Press, 1969), 306.
47. Ibid., 314.
48. Igino Giordani, *Pius X: A Country Priest*, trans. Thomas J. Tobin (Milwaukee: Bruce Publishing, 1954), 62–66.
49. Katherine Burton, *The Great Mantle: The Life of Giuseppe Melchiore Sarto, Pope Pius X* (New York: Longmans, Green, 1950), 139.
50. Maynard, *Story of American Catholicism*, 2:171.
51. Burton, *The Great Mantle*, 151.
52. Even the Americanizing John Ireland repeated his desire that America should be made Catholic. See McAvoy, *History of the Catholic Church in the United States*, 284.
53. Pius X, "Pascendi Dominici Gregis," in Claudia Carlen, ed., *The Papal Encyclicals*, vol. 3, 1903–1939, 93 (Wilmington, N.C.: McGrath, 1981).

2. THE CHALLENGE OF PRAGMATISM

1. R. H. Tierney, S.J., "Pragmatism and the Higher Life, II," *America* 6 (February 17, 1912): 442.

2. James J. Fox, "St. Thomas and His Philosophy," *Catholic University Bulletin* 14 (April 1908): 347. On *Aeterni Patris*, see Ralph M. McInerny, "The *Aeterni Patris* of Leo XIII, 1879–1979," *American Journal of Jurisprudence* 24 (1979): 1–2; Gerald A. McCool, "The Centenary of *Aeterni Patris*," *Homiletic and Pastoral Review* 79 (January 1979): 8–15; G. F. Ritzel, "Some Historical Backgrounds of the Encyclical Aeterni Patris," *Nuntius Aulae* 38 (July 1956): 135–55. Also helpful is Jon Alexander, "*Aeterni Patris*, 1879–1979: A Bibliography of American Responses," *Thomist* 43 (July 1979): 480–81.

3. William M. Halsey, *The Survival of American Innocence: Catholicism in an Era of Disillusionment, 1920–1940* (Notre Dame, Ind.: University of Notre Dame Press, 1980), 140–46.

4. George H. Derry, "Unlocking the Medieval Mind," *America* 17 (September 15, 1917): 579; see also James A. Cahill, S.J., "Scholastic Philosophy," *America* 17 (June 2, 1917): 195–96.

5. F. Aveling, "The Neo-Scholastic Movement," *American Catholic Quarterly Review* 31 (January 1906): 33; "With Our Readers," *Catholic World* (October 1916): 137.

6. Leo XIII, "Aeterni Patris," in Claudia Carlen, ed., *The Papal Encyclicals*, vol. 2, *1878–1903*, 25 (Wilmington, N.C.: McGrath, 1981).

7. On neo-Scholasticism, see Joseph Watzlawik, *Leo XIII and the New Scholasticism* (Cebu City, Philippines: University of San Carlos, n.d.).

8. M. De Wulf, "Neo-Scholasticism," *Catholic Encyclopedia*, 2d ed., 1913.

9. "Father Blakely States the Issue," *New Republic* 7 (July 29, 1916): 320.

10. Washington Gladden, *Social Salvation* (Boston: Houghton Mifflin, 1902), 30–31.

11. Robert T. Handy, ed., *The Social Gospel in America, 1870–1920* (New York: Oxford University Press, 1966), 324.

12. It is true that Peirce and James, though good friends, differed on some important philosophical questions—so much so, indeed, that Peirce would later rename his system Pragmaticism—but for our purposes it will suffice to sketch a broad picture of Pragmatism for the sake of describing the Catholic critique and to pass over the more technical and abstruse differences that existed within the Pragmatic movement itself. For a careful discussion of these distinctions, see Charles Morris, *The Pragmatic Movement in American Philosophy* (New York: Braziller, 1970).

13. John Dewey, "The Scholastic and the Speculator," in *The Early Works, 1882–1898*, vol. 3, *Early Essays and Outlines of a Critical Theory of Ethics, 1889–1892*, 149 (Carbondale: Southern Illinois University Press, 1969).

14. John S. Zybura, ed., *Present-Day Thinkers and the New Scholasticism* (St. Louis, Mo.: Herder, 1926), 31.

15. To be sure, James was a well-known anti-imperialist in 1898 and the years that followed.

16. William James, *Pragmatism: A New Name for Some Old Ways of Thinking* (1907; reprint, Indianapolis: Hackett, 1981), 29.

17. Ibid., 27–29.

18. Ibid., 29.

19. James believed that his philosophy had been so poorly understood and wrongly criticized that he published a companion volume responding to others' misconceptions. See William James, *The Meaning of Truth* (New York: Longmans, Green, 1911).

20. James T. Kloppenberg, "Pragmatism: An Old Name for Some New Ways of Thinking?" in Morris Dickstein, ed., *The Revival of Pragmatism: New Essays on Social Thought, Law, and Culture*, 86 (Durham, N.C.: Duke University Press, 1998).

21. For a concise presentation of the older view, see Frederick D. Wilhelmsen, *Man's Knowledge of Reality: An Introduction to Thomistic Epistemology* (Englewood Cliffs, N.J.: Prentice-Hall, 1956).

22. William James, "Remarks on Spencer's Definition of Mind as Correspondence," in *Essays in Philosophy*, 7, 21 (Cambridge: Harvard University Press, 1978).

23. R. H. Tierney, S.J., "Pragmatism and the Higher Life, I," *America* 6 (February 10, 1912): 416. A more tempered discussion can be found in W. R. A. Marron, "Pragmatism in American Philosophy," *Catholic University Bulletin* 10 (April 1904): 211–24.

24. William Turner, "Pragmatism," *Catholic Encyclopedia*, 2d ed., 1913.

25. R. H. T[ierney], review of Emile Boutroux, *William James*, trans. Archibald and Barbara Henderson (New York: Longmans, Green, 1912), *America* 6 (March 2, 1912): 498.

26. Edmund T. Shanahan, S.T.D., "Completing the Reformation, I," *Catholic World* 99 (July 1914): 433–45.

27. Edmund T. Shanahan, S.T.D., "Completing the Reformation, VI," *Catholic World* (December 1914): 308–309.

28. Shanahan, "Completing the Reformation, I," 434–35, 437.

29. Edmund T. Shanahan, S.T.D., "Completing the Reformation, II," *Catholic World* (August 1914): 634.

30. Edmund T. Shanahan, S.T.D., "Completing the Reformation, III," *Catholic World* (September 1914): 761.

31. Ibid., 765.

32. See also these three articles by Edmund T. Shanahan, S.T.D.: "The Genesis of Kant's Criticism, I," *Catholic World* (December 1915): 333–46; "The Genesis of Kant's Criticism, II," *Catholic World* (January 1916): 443–59; "Cutting Truth in Two," *Catholic World* (September 1916): 775–88.

33. Pius X had in mind modern philosophy in general when he observed: "According to this teaching, human reason is confined entirely within the field of phenomena; that is to say, to things that are perceptible to the senses, and the manner in which they are perceptible. It has no right and no power to transgress these limits. Hence it is incapable of lifting itself up to God and of recognizing His existence, even by means of visible things. . . . Yet the Vatican Council has defined: 'If anyone says that the one true God, our Creator and Lord, cannot be known with certainty by the natural light of human reason by means of the things that are made, let him be anathema.'" Pius X, "Pascendi Domenici Gregis," in Henry Denzinger, Sources of Catholic Dogma, trans. Roy J. Deferrari, 514–15 (St. Louis, Mo.: Herder, 1957).

34. Shanahan, "Completing the Reformation, VI," 321.

35. Shanahan, "Completing the Reformation, I," 442.

36. Edmund T. Shanahan, S.T.D., "Completing the Reformation, V," Catholic World (November 1914): 187.

37. Shanahan, "Completing the Reformation, I," 442.

38. See Fulton J. Sheen, God and Intelligence in Modern Philosophy: A Critical Study in the Light of the Philosophy of St. Thomas (New York: Longmans, Green, 1925), 47–61.

39. William James, Varieties of Religious Experience: A Study in Human Nature (New York: Longmans, Green, 1902), 31, 34.

40. William James, A Pluralistic Universe (New York: Longmans, Green, 1909), 318.

41. William Turner, S.T.D., "Pragmatism: What Does It Mean?" Catholic World (November 1911): 185–86.

42. James, Varieties of Religious Experience, 431.

43. Interestingly, for all his emphasis on religious experience, James could not claim to have had such experience himself. "I have no living sense of commerce with God," he wrote in a 1904 letter to James Leuba. On a questionnaire distributed by a scholar interested in the subject of religious experience, when asked if he had ever experienced God's presence James wrote, "No." See Sheen, God and Intelligence in Modern Philosophy, 217n. This latter piece of evidence may require some qualification, since an examination of the questionnaire reveals that the sense in which the term "religious experience" was used appears to have been that of mystical experience, which James had never claimed to have received.

44. A. Vermeersch, "Modernism," Catholic Encyclopedia, 2d ed., 1913.

45. James himself rejected Pascal's wager. But Monsignor Graham argues that James ultimately endorsed a position very close to it. James wrote in The Will to Believe and Other Essays in Popular Philosophy: "If religion be true and the evidence for it be still insufficient, I do not wish, by putting your extinguisher upon my nature (which feels to me as if it had after all some business in this matter), to forfeit my sole chance in life of getting upon the winning side—that chance depending, of course, on my willingness to run the risk of acting as if my passional need of taking the world religiously might be prophetic and right. . . . One who should shut

himself up in snarling logicality and try to make the gods extort his recognition willy-nilly, or not get it at all, might cut himself off forever from his only opportunity to making the gods' acquaintance." George P. Graham, *William James and the Affirmation of God* (New York: Peter Lang, 1992), 164.

46. George Tyrrell, *The Programme of Modernism* (New York: Putnam's, 1908), 17.

47. Vermeersch, "Modernism"; Shanahan, "Completing the Reformation, V," 185; Fox, "St. Thomas and His Philosophy," 345; William Turner, "The Philosophical Bases of Modernism," *Catholic University Bulletin* 14 (May 1908): 447–50 and passim.

48. Pius X, *Sacrorum Antistitum*, September 1, 1910.

49. Pius X, *Our Apostolic Mandate: On the "Sillon,"* apostolic letter, trans. Yves Dupont (Yarra Junction Vic, Australia: Instauratio Press, 1990), 21–22.

50. Daniel A. Dever, "Pius the Tenth: An 'Ecclesiastical' Pope," *American Catholic Quarterly Review* 39 (July 1914): 361–81.

51. Ibid., 366.

52. Ibid., 369.

53. Ibid., 369–70.

54. Ibid., 370.

55. James, *Pragmatism*, 115. Emphasis in original.

56. Dever, "Pius the Tenth," 372–73.

57. James, *Pragmatism*, 134.

58. Ibid., 38.

59. M. P. Smith, C.S.P., "Pope Pius the Tenth," *Catholic World* 100 (October 1914): 96–97.

60. Theodore Maynard, *The Story of American Catholicism*, vol. 2 (New York: Macmillan, 1941; reprint, Garden City, N.Y.: Image Books, 1960), 2:165.

61. R. Scott Appleby, *"Church and Age Unite!": The Modernist Impulse in American Catholicism* (Notre Dame, Ind.: University of Notre Dame Press, 1992), 235.

62. Turner became bishop of Buffalo in 1919.

63. Appleby, *"Church and Age Unite!"* 230–31.

64. Gabriel Daly, O.S.A., *Transcendence and Immanence: A Study in Catholic Modernism and Integralism* (Oxford: Clarendon, 1980), 216.

65. Sheen, *God and Intelligence in Modern Philosophy*, 182 ff.

66 Shanahan, "Completing the Reformation, I," 444.

67. Pius IX, "Syllabus of Errors," in Denzinger, *Sources of Catholic Dogma*, 437.

68. James, *Varieties of Religious Experience*, 171.

69. James, *Pragmatism*, 134.

70. Ibid., 45–52.

71. Ibid., 49–50; cf. "Pragmatism," *America* 1 (July 31, 1909): 438.

72. James, *Pragmatism*, 51.

73. Certainly among the most careful and thought-provoking discussions of James, Pragmatism, and religious belief is Graham, *William James and the Affirmation of God*.

74. William James, *The Will to Believe and Other Essays in Popular Philosophy* (New York: Longmans, Green, 1897; reprint, Cambridge: Harvard University Press, 1978), 25.

75. Graham, *William James and the Affirmation of God*, 181.

76. Ibid., 211–12.

77. Quoted in ibid., 212.

78. Tierney, "Pragmatism and the Higher Life, II," 441.

79. James Bissett Pratt, *What Is Pragmatism?* (New York: Macmillan, 1909), 175.

80. James, *Pragmatism*, 133.

81. Turner, "Pragmatism," *Catholic Encyclopedia*.

82. Pius X, "Pascendi Dominici Gregis," in Carlen, *The Papal Encyclicals*, 3:76.

83. "The Errors of Modernists, on the Church, Revelation, Christ, the Sacraments" (excerpt from the Decree of the Holy Office *Lamentabili Sane*, July 3, 1907), in Denzinger, *Sources of Catholic Dogma*, 510.

84. Fox, "St. Thomas and His Philosophy," 344.

85. Shanahan, "Completing the Reformation, V," 186.

86. Heinrich A. Rommen, *The Natural Law: A Study in Legal and Social History and Philosophy*, trans. Thomas R. Hanley, O.S.B. (Indianapolis: Liberty Fund, 1998), 141.

87. R. H. Tierney, "Pragmatism and the Higher Life, I," 417.

88. Henry Woods, S.J., "Spiritism and Kantism," *America* 24 (October 30, 1920): 37.

89. Tierney, "Pragmatism and the Higher Life, II," 442.

3. SOCIOLOGY AND THE STUDY OF MAN

1. See Harry Elmer Barnes, "Ancient and Medieval Social Philosophy," in Harry Elmer Barnes, ed., *An Introduction to the History of Sociology*, 3–28 (Chicago: University of Chicago Press, 1948). More recently Robert Nisbet has advanced the claim that in fact the idea of a steady progress from the remote past to the present and the future is, if not as pronounced as it would become in later centuries, at least clearly discernible in Greek thought by the fifth century B.C. Robert Nisbet, *History of the Idea of Progress* (New York: Basic Books, 1980), 10–46.

2. Richard Tarnas, *The Passion of the Western Mind* (New York: Ballantine, 1991), 271.

3. See, in particular, Arthur Cushman McGiffert, *The Rise of Modern Religious Ideas* (New York: Macmillan, 1915), 257–60.

4. Nicholas S. Timasheff, *Sociological Theory: Its Nature and Growth* (New York: Random House, 1955), 27–29.

5. Will Durant, *The Story of Philosophy* (1926; reprint, New York: Simon and Schuster, 1961), 353. Comte's saints included Adam Smith and Frederick the Great.

6. Quoted in Vernon K. Dibble, *The Legacy of Albion Small* (Chicago: University of Chicago Press, 1975), 54.

7. C. Joseph Nuesse, "The Introduction of Sociology at the Catholic University of America, 1895–1915," *Catholic Historical Review* 87 (October 2001): 644.

8. See, for example, Lester F. Ward, "Contemporary Sociology," *American Journal of Sociology* 7 (January 1902): 498. Albion Small did attempt to delineate the teleological conceptions that sociologists share, but they were so minimalist ("We regard the ongoing of this life-process as itself sufficient end and reason for intelligent cooperation by thinkers and actors within the process") as to be almost without meaning. Albion W. Small, "The Scope of Sociology," *American Journal of Sociology* 6 (September 1900): 202.

9. McGiffert, *Rise of Modern Religious Ideas*, 260–62. For a concise discussion by a Progressive of the development of the social aspect of religion, see John Dewey, *A Common Faith* (New Haven: Yale University Press, 1934).

10. Walter Rauschenbusch, *A Theology for the Social Gospel* (New York: Macmillan, 1917), 14.

11. The science was still so new, in fact, that article after article appeared in the *American Journal of Sociology* attempting to define sociology and to ascertain its place within social science as a whole. See, for example, Ward, "Contemporary Sociology," 475–500; Albion W. Small, "What Is a Sociologist?" *American Journal of Sociology* 8 (January 1903): 468–77; Albion W. Small, "The Subject-Matter of Sociology," *American Journal of Sociology* 10 (November 1904): 281 ff; Charles A. Ellwood, "Sociology: Its Problems and Its Relations," *American Journal of Sociology* 12 (November 1907): 300–348. Ellwood's article settles on a definition that was more or less satisfactory to most of his colleagues: "Sociology is the science of the organization and evolution of society" (303).

12. John Dewey makes a similar appeal, for example, in *Reconstruction in Philosophy* (New York: Holt, 1920). William James took much less interest in systematic social reform, but the Pragmatic temper as a whole, with its utilitarianism and its emphasis on experimentation, certainly tended in this direction. See James T. Kloppenberg, *Uncertain Victory: Social Democracy and Progressivism in European and American Thought, 1870–1920* (New York: Oxford University Press, 1986), 148–50, 193–94.

13. Charles Macksey, "Taparelli," *Catholic Encyclopedia*, 2d ed., 1913; Georges Goyau, "Ketteler," ibid.; George Metlake [John Laux], *Christian Social Reform: Program Outlined by Its Pioneer, William Emmanuel Baron von Ketteler* (Philadelphia: Dolphin, 1912).

14. See, for example, Edward F. Murphy, M.A., "Simplicity, Sociology, and Religion," *America* 13 (May 1, 1915): 57–58; Murphy, "Comte or Christ?" *America* 21 (September 20, 1919): 588–89.

15. It is true that Comte, unlike the logical positivists of the twentieth century, went to great lengths to distinguish positivism from atheism, but the relationship of the two may have been closer than he cared to admit. See Frederick

Copleston, S.J., A History of Philosophy, vol. 9, Modern Philosophy: From the French Revolution to Sartre, Camus, and Levi-Strauss (New York: Doubleday, 1977), 97–98. Historian Joseph Nuesse likewise notes the difficulties for Catholics in approaching sociology, which "had been tainted from its beginnings by positivist philosophy and, in the theories of the American pioneers, by evolutionary naturalism." Nuesse, "The Introduction of Sociology at the Catholic University of America," 643.

16. Small, "What Is a Sociologist?" 472.

17. See the discussion (680–85) that follows Harald Höffding, "On the Relation Between Sociology and Ethics," American Journal of Sociology 10 (March 1905): 672–79.

18. Paul Blakely, S.J., "The Catholic Charities and the Strong Commission," America 15 (May 6, 1916): 78.

19. J. Harding Fisher, S.J., "What Is the Natural Law?" America 14 (March 25, 1916): 557; cf. James J. Fox, "The 'Evolution' Theory of Morality," Catholic University Bulletin 3 (October 1897): 373–403.

20. Simon N. Patten, The Social Basis of Religion (New York: Macmillan, 1911), 239.

21. Joseph Husslein, S.J., "The Literature of Materialistic Sociology," America 18 (March 29, 1918): 635.

22. Thomas F. Coakley, "Sin or Psychoneurosis?" America 27 (July 1, 1922): 261.

23. John W. Maguire, C.S.V., " 'Modern Sociology' Again," America 17 (April 21, 1917): 47–48.

24. Charles Howard Hopkins, The Rise of the Social Gospel in American Protestantism, 1865–1915 (New Haven: Yale University Press, 1940), 258.

25. Ibid., 272–73.

26. Charles A. Ellwood, The Reconstruction of Religion: A Sociological View (New York: Macmillan, 1922), 127–32.

27. See Patten, Social Basis of Religion, 193–205, 227–47, and passim; see also Hopkins, Rise of the Social Gospel, 273–74.

28. Hopkins, Rise of the Social Gospel, 257–79. The Protestant revivalist preacher Billy Sunday remarked: "The trouble with the church, the YMCA, and the Young People's Societies is that they have taken up sociology and settlement work but are not winning souls to Christ." William G. McLoughlin, Revivals, Awakenings, and Reform: An Essay on Religion and Social Change in America, 1607–1977 (Chicago: University of Chicago Press, 1978), 148.

29. "Father Blakely States the Issue," New Republic 7 (July 29, 1916): 320. Emphasis in original.

30. Henry Pratt Fairchild, Outline of Applied Sociology (New York: Macmillan, 1916), 251.

31. Pius IX, "Syllabus of Errors," in Henry Denzinger, The Sources of Catholic Dogma, trans. Roy J. Deferrari, 441 (Powers Lake, Md.: Marion House, 1955).

32. Paul L. Blakely, S.J., "A Page of Modern Sociology," America 16 (March 3, 1917): 504.

33. Cf. Murphy, "Comte or Christ?" 588–89.

34. Blakely, "A Page of Modern Sociology," 504; Pius IX, "Syllabus of Errors," in Denzinger, The Sources of Catholic Dogma, 436.

35. Paul L. Blakely, S.J., "Cooperation Without Compromise," America 16 (November 18, 1916): 125.

36. Paul L. Blakely, S.J., "A Neglected Faculty," America 13 (September 4, 1915): 527.

37. Coakley, "Sin or Psychoneurosis?" 262.

38. Joseph Husslein, S.J., The Catholic's Work in the World: A Practical Solution of Religious and Social Problems of Today (New York: Benziger Brothers, 1917), 190.

39. Maguire, " 'Modern Sociology' Again," 48.

40. On Kerby, see Timothy N. Dolan, "Prophet of a Better Hope: The Life and Work of Monsignor William Joseph Kerby" (master's thesis, Catholic University of America, 1981); Mary M. Klein, "A Bio-Bibliography of William J. Kerby, 1870–1936" (Ph.D. diss., Catholic University, 1955); Bruce H. Lescher, "William J. Kerby: A Lost Voice in American Catholic Spirituality," Records of the American Catholic Historical Society of Pennsylvania 102 (Spring 1991): 1–16.

41. Frank Kuntz, Undergraduate Days, 1904–1908 (Washington, D.C.: Catholic University Press, 1958), 97.

42. Nuesse, "Introduction of Sociology at the Catholic University of America," 653.

43. Patrick W. Carey, The Roman Catholics (Westport, Conn.: Greenwood, 1993), 256–57.

44. William J. Kerby, "Sociology," Catholic Encyclopedia, 2d ed., 1913.

45. William J. Kerby, The Social Mission of Charity: A Study of Points of View in Catholic Charities (New York: Macmillan, 1921), 52–53.

46. William J. Kerby, "The Literature of Relief," Catholic World 96 (October 1912): 81.

47. Kerby, "Sociology."

48. Ibid.

49. Paul L. Blakely, S.J., "A Mystical Sociologist," America 27 (May 13, 1922): 94.

50. Il Fermo Proposito (June 1905): 190; cited in Edward Cahill, S.J., The Framework of a Christian State (Dublin: M. H. Gill, 1932), 1.

51. Quoted in C. Joseph Nuesse, "The Introduction of the Social Sciences in the Catholic University of America 1895–1909," Social Thought 12 (Spring 1986): 40–41.

52. Loretto R. Lawler, Full Circle: The Story of the National Catholic School of Social Service, 1918–1947 (Washington, D.C.: Catholic University of America Press, 1951), 36–37. In 1947 the school merged with the School of Social Service of the Catholic University of America.

53. In a frequently quoted passage, Lester Frank Ward said of sociology: "It is not quite enough to say that it is a synthesis of them [the special social sciences] all. It is the new compound which their synthesis creates. It is not any of them and

it is not all of them. It is that science which they spontaneously generate. It is a genetic product, the last term in the genesis of science. The special social sciences are the units of aggregation that organically combine to create sociology, but they lose their individuality as completely as do chemical units, and the resultant product is wholly unlike them and is of a higher order." Lester Frank Ward, *Pure Sociology* (New York: Macmillan, 1903), 91.

54. Small, "What Is a Sociologist?" 471.

55. Henry J. Ford, "The Pretensions of Sociology," *American Journal of Sociology* 15 (1909–1910): 96–104; Charles A. Ellwood, "The Science of Sociology: A Reply," ibid., 105–10.

56. Albion Small, "Scholarship and Social Agitation," *American Journal of Sociology* 1 (1895–96): 581.

57. See Murray N. Rothbard, "World War I as Fulfillment: Power and the Intellectuals," in John V. Denson, ed., *The Costs of War: America's Pyrrhic Victories*, 232 ff. (New Brunswick, N.J.: Transaction, 1997); Murray N. Rothbard, *Individualism and the Philosophy of the Social Sciences* (Washington, D.C.: Cato, 1978).

58. George M. Marsden, *Fundamentalism and American Culture: The Shaping of Twentieth-Century Evangelicalism, 1870–1925* (New York: Oxford University Press, 1980), 92, 254, 255.

59. Cecil E. Greek, *The Religious Roots of American Sociology* (New York: Garland, 1992), 43; all of chapter 2 is very useful.

60. Ibid., 36–37.

61. Marsden, *Fundamentalism and American Culture*, 92.

62. Eugene McCarraher, *Christian Critics: Religion and the Impasse in Modern American Social Thought* (Ithaca: Cornell University Press, 2000), 20–30, 32.

63. Frederick Howard Wines, "Sociology and Philanthropy," *Annals of the American Academy of Political and Social Science* 12 (1898): 49–57.

64. On the origins of scientific charity, see Frank D. Watson, *The Charity Organization Movement in the United States* (New York: Macmillan, 1922).

65. Barbara Howe, "The Emergence of Scientific Philanthropy, 1900–1920: Origins, Issues, and Outcomes," in Robert Arnove, ed., *Philanthropy and Cultural Imperialism*, 28 (Boston: G. K. Hall, 1980).

66. Roy Lubove, *The Professional Altruist: The Development of Social Work as a Career, 1880–1930* (Cambridge: Harvard University Press, 1965).

67. Michael B. Katz, *In the Shadow of the Poorhouse: A Social History of Welfare in America* (New York: Basic Books, 1986).

68. Paul Boyer, *Urban Masses and the Moral Order in America, 1820–1920* (Cambridge: Harvard University Press, 1978). I am indebted to Deborah Skok's *U.S. Catholic Historian* article for familiarizing me with some of the principal sources on scientific charity and the various trends in the historiography of the subject. Deborah S. Skok, "Organized Almsgiving: Scientific Charity and the Society of St. Vincent de Paul in Chicago, 1871–1918," *U.S. Catholic Historian* 16 (Fall 1998): 19–35.

69. The assumptions and ideological background of scientific charity are ably treated in Howe, "Emergence of Scientific Philanthropy," 25–54, and Sheila Slaughter and Edward Silva, "Looking Backwards: How Foundations Formulated Ideology in the Progressive Period," in Arnove, *Philanthropy and Cultural Imperialism*, 55–86; Ellen Condliffe Lagemann, *The Politics of Knowledge: The Carnegie Corporation, Philanthropy, and Public Policy* (Middletown, Conn.: Wesleyan University Press, 1989).

70. Leo XIII, "Rerum Novarum," in Claudia Carlen, ed., *The Papal Encyclicals*, vol. 2, *1878–1903*, 255–56 (Wilmington, N.C.: McGrath, 1981).

71. H.W., "Sociology," *America* 5 (September 16, 1911): 550.

72. H.W., "The Propagation of the Faith," *America* 9 (June 28, 1913): 286.

73. See H.W., "Sociology," *America* 6 (March 16, 1912): 550; John V. Matthews, S.J., "Poverty, Wealth, Ambition," *America* 23 (September 18, 1920): 517–18.

74. Matthews, "Poverty, Wealth, Ambition," 518.

75. H.W., "Sociology," *America* 5 (August 26, 1911): 478; see also Kerby, *Social Mission of Charity*, 113.

76. H.W., "Sociology," *America* 5 (August 26, 1911); Matthews, "Poverty, Wealth, Ambition," 518.

77. The characterization of Burke as a moderate Progressive comes from Carey, *The Roman Catholics*, 183. On Burke, see John B. Sheerin, C.S.P., *Never Look Back: The Career and Concerns of John Burke* (New York: Paulist, 1975), a biography written before Burke's papers were opened to scholars; see also Douglas J. Slawson, "John J. Burke, C.S.P.: The Vision and Character of a Public Churchman," *Journal of Paulist Studies* 4 (1995–96): 47–93. On the NCWC, see Douglas J. Slawson, *The Foundation and First Decade of the National Catholic Welfare Council* (Washington, D.C.: Catholic University of America Press, 1992).

78. John J. Burke, Baccalaureate sermon delivered at the College of Mount Saint Vincent-on-Hudson, New York, May 30, 1915. Copy in box 31, John J. Burke Papers, Paulist Fathers Archives, Washington, D.C. Burke insisted tirelessly on this point. A merely humanistic altruism starved and impoverished the soul; it was devoid of Christian charity, "the union, the life of the soul with and in God . . . the Holy Spirit, living, reigning within us." John J. Burke, "With Our Readers: Father Hecker and Present Problems," *Catholic World* 110 (January 1920): 564–70.

79. John J. Burke, Address to the National Catholic Welfare Council, n.d. Copy in box 54, Burke Papers.

80. John J. Burke, "The Roots of Catholic Organization," address to the National Council of Catholic Men, n.d. Copy in box 54, Burke Papers.

81. Rose Ferguson to John J. Burke, Holy Thursday 1923, box 65, Burke Papers. See also Alice S. Duffy to Burke, Holy Thursday 1923, ibid.

82. Burke to Kerby, September 4, 1912, *Catholic World* correspondence file, Paulist Fathers Archives, Washington, D.C. The file containing this letter is part of a larger collection of *Catholic World* correspondence as yet uncatalogued. I am

indebted to archivist Michael Connolly for bringing to my attention a small amount of Burke's correspondence with Kerby from this collection.

83. Ibid.

84. Ibid.

85. Kerby, Social Mission of Charity, 117.

86. William J. Kerby, "Social Work of the Catholic Church in America," Annals of the American Academy of Political and Social Science 30 (November 1907): 473–74.

87. Kerby, Social Mission of Charity, 117–18; see also H.W., "Almsgiving, Its Enemies and Its Friends," America 9 (June 14, 1913): 239; and Joseph Husslein, "The Science of Charity," America 10 (November 1, 1913): 77.

88. Baccalaureate sermon, Trinity College, June 7, 1914. Copy in box 8, William J. Kerby Papers, Catholic University of America, Washington, D.C.; published as "Prayer," Trinity College Record 8 (June 1914): 153–61.

89. William J. Kerby Foundation, William J. Kerby: Democracy Through Christ (Washington, D.C.: William J. Kerby Foundation, 1943), 11. Copy in reference file, Kerby Papers. See also Kerby, Social Mission of Charity, 92–93.

90. Samuel H. Bishop, "The Church and Charity," American Journal of Sociology 18 (November 1912): 369–80.

91. "Sociology," America 2 (January 15, 1910): 374. Referring to the Guild of Saint Elizabeth, a Catholic charitable organization in Boston, America noted that its achievements "could not be surpassed by any secular institution with ten times its resources." H.W., "Sociology," America 6 (March 30, 1912): 597.

92. Paul L. Blakely, S.J., "The Bad Samaritan," America 12 (November 21, 1914): 154–55.

93. Address to the New York School of Social Work, 1920; quoted in John A. Ryan, Social Doctrine in Action: A Personal History (New York: Harper, 1941), 97.

94. Kerby, Social Mission of Charity, 8.

95. William J. Kerby, "Problems in Charity," Catholic World 91 (September 1910): 792.

96. Kerby, Social Mission of Charity, 192; Kerby, "Problems in Charity," 793.

97. Kerby, Social Mission of Charity, 8.

98. William J. Kerby, "The Passions of Charity," Catholic Charities Review 4 (March 1920): 67.

99. Kerby, Social Mission of Charity, 9.

100. Kerby, "The Passions of Charity," 68; see also Kerby, "Problems in Charity," 794–95.

101. Joseph Husslein, S.J., The Catholic's Work in the World, 187.

102. William J. Kerby, "New and Old in Catholic Charity," Catholic Charities Review 3 (January 1919): 13.

103. Kerby, Social Mission of Charity, 108–9.

104. William J. Kerby, "Spiritual Quality of Social Work," in The Considerate Priest (Philadelphia: Dolphin Press, 1937), 209.

105. Paul L. Blakely, S.J., "A Great Social Reformer: St. Francis Regis," America 17 (June 23, 1917): 280.

106. Murphy, "Simplicity, Sociology, and Religion," 58. This was a common assessment. Daniel Lord wrote that "when all the fine-spun theories of modern utopians are sifted, all the gold that assays from their weave will be found to have been mined from Mount Sinai and the hills of Judea." Daniel A. Lord, S.J., "Heaven on Earth," *America* 14 (December 11, 1915): 581. In an address to the National Catholic Welfare Council, John J. Burke remarked: "From the beginning of her history, there is not a channel of charity work, there is not a channel of what is now known as social welfare that the Church has not sought to use and cultivate. No chapter in the history of social reform, no chapter in the history of social welfare, can begin to touch in value, effectiveness or inspiration that chapter nineteen hundred years long that tells the story of Catholic sacrifice, of Catholic labor and of Catholic devotion." Address to National Catholic Welfare Council, n.d. Copy in box 54, Burke Papers.

107. It was not uncommon for secular sources to cite Saint Vincent de Paul as a forerunner of scientific charity. See, for example, Watson, *Charity Organization Movement in the United States*, 14–18.

108. Archibald J. Dunn, *Frederic Ozanam and the Establishment of the Society of St. Vincent de Paul* (New York: Benziger Brothers, n.d.), 56.

109. A. J. Beck, "Modern Apostles of Charity," *America* 25 (July 16, 1921): 297.

110. Ibid.

111. Skok, "Organized Almsgiving," 27.

112. M. P. Hayne, M.A., "The Society of St. Vincent de Paul," *America* 20 (October 26, 1918): 56. Ozanam was beatified by Pope John Paul II in 1997.

113. Husslein, "The Science of Charity," 78. It should be noted that the spiritual element of charity on which Catholics insisted did not imply that their indigent coreligionists be given priority over the needy of other creeds. An *America* columnist relates an incident in which a Protestant pastor in Paris, having been given a sum by his congregation for charitable purposes, gave it to Ozanam to distribute, having no pressing cases of his own for which to use it. A member of the Society of St. Vincent de Paul suggested that the money first be applied to relieving the Catholic poor, and that only then should any remainder be given to Protestant families. To which an indignant Ozanam exclaimed: "Gentlemen, if this proposal has the misfortune to prevail, if it be not distinctly understood that our members succor the poor without reference to creed or country, I shall this moment return to the Protestants the alms they have entrusted to me, and I shall say, 'Take it back; we are not worthy of your confidence.'" M. P. Hayne, "The Society of St. Vincent de Paul," *America* 19 (October 26, 1918): 57.

114. Husslein, "The Science of Charity," 78.

115. T.V.A., "St. Vincent de Paul Society," *America* 18 (February 9, 1918): 444–45.

116. Beck, "Modern Apostles of Charity," 298.

117. Dunn, *Frederic Ozanam*, 41.

118. Ibid., 62–63, 64.

119. Ibid., 92.

120. An excellent portrait of Vincent's life by a sympathetic author can be found in Henri Daniel-Rops, *The Church in the Seventeenth Century*, trans. J. J. Buckingham (New York: Dutton, 1963), 1–50.

121. Ibid., 49.

122. Henry Somerville, "The Apostle of Organized Charity," *Catholic World* 103 (June 1916): 299.

123. "Sociology," *America* 4 (January 21, 1911): 357. Describing the St. Vincent de Paul Society, the editors of *America* insisted that its work, being Christian and supernatural, was therefore "of the highest efficiency." "Sociology," *America* 2 (April 2, 1910): 680.

124. Joseph Husslein, "Is Charity Work a Sinecure?" *America* 15 (June 3, 1916): 194–95.

125. Burke, "The Roots of Catholic Organization."

126. Lord, "Heaven on Earth," 215. Emphasis added.

127. Address to the New York School of Social Work, 1920; quoted in Ryan, *Social Doctrine in Action*, 97.

128. Husslein, "The Science of Charity," 77.

129. Fairchild, *Outline of Applied Sociology*, 176. Catholic intellectuals often spoke in euphemism on topics they considered delicate, so when Kerby alluded to some of the disagreeable aspects of a scientific charity that was uninformed by the Catholic faith, he may well have had its advocacy of contraception in mind.

130. "The Evils of Birth Control," *America* 23 (June 5, 1920): 159.

131. Dr. John J. Cronin, "The Doctor in the Public School," *American Monthly Review of Reviews* 35 (April 1907): 440.

132. Speaking in a natural-law vein, Ryan explained that "it is on exactly the same moral level and is wrong for precisely the same reason as the practice of solitary vice." Quoted in Paul L. Blakely, S.J., "The 'Birth-Controllers,'" *America* 16 (March 24, 1917): 580–81.

133. Paul L. Blakely, S.J., "Conscious Birth Restriction," *America* 13 (June 5, 1915): 210–11; Blakely, "The Black Vice," *America* 26 (November 5, 1921): 70–71; Blakely, "The 'Birth-Controllers,'" 580–81; J. Harding Fisher, S.J., "What Is the Natural Law?" *America* 14 (March 25, 1916): 557–58.

134. It should perhaps be noted that some Catholic thinkers at this time were departing from the traditional natural-law approach to the question, in favor of newer arguments thought to be more persuasive to modern man. See Elizabeth McKeown, "From *Pascendi* to *Primitive Man*: The Apologetics and Anthropology of John Montgomery Cooper," *U.S. Catholic Historian* 13 (Winter 1995): 1–21, but esp. 14–16 and n. 26.

135. Blakely, "The 'Birth-Controllers,'" 581.

136. Blakely, "The Catholic Charities and the Strong Commission," 78.

137. Lord, "Heaven on Earth," 215. This entire line of thought is in a sense a meditation on the scriptural exhortation "Seek ye first the Kingdom of God, and all these things will be added unto you."

138. Burke, "The Roots of Catholic Organization."

139. Ibid. Emphasis added.

140. Aquinas observed that "nothing can satisfy the will of man but the universal good, and that is not found in any being, but in God alone." See Paul L. Blakely, S.J., "Without God," *America* 17 (April 28, 1917): 72.

141. Ibid., 73.

142. Blakely, "The Catholic Charities and the Strong Commission," 78.

143. "I know of not one text-book," said Blakely, "written by a non-Catholic, which so much as teaches His bare existence—an important and significant omission in these days, when sociology is setting up shifting standards of right and wrong, and attempting to legislate for the multifarious needs of man." Ibid.

144. John J. Burke, incomplete address, n.d. Copy in box 54, Burke Papers.

145. "Behold noble but ill-regulated charity," Vincent de Paul once said. "These poor people, provided with too much now, must allow some to perish, and then they will be again in want as before." John Laux, *Church History* (New York: Benziger Brothers, 1930), 499.

146. Kerby, *Social Mission of Charity*, 53, 119, 194.

147. William J. Kerby Foundation, *William J. Kerby*, 23.

148. John J. Burke, "St. Paul and the Mystery of the Gospel," undated sermon, box 31, Burke Papers.

149. See, for example, Peter Baldwin, "Welfare Work in the Church," *America* 23 (October 16, 1920): 622–23; Kerby, *Social Mission of Charity*, 89, 108–9, 168 ff., and passim; Baldwin, "New and Old in Catholic Charity," 8–13.

150. Blakely, "The Bad Samaritan," 154.

151. Cf. William J. Kerby, "The Aloofness of Catholics in Its Relation to Bigotry," address dated January 7, 1916; copy in box 8, Kerby Papers; Kerby, *Social Mission of Charity*, 132–34.

152. Paul L. Blakely, S.J., "Cooperation Without Compromise," *America* 16 (November 18, 1916): 126.

153. John J. Burke, "The Mission House in Prospect," address of May 25, 1922; copy in box 54, Burke Papers; cf. Burke, address to the National Catholic Welfare Council, ibid.

154. Blakely, "Cooperation Without Compromise," 126.

4. ASSIMILATION AND RESISTANCE: CATHOLICS AND PROGRESSIVE EDUCATION

1. Quoted in James T. Kloppenberg, *Uncertain Victory: Social Democracy and Progressivism in European and American Thought, 1870–1920* (New York: Oxford University Press, 1986), 374.

2. Thus Amy Gutmann, a modern communitarian, speaks of every child's right to

a "nonrepressive education." Amy Gutmann, "The Virtues of Democratic Self-Restraint," in Amitai Etzioni, ed., *New Communitarian Thinking: Persons, Virtues, Institutions, and Communities*, 162 ff. (Charlottesville: University Press of Virginia, 1995).

3. See the old but still valuable work by Paul Monroe, A *Brief Course in the History of Education* (New York: Macmillan, 1908), 284 ff.

4. Ibid., 291–96.

5. Lawrence A. Cremin, *American Education: The Metropolitan Experience, 1876–1980* (New York: Harper and Row, 1988), 388–91.

6. See Lester Frank Ward, *Dynamic Sociology* (2 vols., New York: D. Appleton, 1883); see also Cremin, *American Education*, 394–96.

7. Richard Hofstadter, *Social Darwinism in American Thought* (rev. ed., Boston: Beacon, 1955), 76.

8. M. D. Lawsen and R. C. Petersen, *Progressive Education: An Introduction* (Sydney, Australia: Angus and Robertson, 1972), 7.

9. John Dewey, "Religion in Our Schools," *Hibbert Journal* 6 (1908): 808–9, cited in Jude P. Dougherty, "Dewey and the Value of Religion," *New Scholasticism* 1 (Summer 1977): 311.

10. Cf. Raymond E. Callahan, *Education and the Cult of Efficiency* (Chicago: University of Chicago Press, 1962); Walter Drost, *David Snedden and Education for Social Efficiency* (Madison: University of Wisconsin Press, 1967).

11. John Dewey, *Experience and Education* (New York: Macmillan, 1938), 18, 19, 22.

12. William H. Kilpatrick, *Education for a Changing Civilization* (New York, 1926), 59–60.

13. Charles C. Miltner, "The Importance of 'First Philosophy,'" *America* 27 (July 22, 1922): 321.

14. Quoted in Joseph Ratner, ed., *Intelligence in the Modern World: John Dewey's Philosophy* (New York: Modern Library, 1939), 777.

15. Robert B. Westbrook, *John Dewey and American Democracy* (Ithaca: Cornell University Press, 1991), 165.

16. Ibid., 104–5.

17. One of Dewey's fellow Progressives later suggested that Progressive education might not have enjoyed such overwhelming success if Dewey's underlying philosophy had been better understood by the public. Thus Professor Boyd H. Bode observed: "It is conceded on all hands that John Dewey is our outstanding educational philosopher; his influence on American education has been immense. Perhaps one reason for this is that his philosophy has not been clearly understood. If it had been, the enthusiasm for his teachings would doubtless have been tempered more extensively by fear, or at any rate by misgivings. But neither the language nor the emotional tone of Dewey's writings is of a kind to suggest that his teachings may fairly be described as revolutionary, even in a revolutionary age." Boyd H. Bode, "Pragmatism in Education," *New Republic* (October 17, 1949): 15.

18. Quoted in Paul Blanshard, *American Freedom and Catholic Power* (Boston: Beacon, 1949), 106; see also John A. Hardon, S.J., "John Dewey: Radical Social Educator," *Catholic Educational Review* (October 1952). One should perhaps mention in this connection, though it comes after the period generally designated as the Progressive Era, the Supreme Court case *Pierce v. Society of Sisters* (1925). Here the Supreme Court denounced attacks on private schooling that presumed that all education should be public. "The child is not the mere creature of the state," the Court said. Thanks to James Hitchcock for reminding me of this case.

19. Thomas Edward Shields, "Catholic Teachers and Educational Progress," *Catholic World* 83 (April 1906): 101.

20. P[aul] L. B[lakely], "Christ in the School," *America* 16 (December 23, 1916): 263.

21. See also Archbishop John Ireland, "Catholic Schools for Catholic Youth," *Catholic Educational Review* 10 (September 1915): 97–112; William D. Guthrie, "The Significance of the Catholic School," *Catholic Educational Review* 10 (December 1915): 385–95.

22. William Turner, "Sources of the History of Education," *Catholic Educational Review* 1 (May 1911): 199–211.

23. John J. Tracy, "Why a Catholic History of Education," *Catholic Educational Review* 10 (June 1915): 9.

24. See, for example, Patrick J. McCormick, "Education of the Laity in the Middle Ages," *Catholic Educational Review* 1 (December 1911): 805–15, a series that continues for the next several issues; see also McCormick, "Two Medieval Catholic Educators: I. Vittorino da Feltre," *Catholic University Bulletin* 12 (October 1906): 453–84; McCormick, "Two Catholic Medieval Educators: II. Guarino da Verona," *Catholic University Bulletin* 13 (April 1907): 232–49; E. A. Pace, "St. Thomas' Theory of Education," *Catholic University Bulletin* 8 (July 1902): 290–303; John C. Reville, S.J., "The Monastic Schools," *America* 16 (January 27, 1917): 383–84; Reville, "Alcuin of York," *America* 16 (March 17, 1917): 553–54; Reville, "A Pioneer in Pedagogy," *America* 14 (February 26, 1916): 477–78; James J. Walsh, *Education: How Old the New* (New York: Fordham University Press, 1910).

25. Michael J. Larkin, "Pedagogy: True and False," *Catholic Educational Review* 4 (September 1912): 150.

26. A. C. Brickel, S.J., "The Psychology of the Preconscious," *America* 18 (November 17, 1917): 146–47.

27. Edward A. Pace, "Education," *Catholic Encyclopedia*, 2d ed., 1913.

28. Although in theory the school system was secular, since the schools were still subject to local control it was not uncommon for them to reflect at least a vague Protestantism—perhaps one of the reasons that Protestants were so much less likely than Catholics to establish their own schools. As James Hitchcock points out in a forthcoming book, it was Supreme Court decisions beginning in the late 1940s that really solidified secularism in the public schools.

29. Timothy Brosnahan, S.J., "The Educational Fact," *American Catholic Quarterly Review* 30 (June 1905): 533.

30. Paul Blakely, S.J., "The Catholic School for the Catholic Child," *America* 17 (September 1, 1917): 534.

31. Cited in Paul L. Blakely, S.J., "The Catholic School for the Catholic Child," *America* 27 (August 26, 1922): 454.

32. Paul L. Blakely, S.J., "Scandalizing the Little Ones," *America* 15 (August 19, 1916): 457–58.

33. See Blakely, "Catholic School for the Catholic Child," 534.

34. Joseph Husslein, S.J., "The Modern Peril," *America* 11 (July 18, 1914): 318.

35. Westbrook, *John Dewey and American Democracy*, 169–70n.

36. Ibid., 170.

37. See, for example, A. Hilliard Atteridge, "Industry and Education," *America* 16 (February 17, 1917): 440–41; "Survey of the Field: Liberal and Vocational Education," *Catholic Educational Review* 8 (June 1914): 8–24; Francis P. Donnelly, S.J., "Keep the Classics but Teach Them," *America* 25 (June 11, 1921): 179–81. Against strictly vocational education, Thomas Edward Shields observed that it was difficult for a Christian "to be silent when he is told in the name of science and of progress that the disciplines offered by our educational institutions have value only in so far as they tend to develop the brute instincts and to make each man strong for the brute struggle and forgetful of all the higher things that would disarm him and render him capable of offering himself up for an ideal." Thomas Edward Shields, "The Cultural Aim Versus the Vocational," *Catholic Educational Review* 4 (November 1912): 389–97.

38. For further discussion of this point, see chapter 5.

39. Pace, "Education."

40. Thomas J. Shahan, D.D., "Fifty Years of Catholic Education," *Catholic World* (April 1915): 25.

41. Cf. Thomas J. Shahan, "The Teaching Office of the Catholic Church," *Catholic Educational Review* 6 (September 1916): 108; Robert M. Barry and John D. Fearon, "John Dewey and American Thomism," *American Benedictine Review* 10 (1959): 219–28.

42. John J. Tracy, "The Church as an Educational Factor," *Catholic Educational Review* 6 (October 1913): 213.

43. Dougherty, "Dewey and the Value of Religion," 324–25. Horace Kallen, who was a close associate of Dewey, would later set forth a vision of liberty that "cannot favor any race or cult of man over any other; nor any human doctrine and discipline over any other." The God of the theologians was also ipso facto excluded from this new society, which called for a deity who "brings forth impartially all the infinite diversities of experience and who allows men to survive or to perish by their own dispositions and abilities." Horace M. Kallen, *The Liberal Spirit: Essays on the Problems of Freedom in the Modern World* (Ithaca, N.Y.: Cornell University Press, 1948), 190, 91–127; quoted in Paul Edward

Gottfried, *After Liberalism: Mass Democracy in the Managerial State* (Princeton, N.J.: Princeton University Press, 1999), 60–61.

44. Dewey, "Religion in Our Schools," 800.

45. Ibid., 807.

46. Thomas Edward Shields, *Philosophy of Education* (Washington, D.C.: Catholic Correspondence School, 1917), 24.

47. Francis Louis Meade, "Progressive Education and Catholic Pedagogy" (Ph.D. diss., Niagara University, 1934), 151.

48. T[homas] E[dward] Shields, "Notes on Education," *Catholic University Bulletin* 14 (October 1908): 692–93.

49. Pace, "Education."

50. Thomas Edward Shields, "The Ultimate Aim of Christian Education," *Catholic Educational Review* 12 (November 1916): 304; see also Felix M. Kirsch, O.F.M.Cap., "The Education of the Individual," *Catholic Educational Review* 11 (May 1916): 423–32.

51. Thomas J. Shahan, "God and Morality in Education," *Catholic Educational Review* 6 (December 1913): 394.

52. Thomas Edward Shields, *The Psychology of Education* (Washington, D.C.: Catholic Correspondence School, 1906), 30.

53. John C. Reville, S.J., "The Great Pedagogical Blunder," *America* 26 (April 15, 1922): 623.

54. J[ohn] C. R[eville], review of John Dewey, *Democracy and Education*, *America* 15 (September 30, 1916): 599.

55. J[ohn] C. R[eville], review of Marion G. Kirkpatrick, *The Rural School from Within*; Angelo Patri, *A Schoolmaster of the Great City*; and Randolph Bourne, *Education and Living*, *America* 17 (July 14, 1917): 357.

56. Robert M. Crunden, "Essay," in John D. Buenker, John C. Burnham, and Robert M. Crunden, *Progressivism*, 75–76, 96 (Cambridge: Schenkman, 1977).

57. Thomas Edward Shields, "Some Relations Between the Catholic School and the Public School System," *Catholic Educational Review* 12 (September 1916): 137.

58. John Dewey, *Moral Principles in Education* (Boston: Houghton Mifflin, 1909), 7.

59. "Survey of the Field," *Catholic Educational Review* 1 (March 1911): 259.

60. William P. Braun, C.S.C., "Monsignor Edward A. Pace, Educator and Philosopher" (Ph.D. diss., Catholic University, 1968), 119, 122.

61. Ibid., 121–22.

62. Joseph Husslein, S.J., "The Ferrer Modern School," *America* 11 (June 20, 1914): 224–25.

63. See, for example, Timothy Brosnahan, S.J., "The Educational Fact," *American Catholic Quarterly Review* 30 (April 1905): 211 ff.

64. Ibid., 215–16.

65. Pace, "Education."

66. Edward Francis Mohler, "Recalling a Nursery Tale," *America* 18 (November 24, 1917): 170.

67. P[aul] L. B[lakely], "The Era of Reconstruction," *America* 12 (October 17, 1914): 21.
68. Thomas Edward Shields, "Feeling and Mental Development," *Catholic Educational Review* 5 (February 1913): 105–6.
69. Pace, "Education."
70. Edward A. Pace, "The Papacy and Education," *Catholic Educational Review* 1 (January 1911): 7.
71. Edward A. Pace, "Lessons from the Liturgy," *Catholic Educational Review* 1 (March 1911): 243.
72. Thomas Edward Shields, *Philosophy of Education* (1917; reprint, Washington, D.C.: Catholic Education Press, 1921), 306.
73. Ibid., 307–8.
74. Ibid., 309.
75. Thomas Edward Shields, "Notes on Education," *Catholic University Bulletin* 14 (June 1908): 597.
76. Ibid., 597–98.
77. Ibid., 599–601.
78. Shields, *Philosophy of Education*, 314.
79. Shields, "Feeling and Mental Development," 106.
80. Ibid., 106–7.
81. Lambert Nolle, O.S.B., "A New Problem in Catechetics," *Catholic Educational Review* 1 (February 1911): 126–27.
82. See Francis L. Kerze, "Didactic Materialism and the Teaching of Religion," *Catholic University Bulletin* 14 (June 1908): 552–62.
83. Ibid., 556.
84. Ibid., 561.
85. Patrick J. McCormick, "Christian Education," *Catholic Educational Review* 4 (November 1912): 432 ff.
86. Ibid., 433.
87. Sister M. Generose, O.M.C., "Discussion," *Catholic Educational Review* 1 (June 1911): 555.
88. James A. Burns, *The Catholic School System in the United States: Its Principles, Origin, and Establishment* (New York: Benziger, 1908).
89. See Shields, *Psychology of Education*.
90. Justine Ward, *Thomas Edward Shields: Biologist, Psychologist, Educator* (New York: Charles Scribner's Sons, 1947), 144.
91. Ibid., 143.
92. Ibid., 192.
93. Pius X, "Pascendi Dominici Gregis," in Claudia Carlen, ed., *The Papal Encyclicals*, vol. 3, *1903–1939*, 93 (Wilmington, N.C.: McGrath, 1981).
94. Ward, *Thomas Edward Shields*, 267–68.
95. Thomas Edward Shields, "Catholic Teachers and Educational Progress," *Catholic World* 83 (April 1906): 101.

96. Ward, *Thomas Edward Shields*, 219; John Francis Murphy, "Thomas Edward Shields: Religious Educator" (Ph.D. diss., Columbia University, 1971), 108–9.

97. Murphy, "Thomas Edward Shields," 104.

98. Shields, "Catholic Teachers and Educational Progress," 98.

99. A lengthy series of quotations from educators and school officials startled at the effectiveness of Shields's method appears in Ward, *Thomas Edward Shields*, 250–58.

100. Ibid., 255–57.

101. Ibid., 294–300.

102. Ibid., 252.

103. Ibid., 253.

104. Ibid., 263.

105. Thomas Edward Shields, *The Teaching of Religion* (Washington: Catholic Correspondence School, 1908), 21.

106. Edward A. Pace, "Modern Psychology and Catholic Education," *Catholic World* 81 (September 1905): 737.

107. Braun, "Monsignor Edward A. Pace," 121.

108. Lambert Nolle, O.S.B., "The Formal Steps in Religious Education," *Catholic Educational Review* 7 (January 1914): 5.

109. See Meade, "Progressive Education and Catholic Pedagogy," 146.

110. Thomas Edward Shields, "The Teaching of Religion," *Catholic Educational Review* 1 (January 1911): 56.

111. Larkin, "Pedagogy," 146–47. Emphasis added.

5. ECONOMICS AND THE SOCIAL QUESTION

1. Journal, 43, in box 32, John A. Ryan Papers, Catholic University of America, Washington, D.C.

2. Dorothy Ross, *Origins of American Social Science* (Cambridge: Cambridge University Press, 1991), 179; see also 390–470.

3. R. Jeffrey Lustig, *Corporate Liberalism: The Origins of Modern American Political Theory, 1890–1920* (Berkeley: University of California Press, 1982), 202.

4. Edward A. Purcell Jr., *The Crisis of Democratic Theory: Scientific Naturalism and the Problem of Value* (Lexington: University Press of Kentucky, 1973), 25; see also Samuel Haber, *Efficiency and Uplift: Scientific Management in the Progressive Era, 1890–1920* (Chicago: University of Chicago Press, 1964).

5. James A. Neuchterlein, "The Dream of Scientific Liberalism: The *New Republic* and American Progressive Thought, 1914–1920," *Review of Politics* 42 (1980): 167. Robert Westbrook has noted "the unsuccessful efforts of historians to characterize progressivism as an ideology grounded simply in either old middle-class Protestant moralism or the new middle-class scientific gospel of effi-

ciency." Some Progressives spoke in the idiom of one of these strains of thought and some the other——and "many spoke both simultaneously." Robert B. Westbrook, *John Dewey and American Democracy* (Ithaca, N.Y.: Cornell University Press, 1991), 184.

6. Morton G. White, *Social Thought in America: The Revolt Against Formalism* (New York: Viking Press, 1949).

7. John McGreevy, "Catholics and Civic Engagement in the United States" (paper presented at the Spring 2000 Joint Consultation: Commonweal Foundation and Faith and Reason Institute). The paper is an excerpt from McGreevy's forthcoming *Catholicism and American Freedom: A History from Slavery to Abortion* (New York: Norton, 2003).

8. On the Bishops' Program, see Joseph M. McShane, S.J., *"Sufficiently Radical": Catholicism, Progressivism, and the Bishops' Program of 1919* (Washington, D.C.: Catholic University of America, 1986), esp. 57–69. Father McShane's book is noticeably biased in favor of the Bishops' Program (a bias made obvious in the author's use of the words "fortunately" and "unfortunately"). For an alternative view, see Thomas E. Woods Jr., "Catholic Social Teaching and Economic Law: An Unresolved Tension," *Journal des Economistes et des Etudes Humaines* 13 (Spring 2003, forthcoming); see also Woods, "Why Wages Used to Be So Low," *Ideas on Liberty* (June 2003), 38–41.

9. McGreevy, "Catholics and Civic Engagement in the United States."

10. Eugene McCarraher, *Christian Critics: Religion and the Impasse in Modern American Social Thought* (Ithaca: Cornell University Press, 2000), 20.

11. Ibid., 26.

12. John A. Ryan, moral theology notes, 1915, 115, in box 34, Ryan Papers.

13. James Lyman Nash, "Questioning the Efficacy of One Hundred Years of Catholic Social Teaching: The Intrinsic Connection Between Faith and Justice," *Social Thought* 17, no. 2 (1991): 54.

14. See, for example, Marcel Chappin, "Rerum Novarum, The Encyclical in Its Historical Context," in *Rerum Novarum: New Conditions of Life in a Changing World*, 39 (Ankara, Turkey: Ankara University Press, 1993).

15. References to Leo XIII's teaching in this area appear throughout Michael Davies, *The Second Vatican Council and Religious Liberty* (Long Prairie, Minn.: Neumann, 1992).

16. Joseph Watzlawik, *Leo XIII and the New Scholasticism* (Cebu City, Philippines: University of San Carlos, n.d.).

17. Emile Poulat, "Réflexions sur un Centenaire," in Paul Furlong and David Curtis, eds., *The Church Faces the Modern World: Rerum Novarum and Its Impact*, 21–26, but esp. 23–24 (N. Humberside, Great Britain: Earlsgate Press, 1994).

18. John A. Ryan, *A Living Wage: Its Ethical and Economic Aspects* (New York: Macmillan, 1906).

19. George M. Sauvage, review of *A Living Wage*, by John A. Ryan, in *Catholic University Bulletin* 13 (July 1907): 470–75; quotation on 474.

20. John A. Ryan, "The Wage-Contract and Strict Justice," *Catholic University Bulletin* 14 (January 1908): 50–56.

21. Quoted in Katherine Burton, *Leo the Thirteenth: The First Modern Pope* (New York: David McKay, 1962), 171.

22. See, for example, T. J. Flaherty, "Economics Without Ethics," *America* 26 (January 14, 1922): 300.

23. A student of Ryan's work observes that this idea "of an absolute moral obligation was probably unfamiliar to Protestant America, at least in its Roman Catholic form." Patrick Bernard Lavey, "William J. Kerby, John A. Ryan, and the Awakening of the Twentieth-Century American Catholic Social Conscience, 1899–1919" (Ph.D. diss., University of Illinois, Urbana-Champaign, 1986), 229n.

24. Charles R. Morris, *American Catholic: The Saints and Sinners Who Built America's Most Powerful Church* (New York: Random House, 1997), 152.

25. John A. Ryan, D.D., "The Nature of the State," *America* (July 2, 1921): 252.

26. John A. Ryan, "Family," *Catholic Encyclopedia*, 2d ed., 1913.

27. Leo XIII, "Rerum Novarum,"in Claudia Carlen, ed., *The Papal Encyclicals*, vol. 2, *1878–1903*, 250 (Wilmington, N.C.: McGrath Publishing, 1981).

28. Cited in Charles Rice, *50 Questions on the Natural Law* (San Francisco: Ignatius Press, 1993), 27.

29. Ryan journal, 43, in box 32, Ryan Papers.

30. Charles F. Aiken, S.T.D., "The Doctrine of the Fathers of the Church on the Right of Private Property," *Catholic World* (May 1912): 197–211.

31. Leo XIII, "Rerum Novarum," in Carlen, *The Papal Encyclicals*, 2:244.

32. Ibid., 254.

33. John Ryan, *Distributive Justice: The Right and Wrong of Our Present Distribution of Wealth* (New York: Macmillan, 1916), 359–60.

34. Ibid., 361–62.

35. Ryan, *A Living Wage*, 50–52. Also worth consulting is Ryan's chapter "Some Unacceptable Theories of Wage Justice," in Ryan, *Distributive Justice*, 323–55.

36. Ryan, *Distributive Justice*, 361–62.

37. Ryan, "Family."

38. For a good summary of Father Ryan's case against socialism, see Lavey, "William J. Kerby, John A. Ryan, and the Awakening of the Twentieth-Century American Catholic Social Conscience," 140–82.

39. George M. Searle, C.S.P., "Why the Catholic Church Cannot Accept Socialism," *Catholic World* (July 1913): 449–50.

40. *America* magazine was at the forefront of warning Catholics of both the explicit hostility toward religion that existed among many socialists and the inherent danger to revealed religion present in the materialist philosophy undergirding socialism. See, for example, Joseph Husslein, S.J., "Wage System in the Gospel," *America* 7 (August 10, 1912): 415; Husslein, "The Economic Fetish," *America* 14 (October 23, 1915): 46–47; Husslein, "Varieties of American

Socialism," *America* 9 (September 20, 1913): 557–58; Husslein, "The Christ of Socialism," *America* 6 (April 6, 1912); Husslein, "Christian Socialism," *America* 6 (March 30, 1912): 582–84; H. J. Maeckel, S.J., "Socialism and Christian Marriage," *America* 6 (February 24, 1912): 464–65; Maeckel, "Socialism and Religion," *America* 6 (January 20, 1912): 345–47; "Socialists and the Eucharistic Congress," *America* 7 (September 14, 1912): 543; Richard Dana Skinner, "Socialism and Present-Day Indifference," *America* 7 (May 4, 1912): 79–80.

41. See William J. Kerby, "Atheism and Socialism," *Catholic University Bulletin* 11 (July 1905): 315–26; [John J. Burke], "With Our Readers," *Catholic World* (September 1914): 861–62; see also the discussion in Lavey, "William J. Kerby, John A. Ryan, and the Awakening of the Twentieth-Century American Catholic Social Conscience," 90–139.

42. See, for example, John A. Ryan, D.D., "The State and Labor," *America* 25 (July 30, 1921): 344.

43. Joseph Husslein, "The State and Labor," *America* 18 (March 23, 1918): 595–96.

44. Richard H. Tierney, S.J., "The Religious Element in the Medieval Guilds," *American Catholic Quarterly Review* 30 (October 1905): 656.

45. Hilaire Belloc, "The Results of the Reformation, I. Material," *Catholic World* (January 1912): 523.

46. Edward F. Murphy, "The Church and Some Social Problems," *America* 14 (February 26, 1916): 464.

47. Joseph Husslein, S.J., "Suppressed Catholicism of Labor," *America* 18 (March 2, 1918): 533.

48. Godefroid Kurth, *The Workingmen's Guilds of the Middle Ages* (reprint, Hawthorne, Calif.: Omni Publications, 1987); Edward Cahill, S.J., *The Framework of a Christian State* (Dublin: M. H. Gill and Son, 1932), 71–81.

49. Leo XIII, "Rerum Novarum," in Carlen, ed., *The Papal Encyclicals*, 2:253–54.

50. Pius X, *Our Apostolic Mandate* [Letter to the French Bishops and Archbishops on the "Sillon"], trans. Yves Dupont (Hawthorn, Vic, Australia: Tenet Books, 1974; reprint, Yarra Junction Vic, Australia, Instauratio Press, 1990), 24.

51. Kurth, *Workingmen's Guilds*, 52–53.

52. Joseph Husslein, S.J., "A Scotch Merchant Guild," *America* 10 (February 28, 1914): 488.

53. This was a common theme of Father Joseph Husslein, for example.

54. Joseph Husslein, S.J., "Origin of Medieval Guilds," *America* 10 (December 6, 1913): 198–99.

55. Theodore Maynard, "The Guild Idea," *Catholic World* 106 (March 1918): 723 ff.

56. Tierney, "Religious Element in the Medieval Guilds," 653–54, quotation on 653.

57. Joseph Husslein, S.J., "Live and Let Live," *America* 21 (September 27, 1919): 612.

58. Murphy, "The Church and Some Social Problems," 464.

59. Joseph Husslein, S.J., "Social Concept of Christ's Kingdom, II," *America* 7 (July 13, 1912): 323.

60. Joseph Husslein, S.J., "Catholic Church and Labor Organizations," *America* 7 (May 25, 1912): 149.

61. Leo XIII, "Rerum Novarum," in Carlen, ed., *The Papal Encyclicals*, 2:241–42.

62. Cf. the interesting points raised in F. A. Hayek, "History and Politics," in F. A. Hayek, ed., *Capitalism and the Historians* (Chicago: University of Chicago Press, 1954), 3–29.

63. See his lecture notes on moral theology, 1915, in box 34, Ryan Papers, 117, 119, 121.

64. John A. Ryan, "The Morality of the Aims and Methods of the Labor Union," *American Catholic Quarterly Review* 29 (April 1904): 353.

65. On guild socialism, see Christopher Lasch, *The True and Only Heaven: Progress and Its Critics* (New York: Norton, 1991), esp. 317 ff.

66. McCarraher, *Christian Critics*, 29.

67. On Walsh, see William M. Halsey, *The Survival of American Innocence: Catholicism in an Era of Disillusionment, 1920–1940* (Notre Dame, Ind.: University of Notre Dame Press, 1980), 66–67.

68. James J. Walsh, "Luther and Social Service," *Catholic World* (March 1917): 781–91; Walsh, "The Care of the Dependent Poor," *Catholic World* 103 (September 1916): 721–32; Walsh, "The Care of Children and the Aged," *Catholic World* (October 1916): 56–65; Walsh, "The Story of Organized Care of the Insane and Defectives," *Catholic World* (November 1916): 226–34.

69. Walsh, "Luther and Social Service," 782.

70. Belloc, "The Results of the Reformation," 516.

71. John A. Ryan, D.D., "The Church and Economics," *America* 22 (April 17, 1920): 593.

72. Joseph Husslein, S.J., "Rise and Fall of Protestant Prosperity," *America* 18 (February 23, 1918): 489.

73. On this development in modern political philosophy, see J. N. Figgis, *Studies of Political Thought from Gerson to Grotius* (Cambridge: Cambridge University Press, 1907); and Robert A. Nisbet, *The Quest for Community: A Study in the Ethics of Order and Freedom* (New York: Oxford University Press, 1953).

74. Ryan, "The Morality of the Aims and Methods of the Labor Union," 352–53.

75. Lillian Parker Wallace, *Leo XIII and the Rise of Socialism* (Durham, N.C.: Duke University Press, 1966), 274.

76. Ralph Brown, *German Theories of the Corporative State* (New York: McGraw-Hill, 1947), 19, 53–57, 79, 80–81.

77. M. Kenny, S.J., "How Two Extremes Rose and Met," *America* 6 (March 2, 1912): 486–87.

78. Joseph Husslein, S.J., "An Aristocratic Pillage," *America* 21 (September 6, 1919): 553.

79. Ryan, "The Morality of the Aims and Methods of the Labor Union," 352.

80. Murray N. Rothbard, *An Austrian Perspective on the History of Economic Thought*, vol. 1, *Economic Thought Before Adam Smith* (Hants, Eng.: Edward Elgar, 1995), 67–145.
81. Richard H. Tawney, *Religion and the Rise of Capitalism* (New York: New American Library, 1954), 80.
82. Husslein, "Rise and Fall of Protestant Prosperity," 490.
83. Husslein, "Catholic Church and Labor Organizations," 150.
84. John A. Ryan, "The Church and the Social Question," in box 24, Ryan Papers. See also John A. Ryan, "The Church and Radical Social Movements," in ibid.
85. Ryan journal, 43–45, in box 32, Ryan Papers.
86. Quoted in McCarraher, *Christian Critics*, 25.
87. Husslein, "Suppressed Catholicism of Labor," 534.
88. Maynard, "The Guild Idea," 732.

6. AGAINST SYNCRETISM

1. M.K., review of Charles Brodie Patterson, *What Is New Thought?* (New York: Thomas Y. Crowell Co.), *America* 9 (October 4, 1913): 618.
2. " 'Everybody's' Christian," *America* 12 (April 10, 1915): 654.
3. Henry Woods, S.J., "Antichrist," *America* 5 (September 16, 1911): 536–37.
4. Eisenach contends that "The Bonds of Nationality," Small's 1915 essay in the *American Journal of Sociology*, in which, among other things, the Chicago sociologist discussed the foundations of "national bonds," can "stand as a fair copy of the larger intellectual framework of Progressive discussion of American nationality, not only because of Small's standing, but because he integrated writings of so many of his fellow sociologists and political economists from the previous twenty-five years into this essay." Eldon J. Eisenach, *The Lost Promise of Progressivism* (Lawrence: University Press of Kansas, 1994), 54.
5. Ibid., 58–59.
6. Dudley G. Wooten, "The Propaganda of Paganism, II," *Catholic World* 106 (November 1917): 164.
7. Henry Woods, S.J., "The Protestant Movement for Unity," *America* 8 (December 14, 1912): 222.
8. Walter Rauschenbusch, *Christianity and the Social Crisis* (New York: Macmillan, 1907), 178–79.
9. Ibid., 65, 176–77.
10. John J. Ming, S.J., "The Socialistic Kingdom of God, I," *America* 2 (January 15, 1910): 362; see also Ming, "The Socialistic Kingdom of God, II," *America* 2 (January 22, 1910): 388–89; Ming, "Christianity and Christian Socialism," *America* 2 (November 27, 1909): 169–71; "Gospels of Socialism and of Christ," *America* 2 (January 22, 1910): 396–97; Joseph Husslein, S.J., "Social Concept

of Christ's Kingdom, I," *America* 7 (July 6, 1912): 293–95; "A Secularized Pulpit," *America* 14 (March 25, 1916): 566–67; Woods, "Antichrist," 536–37.

11. Edmund T. Shanahan, S.T.D., "Making Dogma Useless," *Catholic World* (August 1916): 605.

12. "Deconstructionists vs. Dogma," *America* 1 (August 21, 1909): 508.

13. On Eliot, see William Allan Neilson, ed., *Charles W. Eliot: The Man and His Beliefs* (New York: Harper and Bros., 1926).

14. Charles W. Eliot, *A Late Harvest: Miscellaneous Papers Written Between Eighty and Ninety* (Boston: Atlantic Monthly Press, 1924), 231.

15. Edward S. Bergin, S.J., "The Latest New Religion," *America* 2 (October 30, 1909): 58.

16. Ibid., 60.

17. R. H. Tierney, S.J., "Another Remarkable Invention," *America* 10 (January 17, 1914): 341.

18. Edward F. Murphy, "The Religion of the Future," *America* 13 (June 12, 1915): 217.

19. Ibid.

20. Tierney, "Another Remarkable Invention," 341.

21. Murphy, "The Religion of the Future," 217.

22. Wooten, "The Propaganda of Paganism," 160.

23. "With Our Readers," *Catholic World* (February 1918): 717; see also "Varying Morality," *America* 6 (February 24, 1912): 470–71.

24. Paul L. Blakely, S.J., "A New Morality Code," *America* 18 (April 6, 1918): 662.

25. Howard B. Radest, *Felix Adler: An Ethical Culture* (New York: Peter Lang, 1998), 11.

26. Ibid., 12–13.

27. See J. B. Culemans, "The Passing of the Ethical Culture Movement," *America* 24 (February 19, 1921): 427–28.

28. Cf. Radest, *Felix Adler*, 21. Radest, himself a proponent of ethical culture, is very sympathetic to Adler. An interesting Catholic critique of ethical culture appears in Samuel Frederick Bacon, *An Evaluation of the Philosophy and Pedagogy of Ethical Culture* (Washington, D.C.: Catholic University of America Press, 1933).

29. Alfred Martin, "A New Creed for Americans," *New York Evening Post*, December 31, 1910.

30. Quoted in Thomas McMillan, C.S.P., "A School for Ethical Culture," *Catholic Educational Review* 6 (June 1913): 19.

31. E. Spillane, S.J., "Morality Without Religion," *America* 5 (September 23, 1911): 557.

32. Timothy Brosnahan, S.J., "The Educational Fact," *American Catholic Quarterly Review* 30 (April 1905): 221. See also Mark S. Gross, S.J., "The God of the Ethical Societies," *America* 13 (August 28, 1915): 489–90.

33. Cited in Sister Mary Ruth, "The Inefficiency of Moral Education Without a Religious Basis: Ethical Culture Schools in the United States and in England," *Catholic Educational Review* 7 (February 1914): 312.

34. Shanahan, "Making Dogma Useless," 609–10.
35. "Archbishop Ryan on 'New Religion,'" *America* (July 31, 1909): 422.
36. Timothy Brosnahan, S.J., "The Educational Fact," *American Catholic Quarterly Review* 30 (July 1905): 517.
37. Quoted in John F. Duston, S.J., "Back to Bethlehem," *America* 20 (November 21, 1918): 275.
38. Sister Mary Ruth, "The Inefficiency of Moral Education," 306–12.
39. Ibid., 310.
40. Ibid., 311–12. See also Shanahan, "Making Dogma Useless," 611.
41. Cited in Shanahan, "Making Dogma Useless," 311.
42. James Fox, cited in ibid.
43. Sister Mary Ruth, "The Inefficiency of Moral Education," 311–12.
44. Sister Mary Ruth, "The Inefficiency of Moral Education without a Religious Basis," *Catholic Educational Review* 7 (May 1914): 405. Emphasis added.

EPILOGUE: INTO THE FUTURE

1. Quoted in Alfred Kazin, *On Native Grounds* (Garden City, N.Y.: Doubleday, 1956), 150.
2. See, for example, Herbert F. Margules, "Recent Opinion of the Decline of the Progressive Movement," *Mid-America* 45 (1963): 250–68.
3. William M. Halsey, *The Survival of American Innocence: Catholicism in an Era of Disillusionment, 1920–1940* (Notre Dame, Ind.: University of Notre Dame Press, 1980), 17.
4. Hilaire Belloc, *The Great Heresies* (Rockford, Ill.: TAN, 1991), 160.
5. Charles R. Morris, *American Catholic: The Saints and Sinners Who Built America's Most Powerful Church* (New York: Random House, 1997), 162.
6. Peter A. Huff, *Allen Tate and the Catholic Revival: Trace of the Fugitive Gods* (New York: Paulist, 1996), 28–29.
7. Ibid., 23.
8. Halsey, *Survival of American Innocence*, 56–57.
9. Ibid., 57.
10. Christopher Dawson, *Religion and the Modern State* (New York: Sheed and Ward, 1935), 57.
11. Ibid., 58; Geoffrey O'Connell, *Naturalism in American Education* (Washington, D.C.: Catholic University, 1936), 184.
12. Joseph A. Varacalli, "A Catholic Plausibility Structure," *Homiletic and Pastoral Review* (November 1988), pp. 63–67; see also Varacalli, *Bright Promise, Failed Community: Catholics and the American Public Order* (Lanham, Md.: Lexington, 2000).
13. Peter L. Berger, *The Sacred Canopy* (New York: Anchor, 1969), 45; cited in Varacalli, "A Catholic Plausibility Structure," 65.

14. Joseph A. Varacalli, "Secular Sociology's War Against *Familiaris Consortio* and the Traditional Family: Whither Catholic Higher Education and Catholic Sociology?" in Rev. Anthony Mastroeni, ed., *The Church and the Universal Catechism: Proceedings from the 15th [Fellowship of Catholic Scholars] Convention* (Fellowship of Catholic Scholars, 1992), 162.

15. Varacalli, "A Catholic Plausibility Structure," 67. Emphasis in original. By contrast, Varacalli examines the condition of the postconciliar American Church in *Bright Promise, Failed Community*.

16. Monsignor George A. Kelly, *The Battle for the American Church* (New York: Doubleday, 1979), 18; cited in Varacalli, "A Catholic Plausibility Structure," 66.

17. Varacalli, "Secular Sociology's War," 164.

18. Ibid., 167.

19. Much of this analysis appears in Joseph A. Varacalli, "Toward the History and Promise of Roman Catholic Sociologies," unpublished monograph, ca. 1987–89. I am grateful to Professor Varacalli for making this manuscript available to me.

20. "The Pastoral Constitution on the Church in the Modern World" [*Gaudium et Spes*], in Walter M. Abbott, S.J., ed., *The Documents of Vatican II*, 243 (New York: America Press, 1966).

21. Patricia Byrne, "In the Parish but Not of It: Sisters," in Jay P. Dolan, R. Scott Appleby, Patricia Byrne, and Debra Campbell, eds., *Transforming Parish Ministry: The Changing Roles of Catholic Clergy, Laity, and Women Religious*, 166 (New York: Crossroad, 1990).

22. Arnold Sparr, *To Promote, Defend, and Redeem: The Catholic Literary Revival and the Cultural Transformation of American Catholicism, 1920–1960* (New York: Greenwood, 1990), 163–70.

23. Paul Blanshard, *American Freedom and Catholic Power* (Boston: Beacon, 1949).

24. "Pope John's Opening Speech to the Council," in Abbott, *The Documents of Vatican II*, 716.

25. Vatican Council II, "Constitution on the Sacred Liturgy," par. 36 and 116, in Abbott, *The Documents of Vatican II*, 150, 172.

26. Quoted in Michael Davies, *Pope John's Council* (Kansas City, Mo.: Angelus, 1977), 56.

27. Professor James Hitchcock has suggested to me that in its own way *Gaudium et Spes* was highly "triumphalistic," especially by current standards, in that it suggests that the world, floundering in a well-intentioned muddle, needs the Church and the Gospel to find its way.

28. Quoted in Romano Amerio, *Iota Unum: A Study of Changes in the Catholic Church in the XXth Century*, trans. John Parsons (Kansas City, Mo.: Sarto House, 1996), 355n.

29. Quoted in "If Pius XI Had Only Understood," *The Latin Mass*, Summer 2000, 7–8.

30. Thus see the extraordinary book by Stanley L. Jaki, *Science and Creation: From Eternal Cycles to an Oscillating Universe* (Edinburgh: Scottish Academic Press, 1986).

31. Theodore Maynard, *The Story of American Catholicism* (New York: Macmillan, 1941; reprint, Garden City, N.Y.: Image Books, 1960), 2:148.

32. George A. Kelly, *The Battle for the American Church* (Garden City, N.Y.: Doubleday, 1979), 7.

33. Garry Wills, *Bare Ruined Choirs* (Garden City, N.Y.: Doubleday, 1972), 15–16; quoted in Kelly, *Battle for the American Church*, 13.

34. Quoted in Amerio, *Iota Unum*, 6–7.

35. James Hennesey, *American Catholics: A History of the Roman Catholic Community in the United States* (New York: Oxford University Press, 1981), 327.

36. Allan Carlson, *The New Agrarian Mind: The Movement Toward Decentralist Thought in Twentieth-Century America* (New Brunswick, N.J.: Transaction, 2000), 209–10. On this topic see also William D. Mosher, David P. Johnson, and Marjorie C. Horn, "Religion and Fertility in the United States: The Importance of Marriage Patterns and Hispanic Origin," *Demography* 23 (August 1986): 367–69; Lincoln H. Day, "Natality and Ethnocentrism: Some Relationships Suggested by an Analysis of Catholic-Protestant Differentials," *Population Studies* 22 (1968): 27–30; and Leon Bouvier and S. L. N. Rao, *Socio-religious Factors in Fertility Decline* (Cambridge: Ballinger, 1975).

37. Edward F. Murphy, "The Religion of the Future," *America* 13 (June 12, 1915): 218.

SELECTED BIBLIOGRAPHY

MANUSCRIPT COLLECTIONS

Burke, John J. Papers. Paulist Fathers Archives, Washington, D.C.
Pace, Edward A. Papers. Catholic University of America, Washington, D.C.
Ryan, John A. Papers. Catholic University of America, Washington, D.C.

PERIODICALS

America
American Catholic Quarterly Review
American Ecclesiastical Review
American Journal of Sociology
Catholic Charities Review
Catholic Educational Review
Catholic University Bulletin
Catholic World

OTHER PRIMARY SOURCES

Abbott, Walter M., S.J., ed. *The Documents of Vatican II.* New York: America Press, 1966.
Burns, James A. *The Catholic School System in the United States: Its Principles, Origin, and Establishment.* New York: Benziger, 1908.
Carlen, Claudia, ed. *The Papal Encyclicals.* 5 vols. Wilmington, N.C.: McGrath, 1981.
Cronin, Dr. John J. "The Doctor in the Public School." *American Monthly Review of Reviews* 35 (April 1907): 440.
De Wulf, M. "Neo-Scholasticism." *Catholic Encyclopedia*, 2d ed., 1913.

Denzinger, Henry. *The Sources of Catholic Dogma.* Translated by Roy J. Deferrari. Powers Lake, Md.: Marion House, 1955.

Dewey, John. *The Early Works, 1882–1898.* 3 vols. Carbondale: Southern Illinois University Press, 1969.

———. *Experience and Education.* New York: Macmillan, 1938.

———. *Moral Principles in Education.* Boston: Houghton Mifflin, 1909.

Eliot, Charles W. *A Late Harvest: Miscellaneous Papers Written Between Eighty and Ninety.* Boston: Atlantic Monthly Press, 1924.

Ellwood, Charles A. *The Reconstruction of Religion: A Sociological View.* New York: Macmillan, 1922.

Fairchild, Henry Pratt. *Outline of Applied Sociology.* New York: Macmillan, 1916.

"Father Blakely States the Issue." *New Republic* 7 (July 29, 1916): 320–21.

Gladden, Washington. *Social Salvation.* Boston: Houghton Mifflin, 1902.

Goyau, Georges. "Ketteler." In *Catholic Encyclopedia,* 2d ed., 1913.

Handy, Robert T., ed. *The Social Gospel in America, 1870–1920.* New York: Oxford University Press, 1966.

Husslein, Joseph, S.J. *The Catholic's Work in the World: A Practical Solution of Religious and Social Problems of Today.* New York: Benziger Brothers, 1917.

Ireland, John. "The Dogmatic Authority of the Papacy." *North American Review* 187 (1908): 486–87.

____. "Three and a Half Years of Pius X." *North American Review* 184 (1907): 35–45.

James, William. *Essays in Philosophy.* Cambridge: Harvard University Press, 1978.

———. *A Pluralistic Universe.* New York: Longmans, Green, 1909.

____. *Pragmatism: A New Name for Some Old Ways of Thinking.* 1907. Reprint, Indianapolis: Hackett, 1981.

____. *Varieties of Religious Experience: A Study in Human Nature.* New York: Longmans, Green, 1902.

———. *The Will to Believe and Other Essays in Popular Philosophy.* Cambridge: Harvard University Press, 1978.

Kerby, William J. *The Considerate Priest.* Philadelphia: Dolphin Press, 1937.

———. *The Social Mission of Charity: A Study of Points of View in Catholic Charities.* New York: Macmillan, 1921.

____. "Social Work of the Catholic Church in America." *Annals of the American Academy of Political and Social Science* 30 (November 1907).

____. "Sociology." *Catholic Encyclopedia,* 2d ed., 1913.

Kilpatrick, William H. *Education for a Changing Civilization.* New York: Macmillan, 1926.

Kuntz, Frank. *Undergraduate Days, 1904–1908.* Washington, D.C.: Catholic University Press, 1958.

Lasch, Christopher. *The True and Only Heaven: Progress and Its Critics.* New York: Norton, 1991.

Macksey, Charles. "Taparelli." *Catholic Encyclopedia,* 2d ed., 1913.

Metlake, George [John Laux]. *Christian Social Reform: Program Outlined by Its Pioneer, William Emmanuel Baron von Ketteler.* Philadelphia: Dolphin, 1912.

Pace, Edward A. "Education." *Catholic Encyclopedia*, 2d ed., 1913.

Patten, Simon N. *The Social Basis of Religion*. New York: Macmillan, 1911.

Pius X. *Our Apostolic Mandate: On the Sillon*. Apostolic Letter. Translated by Yves Dupont. Yarra Junction Vic, Australia: Instauratio, 1990.

Pratt, James Bissett. *What Is Pragmatism?* New York: Macmillan, 1909.

Rauschenbusch, Walter. *Christianity and the Social Crisis*. New York: Macmillan, 1907.

____. *A Theology for the Social Gospel*. New York: Macmillan, 1917.

Ryan, John A. *Distributive Justice: The Right and Wrong of Our Present Distribution of Wealth*. New York: Macmillan, 1916.

____. *A Living Wage: Its Ethical and Economic Aspects*. New York: Macmillan, 1906.

____. "Poverty." *Catholic Encyclopedia*, 2d ed., 1913.

____. *Social Doctrine in Action: A Personal History*. New York: Harper, 1941.

Shields, Thomas Edward. *Philosophy of Education*. Washington, D.C.: Catholic Correspondence School, 1917.

____. *The Psychology of Education*. Washington, D.C.: Catholic Correspondence School, 1906.

____. *The Teaching of Religion*. Washington, D.C.: Catholic Correspondence School, 1908.

Turner, William. "Pragmatism." *Catholic Encyclopedia*, 2d ed., 1913.

Tyrrell, George. *The Programme of Modernism*. New York: Putnam's, 1908.

Vermeersch, A. "Modernism." *Catholic Encyclopedia*, 2d ed., 1913.

Walsh, James J. *Education: How Old the New*. New York: Fordham University Press, 1910.

Ward, Lester Frank. *Dynamic Sociology*. 2 vols. New York: D. Appleton, 1883.

Wines, Frederick Howard. "Sociology and Philanthropy." *Annals of the American Academy of Political and Social Science* 12 (1898): 49–57.

SECONDARY SOURCES

Alexander, Jon. "Aeterni Patris, 1879–1979: A Bibliography of American Responses." *Thomist* 43 (July 1979): 480–81.

Amerio, Romano. *Iota Unum: A Study of Changes in the Catholic Church in the XXth Century*. Translated by Fr. John Parsons. Kansas City, Mo.: Sarto House, 1996.

Appleby, R. Scott. *"Church and Age Unite!": The Modernist Impulse in American Catholicism*. Notre Dame, Ind.: University of Notre Dame Press, 1992.

Arnove, Robert, ed. *Philanthropy and Cultural Imperialism*. Boston: G. K. Hall, 1980.

Bacon, Samuel Frederick. *An Evaluation of the Philosophy and Pedagogy of Ethical Culture*. Washington, D.C.: Catholic University of America Press, 1933.

Barnes, Harry Elmer, ed. *An Introduction to the History of Sociology*. Chicago: University of Chicago Press, 1948.

Barry, Robert M., and John D. Fearon. "John Dewey and American Thomism." *American Benedictine Review* 10 (1959): 219–28.

Belloc, Hilaire. *The Great Heresies.* Rockford, Ill.: TAN, 1991.

Blanshard, Paul. *American Freedom and Catholic Power.* Boston: Beacon, 1949.

Boyer, Paul. *Urban Masses and the Moral Order in America, 1820–1920.* Cambridge: Harvard University Press, 1978.

Brown, Ralph. *German Theories of the Corporative State.* New York: McGraw-Hill, 1947.

Buenker, John D., John C. Burnham, and Robert M. Crunden. *Progressivism.* Cambridge: Schenkman, 1977.

Burton, Katherine. *The Great Mantle: The Life of Giuseppe Melchiore Sarto, Pope Pius X.* New York: Longmans, Green, 1950.

———. *Leo the Thirteenth: The First Modern Pope.* New York: David McKay, 1962.

Byrne, Patricia. "In the Parish but Not of It: Sisters." In Jay P. Dolan, R. Scott Appleby, Patricia Byrne, and Debra Campbell, eds., *Transforming Parish Ministry: The Changing Roles of Catholic Clergy, Laity, and Women Religious.* New York: Crossroad, 1990.

Cahill, Edward, S.J. *The Framework of a Christian State.* Dublin: M. H. Gill, 1932.

Callahan, Raymond E. *Education and the Cult of Efficiency.* Chicago: University of Chicago Press, 1962.

Carey, Patrick W. *The Roman Catholics.* Westport, Conn.: Greenwood, 1993.

Carlson, Allan. *The New Agrarian Mind: The Movement Toward Decentralist Thought in Twentieth-Century America.* New Brunswick, N.J.: Transaction, 2000.

Cole, Stewart G. *The History of Fundamentalism.* New York: Harper and Row, 1931.

Copleston, Frederick, S.J. *A History of Philosophy.* 9 vols. New York: Doubleday, 1977.

Cremin, Lawrence A. *American Education: The Metropolitan Experience, 1876–1980.* New York: Harper and Row, 1988.

Cross, Robert D. *The Emergence of Liberal Catholicism in America.* Cambridge: Harvard University Press, 1958.

Daly, Gabriel, O.S.A. *Transcendence and Immanence: A Study in Catholic Modernism and Integralism.* Oxford: Clarendon, 1980.

Davies, Michael. *Pope John's Council.* Kansas City, Mo.: Angelus, 1977.

———. *The Second Vatican Council and Religious Liberty.* Long Prairie, Minn.: Neumann, 1992.

Dawson, Christopher. *Religion and the Modern State.* New York: Sheed and Ward, 1935.

Dibble, Vernon K. *The Legacy of Albion Small.* Chicago: University of Chicago Press, 1975.

Dickstein, Morris, ed. *The Revival of Pragmatism: New Essays on Social Thought, Law, and Culture.* Durham, N.C.: Duke University Press, 1998.

Dolan, Timothy N. "Prophet of a Better Hope: The Life and Work of Monsignor William Joseph Kerby." Master's thesis, Catholic University of America, 1981.

Dougherty, Jude P. "Dewey and the Value of Religion." *New Scholasticism* 1 (Summer 1977).

Drost, Walter. *David Snedden and Education for Social Efficiency.* Madison: University of Wisconsin Press, 1967.

Dunn, Archibald J. *Frederic Ozanam and the Establishment of the Society of St. Vincent de Paul.* New York: Benziger Brothers, n.d.

Durant, Will. *The Story of Philosophy.* 1926. Reprint, New York: Simon and Schuster, 1961.

Eisenach, Eldon J. *The Lost Promise of Progressivism.* Lawrence: University Press of Kansas, 1994.

Ellis, John Tracy. "The Formation of the American Priest: An Historical Perspective." In John Tracy Ellis, ed., *The Catholic Priest in the United States: Historical Investigations.* Collegeville, Minn.: St. John's University Press, 1961.

Fogarty, Gerald P., S.J. "The Catholic Hierarchy in the United States Between the Third Plenary Council and the Condemnation of Americanism." *U.S. Catholic Historian* 11 (Summer 1993): 19–35.

Giordani, Igino. *Pius X: A Country Priest.* Translated by Thomas J. Tobin. Milwaukee: Bruce Publishing, 1954.

Gleason, Philip. "The New Americanism in Catholic Historiography." *U.S. Catholic Historian* 11 (Summer 1993): 1–18.

Gottfried, Paul Edward. *After Liberalism: Mass Democracy in the Managerial State.* Princeton, N.J.: Princeton University Press, 1999.

Graham, George P. *William James and the Affirmation of God.* New York: Peter Lang, 1992.

Greek, Cecil E. *The Religious Roots of American Sociology.* New York: Garland, 1992.

Gutmann, Amy. "The Virtues of Democratic Self-Restraint." In Amitai Etzioni, ed., *New Communitarian Thinking: Persons, Virtues, Institutions, and Communities,* 154–69. Charlottesville: University Press of Virginia, 1995.

Halsey, William M. *The Survival of American Innocence: Catholicism in an Era of Disillusionment, 1920–1940.* Notre Dame, Ind.: University of Notre Dame Press, 1980.

Hennesey, James, S.J. *American Catholics: A History of the Roman Catholic Community in the United States.* New York: Oxford University Press, 1981.

Hofstadter, Richard. *Social Darwinism in American Thought.* Rev. ed. Boston: Beacon, 1955.

Hopkins, Charles Howard. *The Rise of the Social Gospel in American Protestantism, 1865–1915.* New Haven: Yale University Press, 1940.

Huff, Peter. *Allen Tate and the Catholic Revival: Trace of the Fugitive Gods.* New York: Paulist, 1996.

Katz, Michael B. *In the Shadow of the Poorhouse: A Social History of Welfare in America.* New York: Basic Books, 1986.

Kelly, George A. *The Battle for the American Church.* Garden City, N.Y.: Doubleday, 1979.

Killen, David P. "Americanism Revisited: John Spalding and *Testem Benevolentiae.*" *Harvard Theological Review* 66 (October 1973): 413–54.

Klein, Mary M. "A Bio-Bibliography of William J. Kerby, 1870–1936." Ph.D. diss., Catholic University, 1955.

Kloppenberg, James T. *Uncertain Victory: Social Democracy and Progressivism in European and American Thought, 1870–1920*. New York, Oxford University Press, 1986.

Kurth, Godefroid. *The Workingmen's Guilds of the Middle Ages*. Reprint. Hawthorne, Calif.: Omni Publications, 1987.

Lagemann, Ellen Condliffe. *The Politics of Knowledge: The Carnegie Corporation, Philanthropy, and Public Policy*. Middletown, Conn.: Wesleyan University Press, 1989.

Laux, John. *Church History*. New York: Benziger Brothers, 1930.

Lavey, Patrick Bernard. "William J. Kerby, John A. Ryan, and the Awakening of the Twentieth-Century American Catholic Social Conscience, 1899–1919." Ph.D. diss., University of Illinois, Urbana-Champaign, 1986.

Lawler, Loretto R. *Full Circle: The Story of the National Catholic School of Social Service, 1918–1947*. Washington, D.C.: Catholic University of America Press, 1951.

Lawsen, M. D., and R. C. Petersen. *Progressive Education: An Introduction*. Sydney, Australia: Angus and Robertson, 1972.

Lears, T. J. Jackson. *No Place of Grace: Antimodernism and the Transformation of American Culture, 1880–1920*. New York: Pantheon, 1981.

Lescher, Bruce H. "William J. Kerby: A Lost Voice in American Catholic Spirituality." *Records of the American Catholic Historical Society of Pennsylvania* 102 (Spring 1991): 1–16.

Lubove, Roy. *The Professional Altruist: The Development of Social Work as a Career, 1880–1930*. Cambridge: Harvard University Press, 1965.

Lustig, R. Jeffrey. *Corporate Liberalism: The Origins of Modern American Political Theory, 1890–1920*. Berkeley: University of California Press, 1982.

MacIntyre, Alasdair. *A Short History of Ethics: A History of Moral Philosophy from the Homeric Age to the Twentieth Century*. New York: Macmillan, 1966.

Maritain, Jacques. *Moral Philosophy: An Historical and Critical Survey of the Great Systems*. New York: Scribner's, 1964.

Marsden, George. *Fundamentalism and American Culture: The Shaping of Twentieth Century Evangelicalism, 1870–1925*. New York: Oxford University Press, 1980.

Maynard, Theodore. *The Story of American Catholicism*. 2 vols. New York: Macmillan, 1941.

McAvoy, Thomas T., C.S.C. *The Great Crisis in American Catholic History, 1895–1900*. Chicago: Henry Regnery, 1957.

——. *A History of the Catholic Church in the United States*. Notre Dame, Ind.: University of Notre Dame Press, 1969.

McCarraher, Eugene. *Christian Critics: Religion and the Impasse in Modern American Social Thought*. Ithaca: Cornell University Press, 2000.

McCool, Gerald A. "The Centenary of *Aeterni Patris*." *Homiletic and Pastoral Review* 79 (January 1979): 8–15.

McGiffert, Arthur Cushman. *The Rise of Modern Religious Ideas*. New York: Macmillan, 1915.

McInerny, Ralph M. "The *Aeterni Patris* of Leo XIII, 1879–1979." *American Journal of Jurisprudence* 24 (1979): 1–2.

McKeown, Elizabeth. "From *Pascendi* to *Primitive Man*: The Apologetics and Anthropology of John Montgomery Cooper." *U.S. Catholic Historian* 13 (Winter 1995): 1–21.

McLoughlin, William G. *Revivals, Awakenings, and Reform: An Essay on Religion and Social Change in America, 1607–1977.* Chicago: University of Chicago Press, 1978.

McShane, Joseph M., S.J. *"Sufficiently Radical": Catholicism, Progressivism, and the Bishops' Program of 1919.* Washington, D.C.: Catholic University of America, 1986.

Meade, Francis Louis. "Progressive Education and Catholic Pedagogy." Ph.D. diss., Niagara University, 1934.

Monroe, Paul. *A Brief Course in the History of Education.* New York: Macmillan, 1908.

Morris, Charles. *American Catholic: The Saints and Sinners Who Built America's Most Powerful Church.* New York: Random House, 1997.

———. *The Pragmatic Movement in American Philosophy.* New York: Braziller, 1970.

Murphy, John Francis. "Thomas Edward Shields: Religious Educator." Ph.D. diss., Columbia University, 1971.

Neilson, William Allan, ed. *Charles W. Eliot: The Man and His Beliefs.* 2 vols. New York: Harper, 1926.

Neuchterlein, James A. "The Dream of Scientific Liberalism: The New Republic and American Progressive Thought, 1914–1920." *Review of Politics* 42 (1980).

Nichols, Aidan, O.P. *Looking at the Liturgy: A Critical View of Its Contemporary Form.* San Francisco: Ignatius Press, 1996.

Nisbet, Robert. *History of the Idea of Progress.* New York: Basic Books, 1980.

Nuesse, C. Joseph. "The Introduction of Sociology at the Catholic University of America, 1895–1915." *Catholic Historical Review* 87 (October 2001).

O'Connell, Geoffrey. *Naturalism in American Education.* Washington, D.C.: Catholic University, 1936.

O'Connell, Marvin R. *John Ireland and the American Catholic Church.* St. Paul: Minnesota Historical Society Press, 1988.

Poulat, Emile. "Réflexions sur un Cententaire." In *The Church Faces the Modern World: Rerum Novarum and Its Impact,* ed. Paul Furlong and David Curtis, 21–26. N. Humberside, Great Britain: Earlsgate Press, 1994.

Purcell, Edward A. Jr. *The Crisis of Democratic Theory: Scientific Naturalism and the Problem of Value.* Lexington: University Press of Kentucky, 1973.

Radest, Howard B. *Felix Adler: An Ethical Culture.* New York: Peter Lang, 1998.

Ratner, Joseph, ed. *Intelligence in the Modern World: John Dewey's Philosophy.* New York: Modern Library, 1939.

Reher, Margaret Mary. "Americanism and Modernism: Continuity or Discontinuity?" *U.S. Catholic Historian* 1 (Summer 1981): 87–103.

———. *Catholic Intellectual Life in America.* New York: Macmillan, 1989.

———. "The Church and the Kingdom of God in America: The Ecclesiology of the Americanists." Ph.D. diss., Fordham University, 1972.

Ritzel, G. F. "Some Historical Backgrounds of the Encyclical Aeterni Patris." *Nuntius Aulae* 38 (July 1956): 135–55.

Rommen, Heinrich A. *The Natural Law: A Study in Legal and Social History and Philosophy*. Translated by Thomas R. Hanley, O.S.B. Indianapolis, Ind.: Liberty Fund, 1998.

Ross, Dorothy. *Origins of American Social Science*. Cambridge: Cambridge University Press, 1991.

Rothbard, Murray N. "World War I as Fulfillment: Power and the Intellectuals." In John V. Denson, ed., *The Costs of War: America's Pyrrhic Victories*, 203–53. New Brunswick, N.J.: Transaction, 1997.

Sheen, Fulton J. *God and Intelligence in Modern Philosophy: A Critical Study in the Light of the Philosophy of St. Thomas*. New York: Longmans, Green, 1925.

Sheerin, John B., C.S.P. *Never Look Back: The Career and Concerns of John Burke*. New York: Paulist, 1975.

Skok, Deborah S. "Organized Almsgiving: Scientific Charity and the Society of St. Vincent de Paul in Chicago, 1871–1918." *U.S. Catholic Historian* 16 (Fall 1998): 19–35.

Slawson, Douglas J. "John J. Burke, C.S.P.: The Vision and Character of a Public Churchman." *Journal of Paulist Studies* 4 (1995–96): 47–93.

Sparr, Arnold. *To Promote, Defend, and Redeem: The Catholic Literary Revival and the Cultural Transformation of American Catholicism*. New York: Greenwood, 1990.

Tarnas, Richard. *The Passion of the Western Mind*. New York: Ballantine, 1991.

Tawney, Richard H. *Religion and the Rise of Capitalism*. New York: New American Library, 1954.

Timasheff, Nicholas S. *Sociological Theory: Its Nature and Growth*. New York: Random House, 1955.

Twelve Southerners. *I'll Take My Stand: The South and the Agrarian Tradition*. 1930. Reprint, Baton Rouge: Louisiana State University Press, 1977.

Varacalli, Joseph A. *Bright Promise, Failed Community: Catholics and the American Public Order*. Lanham, Md.: Lexington, 2000.

———. "A Catholic Plausibility Structure." *Homiletic and Pastoral Review* (November 1988), pp. 63–67.

Wallace, Lillian Parker. *Leo XIII and the Rise of Socialism*. Durham, N.C.: Duke University Press, 1966.

Ward, Justine. *Thomas Edward Shields: Biologist, Psychologist, Educator*. New York: Charles Scribner's Sons, 1947.

Watson, Frank D. *The Charity Organization Movement in the United States*. New York: Macmillan, 1922.

Watzlawik, Joseph. *Leo XIII and the New Scholasticism*. Cebu City, Philippines: University of San Carlos, n.d.

Westbrook, Robert B. *John Dewey and American Democracy*. Ithaca, N.Y.: Cornell University Press, 1991.

White, Morton G. *Social Thought in America: The Revolt Against Formalism*. New York: Viking, 1949.

William J. Kerby Foundation. *William J. Kerby: Democracy Through Christ.* Washington, D.C.: William J. Kerby Foundation, 1943.

Zybura, John S., ed. *Present-Day Thinkers and the New Scholasticism.* St. Louis, Mo.: Herder, 1926.

INDEX

RELIGION AND AMERICAN CULTURE

MICHAEL E. STAUB
Torn at the Roots: The Crisis of Jewish Liberalism in Postwar America

AMY DEROGATIS
Moral Geography: Maps, Missionaries, and the American Frontier

ARLENE M. SÁNCHEZ WALSH
Latino Pentecostal Identity: Evangelical Faith, Self, and Society

JULIE BYRNE
O God of Players: The Story of the Immaculata Mighty Macs

CLYDE R. FORSBERG
*Equal Rights: The Book of Mormon, Masonry,
Gender, and American Culture*

ANDREW C. RIESER
*The Chautauqua Moment: Protestants, Progressives,
and the Culture of Modern Liberalism*

CRAIG D. TOWNSEND
*Faith in Their Own Color: Black Episcopalians
in Antebellum New York City*